Families that Flourish

Families that Flourish

Facilitating Resilience in Clinical Practice

Dorothy S. Becvar

W. W. Norton & Company
New York • London

For information about permission to
reproduce selections from this book, write to
Permissions, W. W. Norton & Company, Inc.,
500 Fifth Avenue, New York, NY 10010

Production Manager: Leeann Graham
Manufacturing by Malloy Printing

Library of Congress Cataloging-in-Publication Data

Becvar, Dorothy Stroh.
    Families that flourish: facilitating resilience in clinical practice / Dorothy S. Becvar.
        p.   cm.
"A Norton professional book."
Includes bibliographical references and index.
ISBN-13: 978-0-393-70488-4
ISBN-10: 0-393-70488-2
1. Family psychotherapy I. Title.

RC488.5.B387   2006
616.89'156—dc22   2006047313

W. W. Norton & Company, Inc., 500 Fifth Avenue, New York, N.Y. 10110
www.wwnorton.com

W. W. Norton & Company Ltd., Castle House, 75/76 Wells St., London W1T 3QT

1 3 5 7 9 0 8 6 4 2

For my daughter, Lynne, my husband, Ray
and in loving memory of my son, John

Contents

Foreword

The revolution that is Family Therapy began almost 50 years ago. There was no explosion, commotion, or overturning of the status quo. Yet a revolution it was—beginning with the simple act of bringing family members into a therapy room at the same time. Having more than one person there inevitably changed the focus of treatment from what goes on *within* individual people to what goes on *among* people.

The stir created by this revolutionary practice has subsided as the insights of the family therapy movement have been integrated into mainstream psychotherapy. Many of the principles that emerged in the family therapy world have, however, lost their multiperson system importance. *The Family Therapy Networker* changed its name to *The Psychotherapy Networker*. "Family therapy" has become a standard modality of care on the list of every treatment plan for children and adolescents. The American Family Therapy Academy evolved its focus from ways of thinking about families, family processes, and how to tackle more challenging family problems, to larger social concerns such as political, racial, and social injustices, health care disparities, and intervention with victims of torture, terrorism, and mass murder. It can be argued that principles of family systems theory have informed these attentions, but the conviction that families are a source of health and are primary resources for treatment seems to have weakened. The Family Therapy revolution appears to have subsided into a modality—i.e., family therapy.

Having family members together in therapy does inform manualized approaches to family interventions that have been sold to state and local agencies attempting to make a difference with hard-to-treat populations (such as youth with substance abuse, individuals with chronic mental illness). Yet I believe that there is an inherent conflict between the systematic rules in a manual and the systemic process that unfolds while working with families.

Some of the directions taken by family therapy incorporate revolutionary contributions from Family Therapy and applies them in more conventional psychotherapy settings and larger systems. Multisystem therapy (MST) for example, has successfully applied principles of resourcefulness in families, schools, and peer systems to working with youth and substance abuse. Yet the application of MST to severely emotionally disturbed youth and their families has been less successful. More common practice is to include families in treatment to address their "pathological" influence on the identified patient. This practice ignores the essential contributions of the Family Therapy revolution and defines families as dangerous and toxic or weak and powerless, and therefore, needing to be "empowered" or "detoxified."

It is important and timely, therefore, to refresh our memories and our practices regarding the essence of the Family Therapy revolution. There were two fundamental initial features beyond inviting family members into the room: 1) a move from a linear view of behavioral causality to an appreciation of patterns in which behaviors occur; and 2) the view that families are the primary context of health.

I summarized these fundamentals when I articulated four "giant steps" when writing about "therapeutic innovations in child mental health" (Combrinck-Graham, 1990, pp. 12–13). The steps are:

1. *Working with different experiences of reality.* Bringing family members together highlights the fact that different people have different versions of the same situation. The giant step is to understand the meaning of these differences rather than trying to find a single true version of an event.
2. *Identifying how events are parts of patterns.* This giant step moves the focus of inquiry from *why* to *how* something works.
3. *A focus on competence.* This giant step shifts our focus from an investigation of pathology, labeling, and cataloguing liabilities to recognizing strengths and resources within the family and its own contexts.

4. *Defining mental health.* I found that most "mental health" professionals did not work with a definition of *mental health.* I offered my own, as the fourth giant step: "Mental health is found in a system that is organized for the benefit of its individual members" (1990, p. 13).

More recently I have incorporated a relationship to community in my definition of *mental health*: "The outcome of successful child development is an adult who is a contributing member of a community" (Combrinck-Graham, 2001, p. 613).

In *Families that Flourish: Facilitating Resilience in Clinical Practice,* Dorothy Becvar refreshes our memory about the extraordinary contributions of Family Therapy. To begin with, in describing families that flourish Becvar offers a characterization of families that transcends health care and mechanical lingo (e.g., health and sickness, function and dysfunction) and offers us an evocative and organic appreciation of the vitality and complexity of family life. In refreshing the family therapy lexicon, Becvar reviews and explains the developments—tracing, as with the revolutionary thinkers, the path from applying standard theory to family groups to the extraordinary differences that necessarily occurred when considering family systems—vertically through history and horizontally in the present.

In his 1972 book *The Fallacy of Understanding,* psychoanalyst Edgar Levenson identified a progression of three models governing thinking about psychological processes. The progression began at the turn of the 20th century with the mechanistic model. In the 1940s, 1950s, and 1960s, there was the communication model. In the 1960s and beyond the cybernetic model has became predominant. Becvar articulates the elaboration of the cybernetic model through modernistic and postmodern positions. She describes how the language not only changes from one model to another, but how, in the postmodern way of responding, language itself becomes the context of understanding and change.

Ivan Boszormenyi-Nagy, classified by Becvar as a modernist, once observed that his contextual therapy model never took hold in countries such as France, Italy, and Spain, where romance languages translated his key concepts of *trust* and *loyalty* into words that had a vastly different weight and meaning than in German-based languages (including English) in which it was conceived. This observation marked the beginning of the recognition of value in language. Later Paul Dell (1980), in contrasting the predicate-based Hopi language with the object-basis of most Western language, identified a fundamental challenge for "Hopi family therapists" working with "Aristotelian" object-based parents wanting to know what is wrong with their child (e.g. "What does he have?").

Becvar is patient in drawing distinctions while also acknowledging the value of theories and approaches that, if not foundations of Family Therapy, are certainly the springboards for the revolution. Her example as a writer, interpreter of the field, and through her clinical vignettes consistently exhibits her convictions that families can flourish and therapists can and should facilitate flourishing. In doing so, she affirms that Family Therapy is also flourishing.

Lee Combrinck-Graham, M.D.
Stamford, CT
March 2006

References

Combrinck-Graham, L. (1990). *Giant steps: Therapeutic innovations in child mental health.* New York: Basic.

Combrinck-Graham, L. (2001). Children in families in communities. *Child and Adolescent Psychiatric Clinics of North America, 10*(3), 613–624.

Dell, P. F. (1980). The Hopi family therapist and the Aristotelian parents. *Journal of Marital and Family Therapy, 6*(2), 123–130.

Levenson, E. (1972). *The fallacy of understanding.* New York: Basic.

Preface

My desire to work with families and to focus particularly on their strengths, as well as their potential for growth and positive change, has been basic to my professional orientation from the beginning, emerging out of several personal experiences prior to becoming a family therapist. The first of these experiences occurred in the mid-1970s when, as a recently divorced woman with two young children, I became aware of—and deeply resented—being considered a "broken" family. Despite my sadness at the ending of my marriage, I firmly believed that my children and I were still an intact family, albeit one without a husband/father who resided with us. And I was vehemently opposed to the assumption on the part of many that because of the divorce, my children would necessarily have problems.

A second influential experience occurred shortly after my divorce. I had taken a job in a school for children with learning disabilities. Many of the students had developed behavioral problems in addition to, or perhaps as a function of, their inability to read and write. While working in this school, I learned firsthand the frustrations of trying to help these young people become successful without also including their parents in the process. That is, much of the ground that was gained and the positive changes that occurred during school time often were not maintained by the children when they were at home; as a result, each day brought with it the general feeling of having to start anew.

At about the same time, a serendipitous event occurred. I was invited by the pastor of the church I was attending to become a coleader of Family

Clusters (Sawin, 1979, 1982). Family Clustering (Becvar, 1984b, 1984c) is an approach to working with groups of whole families, generally in the context of a church, with the goal of fostering development and enrichment. Although at the time I was very much a novice, it was in this arena that I had my first introduction to working with and helping other families. It was also in this context that I first came to understand how significant an emphasis on the strengths of individuals and families can be.

Although I did eventually receive some formal training to become a Family Cluster leader, it was not long before I realized that I needed to think about going to graduate school in order to fulfill a desire to become professionally qualified to do therapy with families. Subsequently, I pursued a master's degree in social work with an emphasis in family practice, followed immediately by completion of a Ph.D. in the area of family studies. I created my own multidisciplinary curriculum for my doctoral program, including course work in education, social psychology, social work, sociology and anthropology, and theology. Indeed, even then I felt instinctively that in order to be effective in my work, I would need to learn about, and be able to understand, families from many different perspectives. Fortunately, in addition to my formal graduate studies, I also had the opportunity to attend many workshops presented by the seminal theorists and clinicians in the field of family therapy. Today, I am licensed as both a marital and family therapist and as a clinical social worker.

Although immediately upon completion of my doctoral work I went into academia, having discovered a love for teaching during my graduate studies, I also began to practice privately. This is a pattern that has continued throughout my career, with the balance shifting over time almost equally between full-time teaching/part-time private practice, and full-time private practice/part-time teaching. I have found the combination to be extraordinarily useful, with each facet of my professional pursuits enriching the other. And as my life, both personal and professional, has unfolded, I have continued to enhance my knowledge about and understanding of families, focusing, for example, at various times on family therapy (Becvar & Becvar, 1999, 2006), spirituality (Becvar, 1997, 1998), and death, dying, and grief (Becvar, 2000a, 2000b, 2001), as well as on many other aspects of individual and family development (Becvar, 1985; Nichols, Nichols, Becvar, & Napier, 2001). Although I certainly don't feel that I have finished learning, I have reached a point at which it seems appropriate to synthesize how I have pulled together various segments of the knowledge I have gained and to describe my approach in a manner that, ideally, others may find helpful.

This book, therefore, represents an integration of many clusters of knowledge about families and their successful functioning, with the goal of creating a framework containing easily accessible information and useful suggestions for practice. The idea of writing a book on this topic evolved, in part, out of a desire to share with others what long experience as a teacher, researcher, and clinician has taught me about how to enhance my effectiveness as a family therapist. The project also was encouraged at various workshops, where I presented on the topic of facilitating resilience, by participants who repeatedly asked me when I was going to write "the book" about what I had shared. But above all, I wished to join those relatively few spokespersons who have provided a counterpoint to the tendency so common in our society to label negatively and to pathologize families and their members rather than find ways to understand them in context, focus on and access their strengths, and help them to become more successful.

Following this preface and a brief introduction, the rest of the book is divided into two sections. The first section on principles (Chapters 1–4) provides information relative to my theoretical orientation as well as basic knowledge I believe to be essential for working with families (e.g., the characteristics of families that flourish and the concept of resilience). Also included in this section are examples of and discussions about specific expressions of family resilience in response to a variety of challenging situations. The second section of the book on practice (Chapters 5–9) explores various ways to facilitate families' inherent capacity for resilience. Specific topics addressed include relevant practices derived from various therapeutic models; assessment, analysis, and perturbation with a solution focus; supporting a positive self-concept; encouraging effective parenting; and creating supportive contexts. Each chapter in this second section includes a case example to illustrate specific goals and related interventions. (No single client system is described anywhere in this book. All case examples are fictionalized composites of clients and the stories they have shared with me over the course of many years.) The book ends with a conclusion chapter in which I review what has gone before and offer closing reflections on facilitating resilience in clinical practice.

Regardless of the presenting problems, I believe that the effectiveness of the therapeutic process can be enhanced if we therapists focus not only on helping clients attain their desired solutions but also on supporting their ability to flourish as families. Thus, for me, every therapeutic encounter contains a focus on development and enrichment—in other words, the capacity for resilience. However, rather than telling family members how they should act, or what they should look like, the orientation I utilize shifts to a focus on cocreating with them a context in which they experience themselves as competent and successful. Throughout this book, therefore, there is an emphasis on process that parallels the attention given to content. As is explained further, resilience looks different for different families in different contexts, and there are many aspects that are appropriate to keep in mind when the ultimate goal is to help families flourish.

Acknowledgments

My gratitude goes first and foremost to the individuals, couples and families with whom I have had the privilege to work over the course of many years. From them I have learned much about the human spirit and the potential for resilience despite the many challenges with which they were faced. Theirs are the stories that have affirmed my belief in the importance of a focus on strengths, potentials, and the ability to flourish.

It is also essential to acknowledge how important has been the knowledge gained from the seminal theorists in the field of family therapy and related mental health professions as well as from contemporary researchers and clinicians. This body of work represents the foundation for many of the ideas shared in this book. I thus truly feel that I am standing on the shoulders of giants.

In terms of turning my ideas into a book, I am very grateful to all of the staff at Norton Professional Books, and particularly my editor, Michael McGandy. It was Michael who contacted me about writing a book, and who was willing to consider my topic rather than the one he had in mind. Having worked together for more than a year, I am very appreciative of the collegial relationship we have shared as well as all of the assistance and guidance he provided for me.

Finally, I wish to thank the members of my own little flourishing family. My husband, Ray devotes himself tirelessly to caring for and encouraging me, and I will never be able to thank him enough for all of his love and support. And we are both continually amazed, amused, and delighted by the gloriously resilient young woman who is my daughter, Lynne.

Families that Flourish

Introduction

As therapists work with families to support them in the achievement of their goals, while at the same time facilitating resilience, they must be able to access a broad body of information and knowledge regarding both families, in general, and families that flourish, in particular. First, they must understand the important role and function of families relative to the larger society. In addition, they must be familiar with the various kinds of situations that are likely to confront individuals and families as they evolve through time. They also must have knowledge about families with diverse structures, various ethnic backgrounds, and a variety of nontraditional forms—all topics to be discussed in some depth (Chapter 2).

As an integral part of their work, therapists are (ideally) aware of the variety of general processes that have been found both clinically and through research to characterize successful families. That is, in order to help families flourish, therapists need a solid sense of *what a flourishing family looks like*. For just as health in individuals is far more than the absence of illness, well-functioning, flourishing families are distinguished by specific dimensions that go far beyond the absence of dysfunction or pathology (Chapter 3). Consistent with this awareness, therapists recognize the particular importance of resilience, which is one of the most significant qualities characterizing families that flourish.

As will be described in much greater detail (Chapter 4), *resilience* refers to the ability of those who, even under highly stressful circumstances, are able to cope, rebound, and thrive. Resilience in families enables members to regain their balance following a crisis, and to continue to encourage and support one another as they deal with the necessary requirements for accommodation, adaptation, and, ultimately, healthy survival. In order for therapy to provide something more than assistance with only the immediate problem, it is important for therapists to cocreate with clients a context within which they are able to recognize their own strengths and potentials. Thus, clients are empowered not only to land on their feet following the current crisis, but also to better handle whatever challenges the future may bring.

To be successful in facilitating resilience, therapists must know and understand the specific traits and patterns found in resilient individuals and well-functioning families as they respond to a variety of life's challenges. That is, resilience evidences itself in unique ways relative to specific situations, many of which are summarized and discussed in the following chapters. Finally, all of this information must be integrated and find practical expression in a useful and effective manner, strategies for which are described and illustrated in Part II (Chapters 5–9). However, in addition to various clusters of knowledge, and before considering pragmatics, there must be a solid theoretical foundation. While in graduate school, mental health students typically are exposed to, and expected to assimilate, information regarding families and therapy. In addition, they generally have opportunities to work with clients while being supervised. However, translating general theoretical knowledge into a carefully thought-out and well-delineated personal framework for practice often represents a daunting challenge for those new to the field. And once out in practice, difficulties with the integration of new information and the utilization of new skills may continue. Unfortunately, the lack of a meaningful map may lead novice practitioners to a focus on techniques that are not well-grounded in theory or to the choice to become one-model-only devotees. In either case, therapists' ability to access and incorporate new knowledge, as well as to be helpful to clients, may be diminished.

The approach articulated in this book represents a map that allows for both theoretical integration and pragmatic expression. It is a meta-approach—that is, a story about stories (Becvar & Becvar, 1994b)—that is consistent with a postmodern, second-order cybernetics perspective (Becvar & Becvar, 2006), and it speaks as much to the level of process as it does to the level of content. This approach is an evolving framework for working with clients that allows for accommodation of new ideas and information as well as adaptation to changed circumstances and issues. Furthermore, it is an approach *for therapists* themselves that is isomorphic, or parallel, to the process of facilitating resilience in clients (see Chapter 1).

Perhaps the most basic principle on which this approach rests is recognition of the importance of an ethical, respectful stance toward clients. As every code of ethics in the mental health field specifies, the rights and dignity of each client system are to be acknowledged and respected. We as therapists are instructed to avoid value imposition, to support client autonomy, maintain appropriate boundaries, preserve confidentiality, and work within the limits of our competence. However, behaving in an ethical respectful manner also involves a great deal more for those who espouse a postmodern, second-order cybernetics perspective. From such a perspective we recognize that we can never have access to the truth in any absolute sense. As is explained further, we acknowledge self-reference, or our inevitable subjectivity, and the idea that the observer/ therapist is part of the observed/client system. Therefore, whatever the way the therapist sees and then describes regarding a client, the depiction says as much about the therapist as it does about the client. In other words, the story the therapist creates emerges from an interaction between the characteristics of the client system and the therapist's epistemology, or the frame of reference being used in the attempt to understand the client system and its characteristics. Put yet another way, what the therapist *believes* inevitably restricts and influences what the therapist *sees*. Accordingly, it is essential that therapists acknowledge the limits of their knowledge, noting that all they have are stories, some of which may be useful, and none of which necessarily represents the one *true* story.

From such a perspective it also is understood that there is no one right way for all people and families to function. That is, there is no "transcendent criterion of the correct" (Gergen, 1991, p. 111), no singular mold into which all should fit. Rather, we recognize that people and the families in which they live come in all shapes, sizes, and configurations. However, it is not the structure that is the deciding factor when considering the health of the family. Rather, it is the way the family is organized and the degree to which it operates to support the healthy development of the system and its members that become most significant. I am reminded of the movie *Mask*, which is based on a true story. In this movie a single mom (Cher) is rearing her only son (Eric Stoltz), who is dealing with an extremely disfiguring, ultimately terminal condition. Additional problems include the fact that Mom is addicted to drugs and alcohol and is estranged from her parents, and the son is subject to frequent bouts of debilitating headaches. Support for this family comes primarily from the members of a motorcycle gang, of which Mom is a member. This is hardly the ideal scenario one would choose to depict a well-functioning family. Nevertheless, there is incredible love and strength in this family system, and Mom does a remarkable job of parenting despite the personal challenges she faces on a daily basis. Indeed, in many ways this very nontraditional family epitomizes the characteristic of resilience.

Just as there is no one right way for people and families to be in terms of their structure, from a postmodern, second-order cybernetics perspective it is recognized that even though there may be an objective reality, we cannot know it because we, as observers, can perceive solely through our personal frames of reference. Thus, relative to what we can know, there is no one, absolute reality "out there," separate from the observer, and no problems that exist in isolation. Rather, as noted above, ours is understood as a storied reality. Accordingly, facts are replaced by perspectives, and both reality and problems are understood as emerging in the context of relationships as they are languaged, and thus cocreated, in a particular way. An ethical, respectful stance, therefore, requires that therapists beware of formulating stories that pathologize or that participate in creating problems where none previously were perceived.

Another important aspect of an ethical, respectful stance is the idea that both therapists and clients have particular kinds of expertise. Therapists bring to the therapeutic encounter various degrees of general knowledge about people and families, varieties of experience with different client systems, as well as many skills and perhaps much wisdom regarding the process of helping clients. At the same time, clients bring to the therapeutic encounter a great deal of personal wisdom, including knowledge about themselves, their lives, their challenges, their hopes and dreams. Thus it is essential that clients feel validated, that they are able to trust that their expertise is acknowledged and valued and can see that it is their goals rather than the goals of the therapist, or those inherent in various models, that define and influence the design of therapy.

Consistent with this orientation, therapy is viewed as providing a context for conversation, collaboration and the cocreation of new realities in which identified problems no longer are logical responses, or fit within the current structure. This approach does not deny the existence of very real problems, nor does it condone behaviors that harm others in any way. However, rather than focusing on pathology and problems, the emphasis is on articulating solutions and finding ways to achieve them. In order to do so, judgment in a pejorative sense is suspended, or held in abeyance, with all behavior understood as somehow making sense relative to the structure of the client system. Accordingly, the focus shifts to understanding the perhaps hidden logic of the current context, with change for clients equaling a change in context. In order to facilitate such a change, the therapist considers the perceptions, behaviors, and/or feelings of family members, offering questions, reflections, and suggestions as perturbations in an ongoing, recursive, dialogic process.

During the course of such therapeutic conversations, the ethical, respectful therapist is sensitive to what is and is not talked about, how things are languaged, and to the aspects of social control that may be an integral part of everyday conversations (e.g., who is speaking, where they are). Recognizing the privileged discourse that often dominates the therapy dialogue, the therapist is aware of and, as appropriate, comments upon additional topics of conversation that may be equally or more relevant for clients. Thus attention is given to, and the therapeutic process may include, a consideration of both unasked questions and unquestioned answers. For example, issues of the power implicit in various roles, such as those of client and therapist, or those of men and women, which previously might have remained unacknowledged, may become a topic of conversation. Similarly, the labels created by professionals to identify various behaviors (e.g., depressed, antisocial) may be discussed and perhaps deconstructed as they are described and understood as stories that may or may not be useful in terms of clients' abilities to understand themselves and attain their goals. What is more, the therapist becomes transparent, disclosing his or her thinking about what is going on or how he or she is "storying" the therapeutic process, rather than withholding his or her perspective as a private commentary or one to be shared only with other professionals.

Finally, the ethical, respectful therapist seeks to stay abreast of new information about individuals and families, focusing continually on upgrading his or her skills. I am a great believer in Bach's notion that "you teach best what you most need to learn" (1977, p. 60). Accordingly, this book represents an opportunity and an effort both to teach and to learn. In the succeeding chapters, information that I consider to represent essential knowledge about families and their functioning is discussed, and a theoretical framework for its application is provided. The meta-approach that is described offers one way to think about integrating information as well as about how to work with each unique family in ways that are appropriate for that family and its members. And, always, attention is given to the importance of helping families to flourish through a process in which resilience is facilitated.

PART I
Principles

CHAPTER ONE

Theoretical Orientation

More than 25 years ago, as I was just beginning my graduate studies with the goal of one day being able to work with families, I not only immersed myself in the world of social work, but I also took a course in the philosophy of the behavioral sciences. During this course I was introduced to the transcendental phenomenology of Edmund Husserl (1965) and the cybernetic epistemology of Gregory Bateson (1972). These two perspectives immediately resonated for me and have had a profound impact on the subsequent evolution of what I describe as a second-order cybernetics/postmodern theoretical orientation in therapy (Becvar & Becvar, 2006). Early on I learned about the importance of discerning and acknowledging the basic assumptions underlying one's perspective and of acting in a manner consistent with those assumptions. In addition, I became aware of the inevitability of subjectivity and self-reference, or the idea that whatever a person sees or says reveals as much about the observer as it does about that which is observed or described. Hence the need I feel to begin Part I with a delineation of my personal and professional frame of reference, which provides the foundation for all that is described in subsequent chapters.

Self-Referential Consistency

I learned about the transcendental phenomenology of Edmund Husserl (1965) from the perspective of a professor who had been a student of

French philosopher Paul Ricoeur (1981). The professor focused on a system of argumentation involving the identification of the basic assumptions upon which a given theory or perspective is based in order to distinguish the knowledge claims made by that theory or perspective as justifiable or not. Out of this study grew greater recognition on my part of the need for clarity and integrity relative to thought and action. For example, one may believe in the idea of an unconscious and certainly find the construct a useful one. At the same time, it is important to recognize that there is no way that anyone can claim, with absolute certainty, that an unconscious exists inasmuch as, by definition, it is unknowable (i.e., is unconscious). Rather, the most one can claim is that the concept regarding an unconscious provides a story that is potentially useful in a variety of situations.

A dilemma similar to that posed by the idea of an unconscious arises with the notion of a self-fulfilling prophesy. In order to know that a particular outcome was the result of a specific set of beliefs, we would have to be able to go back in time and see if another set of beliefs would, or would not, have led to the same set of circumstances. Because this is not possible, we cannot be certain that it was the beliefs or the prophesy that led to the experience in question. The validity of the explanation, therefore, is suspect. The analysis of many other comparable examples also would suggest the need for caution when making claims about what we call *knowledge* or *truth* in an absolute sense.

A process of analysis such as that suggested by transcendental phenomenology also is consistent with a postmodern viewpoint. In a similar manner, the latter perspective encourages the deconstruction of what have been called *facts* by identifying the assumptions, values, and ideologies upon which they rest. By doing so we are able to distinguish between what are and what are not valid knowledge claims.

As we assume such a stance consistently, we generally become aware of the appropriateness of holding on to our concepts rather lightly. Thus, for example, we may shift to a perspective that sees theories about human behavior as ways of explaining the phenomena we observe, often from a variety of perspectives, rather than ways of describing the one *true* reality, or the way people or families really live. We also are likely to acknowledge the need to consider ourselves and our constructions about life and living with skepticism and perhaps humor. Indeed, this line of thinking explains the choice I make to speak in terms of *stories* when describing theories or points of view. Such a choice serves as a reminder of the limits of certainty possible in relation to any concept or perspective as well as an implementation of my desire to be self-referentially consistent. I might add that this particular view includes the theoretical perspective that I am describing—which, as mentioned previously, also is just my story.

Pathologies of Epistemology

As noted, the creation of my theoretical perspective, or story, also was heavily influenced by Gregory Bateson. Like Husserl, Bateson (1972) emphasized the importance of self-referential consistency, or the prevention of what he referred to as "pathologies of epistemology." It was his belief that, above all, we must be conscious of the individual frame of reference, or personal epistemology, according to which we perceive phenomena, including the assumptions on which this frame of reference is based. Several conceptual pathologies were of particular concern for Bateson. A primary one involved the idea, held by many, that problems exist separate from those who define them as such. By contrast, from Bateson's perspective, it was essential that we recognize that problems do not exist "out there" but rather are created as we choose to label certain behaviors as problematic. One of my favorite illustrations relates to the way that little boys may be perceived in different contexts. That is, the adage that "boys will be boys" often permits and/or excuses actions out of school that in school are likely to be defined as symptoms of a behavior problem, perhaps attention-deficit hyperactivity disorder (ADHD). Similarly, the reading problems described in many societies would not, and do not, exist in cultures that depend on and value only the oral transmission of information, despite the fact that members of such cultures may be unable to read. In other words, problems exist in the eye of the beholder as the beholder defines phenomena as such.

Another pathology of epistemology described by Bateson, related to the above, equates the map with the territory. That is, the set of concepts one uses to describe a situation or support a position represents but one of many possible ways in which that situation may be understood or a position may be taken. Each description provides a framework that may enable one to make sense of, or describe, what is going on, although it is neither the same as, nor necessarily the truth about, what is going on. Although it certainly may be useful, such a description is recognized as a representation, or a map, rather than the thing itself. As this idea relates to therapy, we recognize the need to be wary of thinking that because the theory used to guide practice was effective with a particular client, it therefore described the essence of the client system with whom one was working. Similarly, it is also important to be sensitive to the fact that when the same theory does not prove useful with another client system, it is the theory that may be inappropriate and in need of revision rather than the client who is resistant or unmotivated.

Bateson also believed that a pathology of epistemology occurs when differences are defined in isolation, without reference to the relationship or the context of which they are a part. To explain, all relationships are comprised of logical complements, both of which must be considered when one seeks to define and comprehend either. For example, understanding light or sound or joy requires knowledge of the respective logical complements, darkness, silence, and sadness. The description of each aspect has meaning only in relation to its complement. In the same way, as we describe another person, we also are describing our relationship with that person; that is, the observed requires an observer, and the observer is part of the observed. To say that our clients are resistant speaks as much about the way we were with them when "resistance" occurred as it does about the way they were with us at a particular time. Indeed, all we really can know or describe about others is how they were with us as a complement to the way we were with them, as we interacted in a given context. What is more, as we behave differently in different settings, we are likely to become different people. Thus, for example, the roles of teacher and students complement each other in the context of a classroom setting and are defined by particular sets of behaviors consistent with that context. However, if my students and I meet at an informal social gathering, we are likely to experience each other very differently as we all assume and share the roles of guests and party-goers.

Given the bilateral nature of interpersonal relationships, or the mutual influence and shared creation of experiences just described, Bateson also believed that additional related pathologies of epistemology included the assumptions that (1) control, in general, and unilateral control, in particular, is possible and (2) that we can achieve change by addressing only part of a system. Indeed, illustrations of the dilemmas created in interpersonal as well as larger social relationships as a function of such assumptions abound. That is, when individuals define a problem in isolation and then attempt to change the other without changing themselves, they generally find themselves participating in a set of interactions that at best maintain, and at worst may escalate, an already difficult situation. To illustrate, if inattention is perceived as a problem by one spouse, blaming the other spouse and trying to get him or her to pay more attention without awareness of the blamer's part in the creation of the inattention he or she is perceiving is likely to be less than effective. Similarly, efforts to control the problem of increasing violence among young children without a long hard look, and concomitant attempts to create change, at the level of the society within which this problem is occurring, probably are doomed to failure. In both instances, trying to focus only on a part of a complex system is to fail to recognize that interconnection is the rule, that difference speaks to relationship, and that effective change requires recognition of both.

As another example, consider the side effects of various drugs hurriedly acknowledged following each advertisement on TV or contained (in very small print) as part of the instructions for their use. A drug is prescribed and taken to deal with a particular symptom, perhaps depression. The drug, however, has the potential to affect a person in a variety of ways beyond the reduction of depression (e.g., cause an increase in appetite leading to weight gain, which may increase the depression). The problem is not the drug but how we have chosen to perceive it, defining as a side effect whatever it legitimately does that we do not want it to do. Indeed, a drug, like a person, cannot have just one effect given the essential interdependence and connection in what has been described as a constantly conjoined universe (Bronowski, 1978).

Finally, Bateson noted that because we cannot get outside of ourselves or our frames of reference, "we shall never be able to claim final knowledge of anything whatsoever" (1979, p. 27). The only bad epistemology or personal worldview, he stated, is one that isn't aware of its own existence. This position may seem a bit extreme, given that it certainly is possible to subscribe to a frame of reference that does not serve us well. However, what he was attempting to emphasize was the need to recognize the inevitability of subjectivity and the fact that our observations are always filtered through the lens of our own epistemology.

Further stating that mind and nature were inseparable, given that we can only know reality as a function of our perceptions, or mental processes, Bateson suggested that although what we say may be true, we cannot assert it to be so in an absolute sense. He also was one of the earliest to translate into the behavioral sciences the idea that we participate in the creation of our reality as we attempt to observe it. From such a perspective, the therapist is understood to be part of the therapeutic process, participating with clients in the cocreation of realities from within the system.

Systems Theory/Cybernetics

The assumptions that Bateson (1972, 1979) described are fundamental to what now may be understood as a second-order cybernetics perspective, which represents a radical alteration in our traditional ways of thinking about and working with people. Given that the distinction between first-order and second-order cybernetics is extremely significant, further discussion seems warranted. Although often unrecognized, it is my belief that second-order cybernetics represents the completion of the paradigm shift (Kuhn, 1970) begun when various therapists working in the mental health arena switched from a concern with the individual and his or her internal processes to a consideration of the interactions between people and the families in which they live.

Utilizing the concepts of systems theory and cybernetics, many of the early pioneers in the realm of family therapy began to emphasize the ideas of recursion, or circular causality and mutual influence, as well as feedback and interdependence. With this change in orientation came awareness of the need to think relationally and holistically, to consider the larger context in which behaviors occur. Rather than continuing the traditional focus on intrapsychic processes and content, therapists became more concerned with relational patterns and processes. However, as initially introduced and embraced, the attempt to observe and understand family dynamics, although quite revolutionary, did not include awareness or acknowledgment of the role of the observer; that is, the person trying to understand and help the family. Early systemic family therapists generally worked with clients from a modernist theoretical position that placed them outside the family and focused on their assessments of what was going on inside the family. In this process they employed such concepts as rules and boundaries, positive and negative feedback, morphostasis/morphogenesis, openness/closedness, entropy/ negentropy, equifinality/equipotentiality, communication/information processing, and relationship and wholeness, as they attempted to understand how a family was functioning. However, the models they used tended to be quite mechanistic, the reason frequently given by family therapists who have chosen to reject a systemic perspective (Anderson & Goolishian, 1986; Hoffman, 1993). Indeed, from my perspective, it was not until the definitions of such first-order concepts had evolved or were replaced by those more consistent with the perspective of second-order cybernetics that the paradigm shift of systems theory and cybernetics truly had been completed.

To briefly review the concepts consistent with and characteristic of the perspective of second-order cybernetics (Becvar & Becvar, 2006), we begin with the idea of *autopoiesis* (Maturana & Varela, 1987). This concept was defined to acknowledge the process of self-creation engaged in by all systems, which are understood to be organizationally closed. In other words, when a therapist is working with a family he or she is considered to be part of the system and whatever they create, they create together. Given the closed status of this system, the idea of inputs from without is replaced by the notion of perturbations from within, with all feedback understood as negative, or indicative of system-maintaining behavior at the level of the whole. In other words, although change at one level may occur and be accommodated by the system (positive feedback), such change operates in the service of maintenance of the larger system (negative feedback). According to the concept of *structural determinism*, we understand that the limits of what a system can or cannot do are defined by its structure, and that whatever it does is logical to its structure and thus makes sense for that system. When systems and their members are structured such that they are able to coexist comfortably with each other and their environment, we speak of *structural coupling*. The concept of *non-purposeful drift* refers to the ongoing processes of perturbation and compensation within and between systems, with change occurring as a function of responses to changes in a context for whose creation the systems involved share responsibility. As interconnectedness and mutual influence are thus assumed, we speak of an *epistemology of participation,* with recognition of the degree to which observer and observed are intertwined. Furthermore, rather than a universe, reality is understood as a multiverse comprised of many equally valid, observer-dependent realities. Finally, as living systems, it is understood that we operate in *consensual domains* that are generated through structural coupling in the context of a common language system.

Given such concepts, a cornerstone of a second-order cybernetics perspective is the idea of interdependence, that we all are connected and interact in an ongoing process of recursion, or mutual influence and feedback. As one who embraces such a perspective, my focus, therefore, is on relationships and the patterns of interaction characteristic of these relationships. Whether the client system includes an individual, a couple, a family, or a larger system, I am thinking relationally, attempting to understand people relative to their context rather than in isolation. Consistent with my focus on patterns, process becomes more salient than content in terms of considering human interaction. In other words, I would not think of you as being a certain kind of person; rather, I would attempt to understand the way you are with me as I am with you, in the context of our relationship in a particular place and at a particular time. Context includes who is present, where we or they are, and how each person views what is transpiring. Furthermore, I see therapeutic interaction as one that occurs within a system whose boundary is unbroken, with no reference to an outside environment and within which the observer is assumed to be part of the observed. Thus, I include an awareness of myself as a participant in whatever occurs, including my assessments of clients and their behaviors.

All of the above ideas and concepts support a stance that is consistent with the notion that reality is inevitably subjective, that what a person believes influences what that person will see and therefore how he or she will behave. A basic assumption of this position is that the reality that each person experiences is constructed through the process of observing that perceived reality. Given that each family member has his or her own view, and thus experience, of the family, there are therefore as many "families" as there are family members. And the perspective of the therapist adds an additional story about, or experience of, the family.

From such assumptions flow the awareness that ultimate truth is not accessible to us. Rather, a fundamental paradox of existence is that although we may assume that "truth" exists, we must accept that what we know may or may not be the truth in an absolute sense. Given that we cannot know that what we know is true in any absolute sense, the concept of "theoretical relativity," that is, thinking in both/and rather than either/or terms, is useful. I believe that all perspectives contain some degree of truth and that the crucial issue is the utility of a particular perspective, which can be decided only in relation to context. Therefore, I feel free to pick and choose from a variety of theories, depending on what I believe might be most helpful for each unique client system at a particular point in time.

In other words, I do not reject the classical, more modernist theories of family therapy and subscribe only to those created with a second-order, postmodern awareness. Rather, I assume a postmodern stance and also feel free to incorporate ideas and concepts from a wide variety of models. Thus I believe in the importance of possessing knowledge and understanding of a variety of family therapy approaches, both modernist and postmodernist. Indeed, I believe that therapists' ability to work effectively with families is enhanced to the extent that they understand the evolution of the field of family therapy and are able to make recourse to the vast amount of information provided by its seminal thinkers and contributors (Becvar & Becvar, 2006). In addition, the theories available from related fields may be a rich resource, often providing important and useful information.

Postmodernism

It is my belief that the assumptions of second-order cybernetics that I have just described, as well as the behaviors that flow from them, are quite consistent with what we think of as a postmodern perspective. Postmodernists also take the position that reality is inevitably subjective and that human beings dwell in realities that are constructed through the act of observation. In other words, what we believe influences what we see, which influences how we behave, which influences or participates in the creation of the reality that we experience, which influences what we believe and thus see, and so on. Therefore, each of us creates and lives in a slightly different reality. This idea is perhaps best illustrated by the fact that siblings generally describe the family in which they grew up in very different ways. Indeed, with a postmodern awareness we may say that they did experience, and thus grew up in, different families, despite the fact that all were living under the same roof. Similarly, couples often have very different experiences of, or stories about, the same events. Rather than trying to discern whose view is right or wrong, we recognize that each person's view is true and valid for that person. The view that there is one right way that all people, couples, or families should function is replaced by the notion that such "totalizing discourses" (White & Epston, 1990) may be demeaning and disrespectful if utilized without consideration of their appropriateness for specific clients. Thus, instead of acting according to the role of a social engineer who attempts to help all clients fit a particular model, the therapist/social scientist assumes a more collegial, nonexpert role in terms of helping people get where they want to go. This they do, at least in part, through a focus on language.

Those more involved with the *social constructionist* arm of postmodernism attempt to understand the socialization processes by which people learn to speak and behave in accepted ways. Out of such a focus has come recognition that each of us is born into, and assimilates, preexisting forms of language in a culturally created linguistic system. In the process of learning to speak in accepted ways, individuals simultaneously adopt the shared values and ideology of their particular language system. That is, their words express the conventions, symbols, and metaphors of their particular group. We now understand that people cannot speak in a language separate from that of their community. Indeed, I experienced a striking illustration of this phenomenon several years ago while teaching in what was for me a very different context.

While in Singapore, where I stayed for a month, I was the instructor for a 1-week intensive family therapy class attended by professional social workers. The class was comprised of members of all three ethnic groups indigenous to Singapore—East Indians, Malaysians, and Chinese—each of whom had a primary language and also had learned English more or less well as a second, required language. Early in the week, a young man had emerged as the "class clown," speaking out freely and frequently making very funny comments. His family was Chinese, he had completed his undergraduate degree in the United States, and he spoke English fluently. Interestingly, however, when we came to the topic of social constructionism and the role of language, this young man shared with us the fact that if the class had been conducted in Mandarin, his native tongue, he never could have behaved as he had throughout the week. He said that much more formal behavior would have been required, consistent with the values of his culture and its language, although he had not really thought about it until we began discussing the process of socialization within a particular language system. It is this sort of process that is the particular focus of study for social constructionists.

Those more involved with the *constructivist* arm of postmodernism focus on each individual's utilization of language as the means by which the world comes to be known and is simultaneously constructed. Once again, the idea of *minds* and *objects* as separate is deconstructed: If we can only know reality via our perceptions, then whatever we perceive is recognized as a function of our mental processes, or mind, and thus the two are inseparable. Mind, therefore, is understood as *nonlocal*, as unbounded by skin; it is universal and empowering of all creatures and things (Bateson, 1979). Consistent with this orientation, each person is understood as having a view, or story, about him- or herself, about others in his or her world, about relationships, about family, and about the world, in general. Together, these views, or stories, participate in the creation of the reality experienced by each individual. According to Mair (1988):

> Stories are habitations. We live in and through stories. They conjure worlds. We do not know the world other than as story world. Stories inform life. They hold us together and keep us apart. We inhabit the great stories of our culture. We live through stories. We are lived by stories of our race and place. It is this enveloping and constituting function of stories that is especially important to sense more fully. We are, each of us, locations where the stories of our place and time become partially tellable. (p. 127)

As the function of stories and their participation in the creation of reality is recognized, the emphasis in therapy shifts to an awareness of the story that the therapist is telling him- or herself about the client as well as of what the client may be telling him- or herself about the process. The beauty of such awareness is that if the story the therapist is telling him- or herself about a client, with its attendant suggestions for understanding and intervening/perturbing, does not seem to be working, he or she has the option of searching for a story that might provide a better fit. Likewise, if at some point the process seems to be stuck, the therapist must consider him- or herself as well as the client when attempting to facilitate greater movement. Clients also may be encouraged to consider the degree to which the stories they are telling themselves about other family members as well as about events in their world may be influencing what they are seeing and thus how they are behaving. Indeed, according to Howard, life may be characterized as the "stories we live by"; psychopathology may be defined as "stories gone mad"; and psychotherapy may be understood as "exercises in story repair" (1999, p. 194). Thus, an important focus of therapy may be that of helping clients to rethink their stories, or their perspectives, with an emphasis on *reauthoring* their lives (White & Epston, 1990).

Given a postmodern orientation that is inclusive of the social constructionist as well as the constructivist emphases, it also is important to recognize that both the self and the problems individuals experience take shape and have meaning in the context of specific relationships. As explained above, problems exist in the eye of the beholder; that is, as they are perceived as such by particular individuals at a particular time. What is more, the perceptions of each person are expressed through the language of the consensual domain, or context, within which these relationships occur. Hence the dissonance or tension that often exists between therapists and involuntary clients, for example: The clients do not perceive a problem, whereas the therapists (and the mandating agents) do.

As therapists attempt to help find solutions to the dilemmas their clients are experiencing, whether perceived as such by the clients or others in their world, therapists recognize that there are no decontextualized individuals or problems. With this awareness, the focus shifts from individuals to relationships—and the significance of the coconstruction of problems and proposed solutions, and of respect for individual differences, rises to the forefront of therapists' attention. Accordingly, the process of dialogue is the means by which clients expand their stories; that is, those systems of meaning that define their world as well as their experience of it. An ongoing exchange of thoughts, feelings, and beliefs allows personal histories and worldviews to be articulated, questioned, deconstructed, and reconstructed in the search for solutions to the problems clients are experiencing. And always, throughout this process, the orientation is toward helping people get where they want to go with a recognition of and respect for the expertise that each person brings to the shared conversations.

Development and Enrichment

As my theoretical framework has evolved over time, I have maintained a recognition of the role of developmental issues and the significance of a focus on enrichment that, as noted in the Preface, emerged early in my professional life. Consequently, my basic orientation also is informed by theories of individual and family development (Carter & McGoldrick, 1980, 1988; Nichols, Nichols, Becvar, & Napier, 2001), which are discussed more fully in Chapter 2. For example, I acknowledge that each individual and each family is engaged in an ongoing process of evolution and development that influences, and is influenced by, the movement of each person or system through the life cycle. Each developmental theory, or story, is understood not as a map of how people necessarily are or should be at a particular stage in life, but as providing potentially useful information that may enable the therapist to have greater sensitivity to, and thus understanding of, the clients with whom he or she is working. Indeed, I attempt to integrate a variety of developmental perspectives in a manner that enables me to get the broadest picture possible of the clients with whom I am working. For example, utilizing the "dynamic process model of the family life cycle" (Becvar & Becvar, 2006) enables me to view the members of a family in terms of the stage of individual development of each member from any one of a number of perspectives, the stage of marriage of the couple, and the stage of the family life cycle characterizing the system at a particular point in time. Various developmental perspectives that offer different windows through which to view individuals and/or families include those focused on cognitive (Piaget, 1955) or moral (Gilligan, 1982; Kohlberg, 1981) development. I also integrate and utilize a variety of theories that construe human development as a process of meaning making and reality construction (Becvar, 2000c; Kegan, 1982; Moshman, 1994), perspectives consistent with a postmodernist orientation.

Whatever developmental models or theories inform my thinking, however, a primary issue for me is contextual awareness and sensitivity. Thus, in addition to general theories about individuals and families, it also is important to be aware of the impact of variations in such dimensions as ability, ethnicity, gender, structure, and spirituality or religion. Indeed, each of these dimensions may have an influence on, or be influenced by, individual and family development issues and challenges, both expected and unexpected, as well as by other aspects of family dynamics. They also may provide information about strengths and appropriate ways to focus on enrichment.

For example, one of the strengths of many African-American families is an extensive kin network that provides both economic and emotional support for its members (Billingsley, 1968; Gutman, 1976; Hill, 1971; Martin & Martin, 1975; McAdoo, 1980). Awareness of this potential resource may enhance the therapist's ability to help an African-American single-parent mother, who is working full time and going to school, to provide appropriate supervision for her children. Thus they may explore together the possibilities for assistance within the client's extended family. This might include a request for financial assistance, inviting a responsible family member to join the household, sending one or more of the children to live with grandparents or other blood or "fictive" kin, or moving to be nearer family members.

Relative to enrichment, I have long operated in a manner consistent with the notion that each system is comprised of a finite amount of energy (Becvar & Becvar, 1994a). Therefore, the more that energy is devoted to positive interactions and experiences, the less energy there is available for negative interactions and experiences. A corollary to this concept is the idea that a happy, healthy family is one in which happy, healthy, meaningful experiences are prevalent. Accordingly, to foster enrichment I am likely to recommend various activities as a means of generating energy to solve the problems with which clients have presented in therapy. For example, I might suggest that couples spend time alone together on a daily basis, doing something both would experience as fun. I might suggest whole family outings or one-on-one time between a parent and child at bedtime. Indeed, the creation and revision of family-based rituals may be an important aspect of helping families. However, although the possibilities in this realm are seemingly endless, always there must be a contextual sensitivity and awareness of the degree to which such suggestions are appropriate, given the various cultural dimensions mentioned previously.

Process of Change

Added to the theoretical mix are my knowledge and beliefs about therapist perspective and behavior. I see myself as participating in a pragmatic process grounded in the assumption that change equals a change in context, as described by Watzlawick, Weakland, and Fisch (1974). I therefore subscribe to the notion that problems become embedded within, and are maintained by, the context of attempted solutions. Consistent with the four-step process of change (Watzlawick et al., 1974), therapists first request that clients define the problem they are experiencing in clear and concrete terms. They then request information from clients regarding what they already have tried as part of their effort to resolve the problem. The next step in the process is absolutely essential: Clients are asked to define the changes they desire in clear and concrete terms. Therapists then may begin to focus on helping clients attain their goals by providing information about new and different options for perceiving and behaving that they might consider. As therapists engage in this process, they recognize that change may be either first order or second order in nature.

A first-order change effort occurs within a system, according to the current rules of the system, which itself remains unchanged. It is exemplified by a "change from one behavior to another within a given way of behaving" (Watzlawick et al., 1974, p. 28). For example, a wife is frustrated because her husband doesn't help with household chores to the extent that she would like. Her repeated requests for assistance are met with anger on his part about her lack of understanding of what he does do and a perception that she is nagging. As the wife becomes increasingly frustrated, she decides to change her tactics and stop asking for help, although her frustration continues to be expressed in her overall attitude toward her husband. This change in tactics is an attempt at first-order change. However, although the husband is aware of his wife's frustration, he continues to be angry with her, refuses to provide further assistance, and nothing changes. The spouses are now stuck because they do not have a rule for changing the rules according to which they have been operating.

Although some logical, first-order change strategies (e.g., asking someone to do something) may be effective, in many instances, they do not produce the desired effect: The husband, as we have just seen, does not respond any differently to his wife's silence than he did to her requests for help. The silence is an opposite behavior that equals more of the same—and more of the same, at least in this case, is not helpful. To illustrate further, yelling back at someone who is yelling at you probably will not solve the problem at hand. Similarly, ignoring the person who is doing the yelling—an opposite behavior—probably will not solve the problem either. In fact, it may make the problem worse. In cases such as these, the attempted solution becomes problematic and second-order change may be necessary for solution.

The focus now shifts to the attempted solution and to the consideration that a change in context may require a response that is illogical in relation to the current rules of a relationship in which members have defined themselves as yeller/yeller or yeller/ignorer. Such an illogical response would allow new behaviors to occur and would signify a change in the system itself. For example, if instead of continuing to yell back, the husband responds to his wife's yelling by standing on his head, the rules of the game are broken and the pattern according to which yelling was being maintained is changed. Indeed, the wife probably will not be able to continue to yell for very long and is likely to begin to respond to her husband in a different manner, just as he responded very differently to her.

Strategies that fall into the second-order change category have been compared to the leap of imagination experienced in moments of creativity. That is, they require a response that is illogical in the current context and thus looks paradoxical or crazy when considered within the framework of the existing rules. Although not all change needs to be second-order to be effective, there are many instances in which it offers the only hope of solution. According to Watzlawick and colleagues (1974):

> A system which may run through all its possible internal changes (no matter how many there are) without effecting a systemic change, i.e., second-order change, is said to be caught in a *Game Without End*. It cannot generate from within itself the conditions for its own change; it cannot produce the rules for the change of its own rules. (p. 22)

Consistent with systems theory and cybernetics, which I see as "co-extensive" (Beer, 1974, p. 2), the key to understanding problem formation and resolution from such a perspective is the awareness of the reciprocal nature of behavior as well as of the importance of the context according to which behavior is defined and has particular meaning. Such awareness leads inevitably to the realization that anyone who is part of a context that defines behavior, places blame, and attempts to effect change within the rules of the context, also is a part of the problem rather than of the solution (Haley, 1976). It thus seems more useful to focus on and attempt to help clients achieve their desired solutions with a related goal of helping them to flourish through the facilitation of resilience.

Conclusion

Rather than operating according to a set agenda or a specific theoretical model of therapy, I endeavor to work in a manner that is consistent with the metatheoretical perspective delineated in this chapter. I therefore attempt to respond in the moment in ways that seem most appropriate for each client system, seeing each individual, each couple, and each family as unique. I also focus on understanding people relatively rather than substantively, with consistent consideration of the larger context. More important than the strategies or techniques I may use is my orientation—my way of thinking about, being with, and helping clients to cocreate a change in context.

For me, self-reflection is an essential aspect of such a therapeutic process. Given my assumptions regarding subjectivity—that believing is seeing, that my personal framework or story influences my perceptions—I ask myself questions such as "What am I telling myself about this client?" or "What other stories/theories might I tell myself?" In other words, I am concerned with the kind of influence my perceptions are having on the way things are unfolding, and I attempt to be sensitive to the possibility that a change in perception may be useful in moving the process along.

Further, as I seek to be sensitive to and acknowledge the influence of the observer (myself) on the observed (my clients), to recognize reciprocity and mutual influence, I consider such questions as "How would my having a different story/theory change what I am seeing?" or "How might the client respond differently to my new story/theory?" Thus, I am trying to remain aware of the ways in which my current story may be limiting my ability to understand clients, and how another perspective might be more useful.

Believing that in therapy I am taking part in the cocreation rather than the discovery of realities, I also might reflect on queries such as "Can I recognize how I am participating in creating problems?" or "Can I see how I am participating in creating solutions?" I attempt to be aware of

(1) the issues on which I focus as well as (2) the metaphors I choose to use, or the way I "language" a particular situation. For I believe that all of these considerations may be crucial to the way a client sees, and thus experiences, self and/or situation.

As I attempt to act in a manner consistent with the behaviors desired, I might consider, for example, questions such as "What kind of response would I like to have from the other person?" and "What behaviors on my part would be logical to the responses I desire?" Furthermore, I might communicate to my clients the utility to be found from such an awareness, as well as the ways in which a similar awareness also might be meaningful for them. Indeed, doing so may bring recognition of the bilateral nature and mutual influence that are characteristic of relationships.

To summarize, my overall stance is one of respect for those with whom I am working, as well as curiosity about their lives and what they would experience as meaningful. This stance includes a heightened sensitivity to mutual influence and the inevitability of subjectivity (i.e., all perceptions are subjective experiences). Consideration of questions regarding *what* is going on and *how* problems are being maintained replaces the need to ask *why* or look for causes. More important than context is process, as I seek to help clients achieve their desired solutions, at the same time keeping in mind all of the aspects that I see as essential to helping families flourish. With these ideas as foundation, we move next to a consideration of families in all of their complexity.

CHAPTER TWO

Families

As our focus shifts to an in-depth consideration of families, we first must understand the role and importance of the family—how completely intertwined it is with society, that each is essential for the existence of the other. As sociologist Claude Levi-Strauss noted, "Society belongs to the realm of culture while the family is the emanation on the social level of those natural requirements without which there could be no society and indeed no mankind" (1956, p. 284). Indeed, it is the family that has the major responsibility for the socialization of young people, the transmission from one generation to the next of the norms and values of the society of which it is a part (Lasch, 1975). What is more, it is the family that provides the primary context of support for both the formation of identity (Weigert & Hastings, 1977) and the emotional well-being of its members (Glasser & Glasser, 1970). And it is the family that provides a home base (Abbott, 1981), Lasch's "haven in a heartless world" (1979).

According to Patterson (2002b), the family can be understood as performing four core functions as it serves both individual family members and society. The first of these, family formation and membership, provides individuals with a sense of belonging, with a personal and social identity, and with meaning and direction for life, and, at the same time, serves society by controlling reproduction and assuring continuation of the species. With its second core function, economic support, the family meets the basic needs of individual members for food, shelter, clothing, and other resources necessary to facilitate growth and development. The society is served to the degree that healthy individuals are able to contribute in meaningful ways and are in need of fewer public resources. The third core function—nurturance, education, and socialization—refers to the family's support for the physical, psychological, social, and spiritual development of both children and adults, as well as its role in instilling social norms and values. The family thus prepares and socializes children for productive adult roles in society, supports productive adult members, and controls antisocial behavior, thereby protecting the society from harm. The fourth core function of the family, protection of vulnerable members (i.e., individual members who are young, ill, disabled, or otherwise in need of care), minimizes public responsibility for the care of vulnerable or dependent individuals. It is certainly little wonder that Zimmerman designated the family as "the primary resource for most individuals and society as well" (1979, p. 457).

However, although simultaneously described as "the most cherished institution of our civilization" (Frankel, 1963, p. 3), the family also has long been the object of considerable debate. Although we in this country are not alone in this regard, through the years the United States has had its share of contributors to ongoing conversations about the family. According to Abbott, writing more than two decades ago (1981),

> [Alexis de] Tocqueville observed [during a visit in the 1840s] that there seemed to be an American obsession with reevaluating and remodeling the family. Those who offer guidelines for defining family relationships (from Judge Ben Lindsay to Margaret Mead, from John Noyes to Gay Talese and Nancy Friday, from the Grimké sisters to Betty Friedan) are earnestly discussed by the American public. (p. x)

Similar discussions by the American public continue today in political debates, in the professional literature, and in the media. According to one source,

> Today, no institution elicits more contentious debate than "the American family." On one side are those who argue that "the family" has been seriously degraded by the movement away from marriage and traditional gender roles. . . . On the other side are those who view family life as amazingly diverse, resilient, and adaptive to new circumstances. . . . (Casper & Bianchi, 2002, p. 1)

As the above observation illustrates, one of the recurring themes in debates about the family is the consideration of whether or not it is in crisis, whether it is breaking down or merely in transition. Although the former view has tended to prevail in the public discourse (Featherstone, 1976; Casper & Bianchi, 2002), the same statistics often have been used to support both positions. Various trends cited include great increases in divorce, in nontraditional family forms, in the age at which individuals choose to marry or have children, in the numbers of couples who choose to remain childless, in women in the workplace, in juvenile crime, in the rate of illegitimacy, in family abuse, and in teenage suicide. Also noted are decreases in the birthrate and thus in the size of the family.

Given all of these well-documented patterns, there is no question that the family has changed. As described by a life insurance company:

> Its official: There's no longer anything typical about the "typical" American family. According to the latest census figures, 38 percent of American children are being raised outside the traditional two-parent family. Gone are the days when mom, dad and a couple of kids were the norm. Instead, the definition of family now embraces many different configurations, including, but not limited to: step-parents, single parent households, adoptive parents, same sex marriages with and without kids, foster parents, grandparents or aunts and uncles caring for children, and adult children living with and caring for their parents. (New Solutions for Non-Traditional Families Facing Financial Concerns, 2005, p. 1)

Given the reality of these diverse family patterns, many continue to lament the loss of the traditional nuclear family. However, whether such changes are necessarily good or bad is debatable. For some—for example, members of the Alliance for Marriage—these patterns are indicative of the declining strength of the American family, which therefore has been deemed the most important issue of the new millennium (Boldt, 2000). For others, perceived positive outcomes include significant advancements in the areas of gender equality in families, as well as "individual autonomy and tolerance toward a diversity of personal and family behaviors," with "large and relatively stable fractions of young people believing that marriage and family life are important and planning marriage and the rearing of children" (Thornton & Young-DeMarco, 2001, p. 1009).

Consistent with the latter perspective, I prefer to view the many and continual changes in families as indicators of healthy evolution and growth that are logical responses to changes in the larger context. As we all know well, recent decades have witnessed monumental advances in technology, as a function of which we now live in an increasingly expanded and complex global society. For example, we are able to communicate instantly with people anywhere in the world and have a much broader access to information about the life and daily events of people in countries of whose existence we might not even have been aware just a few decades ago. In addition, as medical science has revolutionized our ability to overcome illness, both greater life expectancy and the tendency of individuals to stay youthful longer have had remarkable impacts on every aspect of society. And these are just a few of the changes that came with us as we entered the 21st century.

The following five demographic trends have all had an impact on, and thus have participated in the creation of the current characteristics of the American family:

1. The delay in forming marriages, increasing the time adults spend outside marriage, often living in their parents' homes, with friends or with unmarried partners
2. The increase in heterosexual cohabitation, either as a precursor or alternative to marriage or as an alternative to living alone, combined with the growing acknowledgment of same sex cohabitation and concerns of gay and lesbian families
3. The growth in single parenting due to widespread divorce (and, more recently, a growing tendency for births to occur outside marriage as marriages are postponed) and the increasing number of years adults and children spend outside of married-couple families
4. The steady increase in women's labor force participation, especially among married women, in the second half of the 20th century and the accompanying decline in the one-wage-earner, two-parent family (what some refer to as the traditional family)
5. Delayed and declining fertility and declining mortality resulting in fewer children, smaller families, and also a lengthening of life, adding to the time adults spend "postchildren," which fueled the growth in married couples without children and elderly who increasingly live independently, apart from their children or extended kin. (Casper & Bianchi, 2002, pp. 7–8)

Given the systemic notion that all behaviors fit, or are logical to context, it makes perfect sense to me that the complexity of family life has increased so drastically. In a similar manner, because problems such as violence and poverty remain unsolved at a societal level, the persistence of these problems at the level of the family also is not surprising. However, as I recognize the mutual influence of the society on the family and the family on society, rather than attempting to find fault or lay blame, my attention shifts to a search for solutions. That is, if our goal is to help or to strengthen families (and thus perhaps society), the potential for success is much greater with a consideration of what works as opposed to our traditional focus on what doesn't work (i.e., problems and pathology) (Combrinck-Graham, 1990). For just as there always have been families with problems, we could not know of their existence except by contrast with those that have been successful. These are the families that, however quietly, continue to flourish.

However, when we begin to consider the incredible number of factors that impinge upon and influence the creation and ongoing evolution of a family, we are faced with the inevitable awareness not only that each family is unique but also that full understanding of any family, including our own, simply is not possible. Each family has its own set of developmental trajectories and distinctive experiences, both for the individual members and for the family as a whole. In addition, as has been noted several times, there are wide variations in the forms and structures into which families may organize themselves, with each type characterized by its particular combination of issues, tasks, and challenges. Further complicating the picture, families also differ in their "cultural histories, ethnic identities, bonds of kinship, patterns of residence, forms of lineage, intergenerational relationships, socioeconomic characteristics, and an array of institutionalized attitudes and beliefs" (Wilkinson, 1999, p. 15).

Although this complexity may seem daunting, it also may enable us as therapists and social scientists to remain modest in our claims of knowledge about families. What is more, awareness of this complexity encourages an anthropological stance, a recognition that as we are invited into a family through the process of therapy, we in essence are entering a foreign culture, and that it will be essential to familiarize ourselves with the rules and norms of that culture before proceeding in either thought or action. Further, true appreciation for the complex nature of families sensitizes us to the need to gather as much information as possible about the various factors that may be impacting a particular family and its members at a particular point in time.

In this chapter we consider some of the more obvious and salient dimensions of families and the ramifications of these dimensions for therapy. In the following discussions we focus on individual development, family development, and a consideration of the dynamic process model of the family life cycle, which facilitates integration of various developmental theories. Next, expected and unexpected developmental challenges are addressed, followed by discussions of variations in both structure and ethnic and cultural dimensions. As these various perspectives are considered, it is important to note that providing a comprehensive survey of these domains is not possible in this context. However, more crucial than complete coverage is the stimulation of a heightened curiosity about, and sensitivity to, each domain, which includes both knowledge about general characteristics as well as a not-knowing stance regarding the specific ways in which various aspects may be interacting with each other and influencing the life of each unique family system.

Individual Development

As we briefly consider some of the ways in which individual development may be understood, we soon recognize that, like the families they comprise, human beings are complicated. According to Koch, "characteristically, psychological events . . . are multiply determined, ambiguous in their human meaning, polymorphous, contextually environed, or embedded in complex and vaguely bounded ways, evanescent and labile in the extreme" (1981, p. 258). In the efforts of many to grasp and make sense of this complexity, numerous aspects of human development have been studied and a variety of models have been described. From my perspective, each of these models represents a story that offers potentially useful information rather than a description of the way that all persons necessarily do or must develop. Thus, we can feel free to pick and choose among theories, utilizing and integrating a variety of concepts as appropriate in the moment.

Cognitive Development

According to Swiss psychologist Jean Piaget's theory of cognitive development, intelligence evolves through several stages that correspond to the age of the child (Phillips, 1969; Singer & Revenson, 1978). The *sensori-motor* stage, described as lasting from birth to approximately 24 months, culminates in the child's ability to distinguish objects as separate from him- or herself; that is, the achievement of object permanence. The *pre-operational* stage, from ages 2–7 years, is characterized by the acquisition of language and the expression of curiosity from an egocentric stance that does not yet include the ability to think logically. From ages 7–11, the child in the stage of *concrete operations* learns how to reverse the direction of thoughts and can "see that objects or quantities remain the same de-spite a change in their physical appearance" (Singer & Revenson, 1978, p. 23), as when the same amount of water is poured into different size containers. However, it is not until the child reaches the stage of *formal operations*, which is said to occur between the ages of 11 and 16, that the ability to think abstractly or hypothetically and to consider the future emerges.

Having a very basic awareness of Piaget's stages enables the thera-pist to recognize the type of cognitive operations or ability a client may be evidencing and to tailor his or her language and interventions, or per-turbations, accordingly. At the same time, it is important to be aware that individual development rarely unfolds as neatly or in as orderly a fash-ion as many models would seem to indicate. Therefore, the fact that a client is an adult does not necessarily mean that the use of abstract con-cepts is going to be experienced by her or him as meaningful or helpful. Nor does it mean that a child may not be able to understand such con-cepts quite well.

Psychosocial Development

Familiarity with Erik Erikson's (1963) psychosocial framework for de-scribing human development, built on the foundation created by Freud with his model of psychosexual development, also sensitizes the thera-pist to a variety of issues with which a client may be dealing at a partic-ular point in time. Keeping in mind the male bias of this theory, it may be useful to be aware of Erikson's idea that as individuals progress through each of eight stages, they must deal with a particular developmental cri-sis. According to this perspective, the degree to which resolution of the task relevant to each crisis is achieved at a particular stage affects all of the following stages, either supporting or impeding subsequent development. The four stages of infancy and childhood and their related development tasks have been defined as follows:

1. *Oral–sensory:* basic trust versus mistrust
2. *Muscular–anal:* autonomy versus shame and doubt
3. *Locomotor–genital:* initiative versus guilt
4. *Latency:* industry versus inferiority

The four stages and related tasks describing individual development from adolescence through old age include:

5. *Puberty and adolescence:* identity versus role confusion
6. *Young adulthood:* intimacy versus isolation
7. *Adulthood:* generativity versus stagnation
8. *Maturity:* ego integrity versus despair

As with Piaget's model, Erikson's theory indicates that each of these stages is also age linked. However, once again, what may be more helpful is awareness of some of the predictable challenges that may characterize various stages of development. In this regard, recognizing the issues with which either a male or a female adolescent (and his or her family) may be struggling allows for normalization of behaviors that otherwise might be perceived as symptomatic of much greater problems. Or, being sensitive to the impact on an older adult of feelings and beliefs about having achieved a sense of meaning and purpose in life may cue the therapist to explore an area of great significance to that person.

Moral Development

Another dimension of individuals that may be important to keep in mind is that of moral development. Lawrence Kohlberg (1981), building on Piaget's theory, created a model according to which the development of moral reasoning, or the basis upon which people make ethical decisions, could be understood as a progression through three levels, each of which was comprised of two stages. At the *preconventional* level, children at the first, or obedience and punishment stage, are said to behave appropriately in response to the directives of those in authority because they fear punishment for noncompliance. At the second stage of this first level—that of individualism, instrumentalism, and exchange—appropriate behavior is chosen because it is perceived as being in one's best interest to do so. At the second or *conventional* level, a third-stage "good boy/girl" orientation is characterized by ethical behavior motivated by a desire for approval from others. At the fourth stage, that of law and order, the individual chooses to be law abiding and to honor his or her duty or obligations. Although Kohlberg believed that most adults never reach the third, *postconventional*, level of moral development, he described those in stage five, that of the social contract, as having attained "an understanding of social mutuality and a genuine interest in the welfare of others" (Barger, 2000, p. 2). At the final stage, that of the principled conscience, behavioral choices are made in response to both universal principles and the dictates of a personal sense of right and wrong.

Although Kohlberg's framework may be useful in identifying how a person makes decisions, it is only part of the story. As with the work of Erikson, the subjects studied by Kohlberg were mainly males. Carol Gilligan's (1982) perspective provides a useful complement with its delineation of the moral development of women, which she saw as different from that of men. For Gilligan, rather than a focus on justice, women are more concerned with relationships, connections, and caring, and with conflicts between self and others. At the *preconventional* stage the goal is individual survival. As the female transitions from this stage to the next, she shifts from selfishness to responsibility to others, or the attainment of the *conventional* stage, with the goal described as self-sacrifice perceived as goodness. As the female moves from the second to the third stage, the internal shift is from self-sacrifice to the realization that she is a person, too. At the third or *postconventional* stage, the goal is characterized by principles of nonviolence and the proviso not to hurt others or oneself.

All of the above frameworks, particularly in combination, may prove useful both in understanding and helping individuals understand themselves and when working with relationships. Indeed, as various ways of construing, making sense of, and responding to one's world can be recognized and acknowledged as valid, differences can be perceived without judgment and their presence may be experienced as potential resources. In addition, the use of stage models of individual development can be supplemented with ideas drawn from the theories of those espousing a more postmodern perspective, with an emphasis on the process of meaning making and reality construction.

Postmodern Perspectives

In the realm of personality development, Kegan (1982) takes a life-span approach to understanding the ways in which relationships between subject and object evolve. He believes that objects are created through a process of differentiation and are related to through a process of integration:

> Subject–object relationships emerge out of a lifelong process of development: a succession of qualitative differentiations of the self from the world, with a qualitatively more extensive object with which to be in relation created each time; a natural history of qualitatively better guarantees to the world of its distinctness; successive triumphs of "relationship to" rather than "embeddedness in." (p. 77)

Whereas this theory also describes a series of stages or types of balance in subject–object relationships, Kegan sees it as a metatheoretical perspective that provides a framework for understanding various other developmental theories. He illustrates his model using a helix, or spiral, to depict the ongoing evolutionary process in which individuals engage as they seek to resolve the tension created by a desire to be both differentiated from (distinctness) and embedded in (inclusion) their context. From a clinical perspective, understanding where a client is in such a process can shed light on his or her efforts to make meaning. Further, according to Kegan, the therapeutic context becomes "a culture of embeddedness in the facilitation of a troubled person's evolution" (1982, p. 262), with both therapist and client engaged in creating a more useful construction of the world and a better sense of what is true.

Relative to cognitive development, Moshman (1994) sees both objectivity and subjectivity as complementary aspects of the process of knowing. Given that one's personal perspective always provides a lens through which one's knowledge is viewed, it is inevitably subjective. At the same time, knowledge also is objective, given the degree to which it is constrained by, and thus is created as a function of, a reality that is separate from the observer. As one's rationality develops, a metasubjective perspective is created through the process of reflecting on and reconstructing subject–object relationships that previously were implicit. According to Moshman (1994):

> We are rational to the extent that our most fundamental conceptions and modes of reasoning enable greater objectivity than did their predecessors. Rationality resides in the developmental process whereby our subjectivity becomes an object of reflection, thereby allowing the construction of a more objective meta-subjectivity. (p. 251)

Thus therapy provides a context for helping clients reflect on their thought processes, with a focus on making changes consistent with good reasoning.

Similarly, Noam (1993) has created a more postmodern approach to moral development that considers "the biographical path in which meanings about the self and other relationships are constructed and transformed" (Becvar, 2000c, p. 75). The self is defined as a process through which one's thoughts, feelings, and actions about self, others, and the world are structured. Noam believes that the lack of a strong sense of self accounts for immoral behavior, and that moral conflict may provide a catalyst for establishing strength in the self. According to his perspective, "moral maturity needs to be judged by the relationship between the complexity of judgments and the capacity to transform judgments into positive adaptations" (Noam, 1993, p. 213).

According to Noam, development occurs as a function of an interactive process in which the evolution and formation of the individual and his or her construction of reality are influenced by all of a person's experiences. As meanings are developed, new abilities and vulnerabilities that relate both to moral development and to the basic development of the self are created. As a person becomes more reflective and decisive, is able to think through decisions carefully, and recognizes the ability to make a difference, moral judgment and moral action are enhanced.

In therapy, Noam suggests a focus on exploring and transforming vulnerabilities into strengths. By creating trustworthy, respectful relationships, therapists participate in strengthening the self of their clients. Self-reflection and the creation of new understanding about past experiences also are important, as is consideration of instances in which a morally courageous position was taken. Thus, "what begins as a rigid application of moral rules can lead to explorations with more flexible evaluations of internal reality and to new relational capacities" (Noam, 1993, p. 236).

Noam's model, as well as the other theories and related approaches described above, provide information that therapists can draw upon as they work with clients. What is more, there certainly are many other perspectives, although not included here, that also might add to therapists' ability to understand and facilitate functioning. In addition, it is extremely important to recognize that individual development represents only one piece of the puzzle, and that for the fullest understanding of any single person, it is essential to consider him or her in context.

Family Development

Inasmuch as individuals are born into, and generally live in, a family unit of one sort or another, recognition of the dynamics, issues, and tasks of the larger system is crucial. The family as a whole also may be understood as characterized by developmental processes that influence, and are influenced by, growth and change among its members. The stage model of family development considered here integrates ideas from several sources (Barnhill & Longo, 1978; Carter & McGoldrick, 1980; Duvall, 1962). However, although it may be helpful with many clients, it is important to be aware that this framework was devised in response to studies of the so-called traditional family in an earlier era. As noted at the outset, because the traditional family is no longer the norm, several limitations and suggestions for revision of this model are considered following its description.

According to the family development framework, the first stage focuses on the point at which the basic emotion issue involves acceptance of a separation between parents and young adults as the latter are concerned primarily with differentiating from their family of origin, developing peer relations, and initiating a career. In the second stage, that of the newly married couple, the basic emotion issue is commitment to the marriage, with specific tasks including the formation of the marital system and making room for one's spouse in relationships with family members and friends. Childbearing defines the third stage, in which accepting new members into the system is the basic emotion issue. The tasks for this stage involve adjusting the marriage to accommodate the child(ren), taking on parenting roles, and incorporating grandparents into the family system. The fourth stage is that of the preschool-age child, and the basic emotion issue involves accepting the new personality; the family is faced with the tasks of adjusting to the needs of each child and coping with the related energy drain and lack of privacy.

In the fifth stage, that of the school-age child, allowing the child to establish relationships outside the family is the basic emotion issue, and the family's tasks include extending interactions with society and encouraging educational achievement. The sixth stage is that of the teenage child, and the basic emotion issue involves the need to increase the flexibility of family boundaries to allow greater independence on the part of the child. For this stage the tasks include shifting parent–child relationships to balance freedom and limits, and refocusing on midlife career and marital issues. The seventh stage focuses on the family as a launching center as it deals with the basic emotion issue of accepting exits from, and entries into, the family. The tasks typical of this stage are those of releasing young adult children into work, college, and marriage, and maintaining a supportive home base. In the eighth stage, that of middle-aged parents, the basic emotion issue is letting go of children and facing each other again; the tasks include rebuilding the marriage, realigning the family to include spouses of children and grandchildren, and dealing with the aging of the older generation. The ninth and final stage in this model is that of retirement, acceptance of which is the basic emotion issue; the tasks involve adjusting to retirement and old age, coping with the death of parents and spouses, closing or adapting the family home, maintaining both couple and individual functioning, and supporting the middle generation.

There are several ways in which such a stage model of family development can be useful. First, we can become sensitive to the fact that it is at the point when a transition from one stage to the next is called for that families are likely to become stuck (Haley, 1973). We therefore may attempt to locate where the family and its members are in the process of development and consider adjustments that may be appropriate for them. For example, tensions may be a function of reluctance on the part of parents to allow their children more freedom and responsibility as the latter move into adolescence. Indeed, to reiterate a point made earlier, having knowledge of specific issues related to normal developmental challenges also may enable the therapist to normalize what family members may be seeing as symptoms of a greater problem. Further, encouraging family members to recognize the interaction between individual and family issues may help to broaden their focus as they search for solutions. Thus, although adolescence is typically seen as presenting great challenges, there often is much more going on in the family that is affecting what members are experiencing than just those issues related to the teenager. This often is a time when parents are confronting their own issues around careers, their relationship, and the older generation.

At the same time, there certainly are several limitations to the stage model of family development that must be kept in mind. The stages tend to describe isolated and static moments in what are, in fact, ongoing, interactive processes in the life of a family. There also is an assumption of progression through the stages in a linear, orderly fashion, which is seldom the way that life actually occurs. In addition, a model such as the one described above probably fits only a small percentage of American families today. What is more, it generally focuses on one child, often the first, and thus is unable to capture the complexity of family interactions. This framework describes only general characteristics that may or may not fit specific families, particularly those in which there are structural or cultural variations. And finally, the framework may or may not be reflective of changes in the larger society.

Thus, although not advocating that we throw the baby of the model out with the bath water of its limitations, it is important to be flexible in its application and sensitive to the need for revision as appropriate. For example, today there are many single-parent families, with some of the most significant changes in family life related to the role of fathers. That is, there is an increasing number of father-only families as well as a greater likelihood of postdivorce custody sharing between fathers and mothers (Casper & Bianchi, 2002). In addition, all parents, whether single, cohabiting, or married, tend to seek employment outside the home—a trend that has had a significant impact on the way that roles and responsibilities in the family are handled. There also has been a great increase in the number of couples who choose to cohabit either prior to, or instead of, marrying, with a concomitant delay in the age at marriage and an increase in nonmarital births. Furthermore, young adults are leaving home at a much later age than did their parents, and nearly half of those who do leave eventually return home for a period of time. In addition, many individuals live in multigenerational households, with members of the older generation generally acting as hosts for those in the younger generations. Although the divorce rate increased dramatically in the 20th century, remarriage was the norm for two-thirds of the women and three-fourths of the men. Thus there are many children who have experienced, or are growing up in, reconstituted (step) families. And all of these factors describe only the tip of the iceberg when we remember the various additional circumstances and the variety of challenges with which families may be faced. Before moving to such a discussion, however, the following section provides a way to make recourse to various models of individual and family development in a pragmatic manner.

Dynamic Process Model

The dynamic process model of the family life cycle (Becvar & Becvar, 2006) is an attempt to integrate a variety of individual developmental models with the stage model of family development, and visually depict a family in a way that acknowledges the movement through time of individual members, the marital couple, and the system as a whole. Included in this model are the unique issues and tasks with which each family may be confronted in the present. To begin, four stages of marriage are created by extrapolating from both the stage model of family development and other relevant information about couples. Stage 1, the honeymoon period, describes the first 2 years of marriage, commitment to which is the emotion issue. The developmental issues specific to this stage include differentiation of the spouses from their families of origin, making room for each other in their relationships with extended family and friends, and adjusting to the demands of their careers. During the early-marriage stage (from 2 to 10 years), the emotion issue is the maturing of the relationship, and the tasks include keeping romance in the marriage, balancing separateness and togetherness, and renewing a commitment to the marriage. The middle-marriage stage (from 10 to 25 years) has as its emotion issue postcareer planning; the tasks include adjusting to midlife changes, renegotiating relationships, and renewing a commitment to the marriage. In the final stage, long-term marriage (25+ years), the emotion issue involves reviews and farewells, and the tasks include maintaining couple functioning, closing or adapting the family home, and coping with the death of one's spouse.

The marriage as well as the aspect of individual development that the therapist wishes to consider are depicted by means of circles on which the various stages of the models are indicated (Figure 2-1). These circles are then overlapped, noting by shading and position where the family members are at a particular point in time relative to the models selected. Thus we can get a graphic sense of the larger context and some of the many family dynamics that may be impacting the situation at hand.

For example, Theresa (age 38) and Michael (age 39) Jones have come to therapy because of concerns about their older daughter, Ellie (age 13).

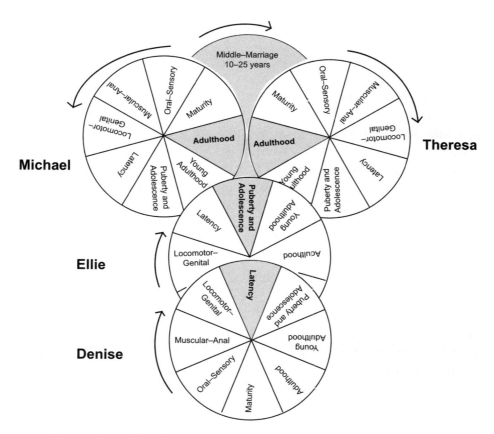

Figure 2-1. The dynamic process model of family development.

At our first meeting, which also includes the Joneses' younger daughter, Denise (age 10), I learn that Theresa and Michael have been married for 15 years. Theresa and Michael both are concerned about recent changes in Ellie's behavior, including lack of follow-through with responsibilities at home and plummeting grades at school. Thinking in terms of both Erikson's model and the stages of marriage, I can immediately see Figure 2-1 in my mind's eye, which gives me some understanding of the family as well as ideas about how to proceed, including questions I might ask when the time is right.

I am tuned in to the fact that Theresa and Michael are in the middle-marriage stage, meaning that postcareer planning, adjusting to midlife changes, renegotiating their relationship, and renewing a commitment to their marriage may be salient issues. In terms of individual development, Theresa and Michael are likely to be dealing with issues and tasks around generativity versus stagnation; Ellie has just entered the stage of puberty and adolescence, with its focus on identity versus role confusion; and Denise is in the latency stage, whose main issue is industry versus inferiority. The arrows next to each circle emphasize the movement that already has occurred in the past as well as what may be expected for the future.

As I learn more about the Joneses, I can expand the picture to include extended family members as well as additional developmental models and related information, as appropriate. The dynamic process model of the family life cycle thus provides some guidance as therapists seek to understand, work with, and help each member of the families with whom they work to achieve their goals. Once again, however, it is important to be sensitive to issues and challenges that may be a part of the fabric of each family but are not represented in this framework, which takes us to a consideration of unexpected developmental challenges.

Expected and Unexpected Developmental Challenges

Each of the models of individual and family development described thus far focuses on what we may think of as expected developmental challenges. That is, regardless of the order or the context in which they occur, there are a variety of tasks and issues with which most individuals and families are likely to be faced as they evolve through time. These are predictable, and therefore relatively manageable, events. However, as life generally teaches us, there are many unexpected challenges that also may confront individuals and families. These are the unpredictable events that often bring clients into therapy. For example, I never expected to be divorced, to remarry and live in a stepfamily, to lose a child, or to be diagnosed with cancer. Nevertheless, all of these events have occurred, and all of them called for significant adjustments in many facets of my world.

Similarly, as other individuals and families are coping with the challenges associated with so-called normal development, they also may experience the loss of a significant relationship through desertion, separation, divorce, death, kidnapping, incarceration, disappearance, mental or physical illness, or substance abuse. The loss of a job, either one's own or that of someone upon whom one depended, also may occur. Individuals and families may experience the loss of a home through intentional relocation, immigration, sudden refugee status, or conditions that culminate in homelessness. In addition, loss of physical capacity may occur as a function of illness, an accident, through the aging process, or because of sterility or infertility. Something of value may be lost through fire, flood, earthquake, or theft. A person or family may be denied membership in an important group. A person may lose respect for, or feel betrayed by, another person, an organization, a religious group, or political groups. A person may lose trust in others as well as self-respect as a function of physical abuse, emotional abuse, or sexual abuse. A parent may be called to active military duty or have to go to war. And any of these experiences also may be associated with the loss of one's belief system.

However, not all unexpected developmental challenges involve loss; some may be anticipated as very positive experiences. For example, a parent may take a job away from home or a grandparent may move in with the family, both of which are seen as welcome events. Perhaps more illustrative is the experience of winning a large amount of money—something that most of us would like to have happen. Similarly, becoming very successful, perhaps famous, generally also is greatly desired. Nevertheless such events tend to be disorienting and require adjustments, often presenting a variety of unanticipated challenges. Indeed, I am reminded of a colleague who, after winning the lottery, had to give up her professional life because of the changes in the way she was perceived by others.

How the various challenges are handled by families and their members is influenced by a variety of factors, such as the absence or presence of meaningful support systems, gender, and religious/spiritual beliefs. Such factors contribute to one's meaning system, which influences the ways in which various events are perceived and thus responded to. Indeed, meanings grow out of social interactions, are modified by personal beliefs, and are interpreted through language. Thus they are constantly emerging, and as such, afford the therapist the opportunity to provide assistance with their creation in the course of conversation. Such conversations may focus on the potential for forgiveness when that might be appropriate, and even when not, the potential for resolution. Always, however, there must be awareness of two additional aspects of the larger context: family structure and family culture and ethnicity.

Structural Variations

We shift now to a consideration of the various forms of family by which clients may be identified and for whom therapists may be called upon to provide assistance. The goal here is to describe aspects on which it may be most important for therapists to focus as they attempt to help clients attain their goals while simultaneously facilitating resilience. Thus this discussion certainly does not provide a full description of what each type of family may be experiencing.

Divorced Families with Young Children

Divorced families with young children are prevalent in our society. Given the enormous burdens associated with childrearing alone, therapists would do well to find ways to support the well-being of the custodial parent and to enhance his or her acceptance of both self and the situation. It also may be important to assess the need to shift and redefine roles, responsibilities, and relationships (Garfield, 1982). Additional significant areas of intervention may include helping family members to mourn the previous family as well as to celebrate the new family. When possible, therapists are advised to encourage effective coparenting with the divorced spouse as part of helping to transform that relationship in a positive manner. Therapists also must assess the need to build new support systems in addition to encouraging the maintenance of appropriate boundaries between parent and child(ren) in order to avoid the latter being seen as the major source of emotional support for the parent. Therapists also may request information about custody and visitation arrangements, and when appropriate, help clients to clarify them. It may be helpful to invite members of these families to *avoid* the assumption that problems necessarily must occur. As with all the other types of families with whom a therapist may work, the bottom line is participating in the cocreation of a context that is supportive of the healthy development of everyone involved.

Single-Parent Families

The needs of single-parent families in which there has been no prior marriage are similar in many ways to those of divorced families with young children. Once again, it is important to find ways to help facilitate the well-being of the parent, especially through the creation of effective support systems. It also may be useful to assess resources available to the family. In terms of relationships, encouraging one-on-one interactions between the parent and each child as a form of nurturing as well as during times of stress may be helpful, always being sensitive to the need for appropriate boundaries between parent and child(ren). Clarification of visitation arrangements may be needed, especially in the absence of legal custody agreements. Specifying roles and responsibilities, avoiding the assumption that problems must necessarily occur, and celebrating the family all may contribute to the creation of a context that supports the healthy development of everyone involved.

Blended Families

When working with blended (or reconstituted) families, it is important for therapists to help them recognize that readjustment takes time, that the nuclear family cannot be recreated (Jacobson, 1979), and that its loss must be mourned (Visher & Visher, 1982). As with any family that has experienced structural change, it also may be useful to focus on the redefinition of roles, responsibilities, and relationships, as well as on the recreation of traditions. Of crucial importance, at least in most instances, is helping the biological parent take responsibility for his or her children while encouraging the stepparent to be a friend to the children of his or her spouse. Doing so may help heighten awareness of the existence of two or more families under the same roof. Respect between stepparents and stepchildren is to be expected, but love is not. Rather, it is important to encourage acceptance of the feelings of everyone involved, with recognition that the various relationships may be characterized by different and inequal amounts of love. Attention to each of these aspects may, once again, help to create a context that supports the healthy development of the family and its members.

Adoptive Families

Very different dynamics may be characteristic of adoptive families, in which the parents tend to be older, married longer, and more financially secure than those in many other forms (Casper & Bianchi, 2002). With adoptive families therapists may be called upon to facilitate attachment even as attention to the birth culture of the child is encouraged and included. Also necessary may be the clarification or finalization of legal arrangements, including (when appropriate) the specification of boundaries with regard to the birth mother. As with any family, it is helpful for parents to assume the best but to be alert to distress signals. Along the way, they may do well to support biracial children in cultural identity formation at the same time that they celebrate difference. It also is important for adoptive parents to be honest with children in age-appropriate ways, and to recognize and support the potential desire of children to seek more information about their birth parents. A healthy, supportive context for all may be facilitated as each of these areas is considered.

Multigenerational Families

Multigenerational families are likely to have their own set of issues and challenges. For example, it may be necessary to help clarify who is in charge of the household and the children. Doing so may require recognition that there is no one right parenting pattern, even as the owner of the home is acknowledged. Parent(s) and children may be living in the grandparents' home, or the grandparents may have moved in with adult children (Casper & Bianchi, 2002). Accordingly, the hierarchy needs to be defined and the creation of appropriate boundaries may need to be supported. These tasks may involve providing assistance with detriangulation and offering information about how to avoid unhealthy coalitions. In addition, specifying the roles and responsibilities for everyone involved and supporting the rule of only two to a relationship may be helpful, even as healthy relationships between members of the different generations are encouraged. This, too, may help with the creation of a context supportive of the healthy development of everyone involved.

Lesbian and Gay Families

When working with lesbian and gay families, therapists must respect the rich variety of constellations that may be possible (Bigner, 2000). It also is crucial for therapists to recognize the impact of homophobia (stigma and nonsupport) on the efforts of such families to be successful. Thus the facilitation of healthy interactions with extended family members and external systems may be useful. Close, flexible, egalitarian partnerships tend to be characteristic of gay and lesbian families; however, members of these families may need assistance in resolving boundary issues. In addition, when taken on, the role of parenting either adopted or biological children often has great significance, although challenges may emerge around stepparenting, particularly in the absence of legal and community sanctions for the blended family. As with adoptive families, therapists are advised to encourage honesty with children in age-appropriate ways. The focus needs to remain on facilitating the normal development of children whose major distinction may be greater tolerance for difference. Indeed, children of lesbians have been found to be less likely to conform to traditional gender roles than children of heterosexual parents (Perrin, 2004). As always, attention to each of these areas may support the creation of a context that is supportive of the healthy development of the family and its members.

Ethnic and Cultural Variations

As is the case with structural diversity, when considering ethnic and cultural diversity the focus is more on the dimensions about which the therapist needs to be sensitive than on detailed characterizations of each group. Further, it is recognized that ethnicity is only one aspect of culture, which has been defined as "a set of shared worldviews, meanings, and adaptive behaviors derived from simultaneous membership and participation in a variety of contexts including language, age, gender, race, ethnicity, religion, socioeconomic status, education, and sexual orientation" (Thomas, 1998, p. 24). And always we must be aware of the possibility for as much difference *within* groups as there may be differences *between* groups. Consciousness of these factors has an important influence on therapists' ability to behave in a culturally competent manner. Other important considerations to which therapists must be sensitive include the facts that (1) therapy may represent a violation of the family's confidentiality, (2) expectations of the therapist may vary, (3) use of the client's native language may differ in importance, and (4) there may be diverse levels of acculturation among members of the same family (Wilson, Kohn, & Lee, 2000).

American-Indian and Alaska-Native Families

American-Indian and Alaska-native families who come to therapy tend to be young, and often are experiencing intergenerational stresses similar to other second- and third-generation Americans, with the older generations seeking to maintain cultural traditions, and the younger generations being more open to becoming part of the larger culture (Attneave, 1982). These families are likely to include three generations and often are headed by a female. Relative to the larger context, therapists are advised to be sensitive to "multigenerational oppression (historical/ideological/ cultural/and economic domination) and current feelings of alienation because of blatant and covert racism and discrimination" (Robbins & Harrist, 2004, p. 24).

It also is important to recognize that the worldview of American-Indian and Alaska-native families tends to be very different from that of mainstream Western society. This worldview embraces a belief in balance and harmony and includes the assumptions that each element in the universe has a place and function; that respect for self, others, and nature is essential; and that exploitation and interference are always to be avoided. The focus is on the here and now, with time viewed as cyclical and seasonal. In addition, a positive view of humanity as well as a respect for the power of places and sacred spaces are characteristics of this worldview, as are the significance of tribal identity and communal sharing and the importance of religion/spirituality (Attneave, 1982; Ho, 1987; Robbins & Harrist, 2004; Sutton & Broken Nose, 1996).

It is appropriate for therapists to request information about each family's unique tribal background, recognizing, for example, that among American Indians there are 500 tribes and 214 reservations (McGoldrick, Giordano, & Pearce, 1996). What is more, inasmuch as family members are likely to be reluctant to seek help (Ho, 1987), a process of mutual

assessment that includes observation and testing of the therapist with little self-disclosure, much silence, a degree of uncertainty, and a tendency
to be indirect is likely (Attneave, 1982). At the same time, there is often an
expectation that the therapist act as an expert who is both culturally sensitive and able to provide concrete and practical advice (Sutton & Broken
Nose, 1996). Important strategies may include the use of open-ended
questions to elicit information and establish relationships. Also useful
may be such postmodern approaches, or perturbations, as metaphors,
externalization, collaborative conversations, an emphasis on possibilities
and strengths, and ongoing reflection and feedback (Ho, 1987; Robbins &
Harrist, 2004). Lastly, searching for support within the community, including enlisting the medicine person as a colleague, may be very useful.

Asian-American Families

Among Asian-Americans, the family takes precedence over the individual, who is understood to be the product of all previous generations (Ho,
1987; Lee, 1996; Shon & Ja, 1982). Formal rules of conduct characterize
various roles and relationships, including expectations for loyalty and
respect, a highly developed sense of obligation, and the use of shame to
reinforce adherence to appropriate behaviors and societal expectations.
The family typically is hierarchical and patriarchal, with marriages
arranged as part of the process of continuing the family line of the male.

Members of Asian-American families tend to value compassion, a respect for life, moderation, self-discipline, patience, modesty, friendliness
and selflessness (Ho, 1987). Often there is a reticence to express feelings
coupled with indirect communication of disagreement. Social, moral,
and organic explanations are preferred for understanding behavioral difficulties, with the individual seen as the victim rather than the cause.
Problem solving generally occurs within the family, with therapy perceived as a last resort and help-seeking behavior to be avoided because
it tends to bring with it a sense of shame and fear of stigma.

Establishing trust is thus essential if therapy with Asian-American
clients is to be effective. Appointments should be made with the family
decision-maker, and it is appropriate for the therapist to provide information about his or her credentials, education, and experience in order
to be accepted as a knowledgeable expert (Ho, 1987; Lee, 1996; Shon & Ja,
1982). Direct confrontation should be avoided, as should ambiguity,
which may create anxiety. Rather, clearly structured, goal-directed work

with concrete, measurable objectives are preferred, especially when these are understood as serving to meet basic needs related to shelter, food, and work. Along the way, it is important to respect the family hierarchy and its roles, and to be polite, formal, accepting and gracious while conveying confidence, empathy, maturity, and other professional behaviors (Lee, 1996).

African-American Families

Creating an atmosphere of trust is also essential when working with African-American families (Boyd-Franklin, 2003; Hines & Boyd-Franklin, 1982; Pinderhughes, 1982). Issues of power and powerlessness tend to be extremely important among members of this population, with an understandable distrust, or what has been called a healthy paranoia (Boyd-Franklin, 2003), regarding the therapeutic process, given long experience with oppression in American society. In addition, African-American clients may have conflicting values relative to their bicultural orientation.

African-American families tend to give great importance to role flexibility and strong kinship bonds, with pressure to maintain close physical proximity as well as to provide financial support within the kin network (Hines & Boyd-Franklin, 1982; Pinderhughes, 1982). The extended family network generally includes both kin and non-kin members, often with great complexity of relationships (Martin & Martin, 1975). Religion and spirituality are likely to play a very important role in the life of the family (Boyd-Franklin, 2003; Jackson, Gregory, & Davis, 2004), and there is likely to be a strong pressure to achieve.

While remaining sensitive to the characteristics of their context, therapists are advised to follow the lead of family members when deciding how much formality is appropriate when working with African-American families (Boyd-Franklin, 2003). The therapy process should be explained in a respectful manner, with differences in ethnicity and culture (if present) addressed early on (Hines & Boyd-Franklin, 1982, 1996; Pinderhughes, 1982). Therapists are advised to avoid intervening in ways that may be experienced as prying; for example, be cautious about the use of such tools as a genogram. They also may need to explore and understand preferred styles of parenting and disciplining children; for example, in African-American families "quick and decisive discipline" (Martin & Martin, 1975, p. 51) often is the rule. Utilizing interventions drawn from a variety of approaches and a multisystemic orientation, including consideration of the families and their members as well as various community and social service agency interactions and potential resources (Boyd-Franklin, 2003), is suggested. Overall, it is important to remain aware that African-American families "are likely to be most responsive to time-limited, problem-solving, child-focused therapy approaches with an active, directive therapist" (Boyd-Franklin, 2003, p. 79).

Latino Families

Regarding therapy with Latino families, there are both general considerations to keep in mind as well as factors of concern that are specific to the various ethnic and cultural groups within this category, for example, Mexican-American families, Puerto Rican-American families, and Cuban-American families. Common to all are the potential significance of migration history as well as the tendency to avoid seeking health care services because of such issues as language barriers, lack of money, problems related to proximity, concerns about being detected by immigration authorities, and fear of misunderstanding and discrimination (Falicov, 1998). On the other hand, when chosen, family therapy tends to be easily accepted because of its compatibility with perceptions of the role that relationship conflicts and financial challenges play in the creation of emotional problems. The process also may be aided as therapists recognize the importance that both various mainstream religious practices and indigenous magical beliefs may have. In addition,

> a consideration of cultural preferences in coping styles that stress quiet acceptance and internal endurance opens the way to questioning instrumental theories of therapeutic change, especially with clients who may already have their own cultural strengths. In the end, what helps is to envision a holistic mind–body connection that allows for emotions to manifest in bodily expressions, and for problems to reside in the mysteries of relational sin and revenge. (Falicov, 1998, p. 155)

Mexican-American Families

Turning to some of the specifics, Mexican-American families tend to have large extended family networks, the members of which live in close proximity (Falicov, 1982). Within the family there is cohesion, respect for authority, and a hierarchical structure based on both gender (male dominance/female submission) and age (parent dominance/child submission). Interdependence or collectivism and a relational focus are assumed, the Catholic religion prevails, and godparents generally play extremely significant roles. Before finally going to therapy, families are likely to turn first to relatives, then to clergy, then friends, followed by godparents, and physicians.

Accordingly, the therapist must take into account the potential for reluctance on the part of clients and understand as normal a tendency to be guarded and tentative (Falicov, 1982). Initial encounters are likely to include respectful, polite interactions with much formality. Taking time to establish rapport with each family member is thus important, as is the need to be respectful of the gender and age hierarchies. It also may be important to inquire about the family's migration history and to be sensitive to issues around isolation, both socially and culturally, as well as lack of knowledge about resources available in the community (Falicov, 1996). In addition, value conflicts between home and other systems, such as work, school, and peers, are likely.

Using a brief, problem-focused approach with a structural orientation may be helpful with Mexican-American families, as may be a focus on both the individuals and the parent–child dyad (Falicov, 1982) rather than the marriage. The therapist may be called upon to mediate intergenerational tensions as a function of different cultural beliefs and expectations (Falicov, 1996). Throughout this process an emphasis on strengths may prove very helpful. Also appropriate is the use of rituals, particularly those that emphasize unity and connection between family members.

Puerto Rican-American Families

The cultural ancestry of Puerto Rican-American families is comprised of a mixture of African, Taino Indian, Corsican, and Spanish influences. A patriarchal family structure is typical, as is a strong sense of commitment and obligation within the extended family and great respect for authority (Garcia-Preto, 1982). The unity, welfare, and honor of the family tend to be highly valued, marriage is understood as a union of two families, and the most important events in the family's life cycle are birth, marriage, and death (Garcia-Preto, 1996). Individuals may fear a loss of impulse control or the expression of violence, and a demeanor that is peaceable is the goal. Further, the dignity of the individual tends to be based on such inner qualities as male *machismo,* which is comprised of virtue, courage, romanticism, and fearlessness (Garcia-Preto, 1982). Although nominally Roman Catholic, there tends to be widespread distrust of organized religion, with spirituality generally expressed through spiritism and a relationship with God that is very personalized (Garcia-Preto, 1996). Time is present-centered and *being* is more important than *doing*; hence a willingness to sacrifice material goals for those that are more spiritual (Garcia-Preto, 1982).

Like Mexican-American families, Puerto Rican-American families tend to turn to social service agencies and therapy only as a last resort, after all other avenues of support have been exhausted. In order to encourage success, it may be important to accommodate language differences and to create relationships that are warm and personal, seeing clients in their home whenever possible (Garcia-Preto, 1982). Respect for the family's hierarchical structure and boundaries is essential. Other characteristics and issues about which the therapist needs to be sensitive are the tendency to somaticize in the face of stress, the possibility that children may be transferred from one nuclear family to another during periods of crisis, and the potential variations in family life and individual behavior based on social class. Although a genogram may prove useful, it should be utilized only after trust and acceptance have been established. In addition, including humor, storytelling, and metaphors in the therapeutic process may all prove very meaningful.

Cuban-American Families

Cuban-American families have an ancestry that includes a blend of Spanish and African cultures (Bernal, 1982). The Spanish language is extremely important. Although folk healing practices are important for some, the Catholic church tends to provide a strong base of both influence and support. In addition, people and persons take precedence over concepts and ideas, and action, doing, and the present, or existence, are considered more important than is one's essence. Familism is a core value, as are male *machismo* and female purity and the need for protection. There is a belief in the specialness of the Cuban culture, although the use of humor, exaggeration, as well as a willingness to be informal and personal also are common.

Therapists are advised to be able to speak Spanish with their Cuban clients and to request information about migration histories and the degree to which individuals are connected to their culture and their families of origin (Bernal & Shapiro, 1996). It also is important to be sensitive to the distinction between problems relating to acculturation and those arising from developmental difficulties. Assessing cultural and relational resources thus may be very useful, while also ascertaining and attempting to understand intergenerational and loyalty conflicts. A broad view of the family context is encouraged, including awareness of the degree to which families may be impacted by various changing political and social realities. Further, the use of structural and strategic interventions to deal with some of these issues has been found to be very helpful (Robbins, Schwartz, & Szapocznik, 2004).

Conclusion

Although this chapter has provided discussions of many ways in which to view families, the theories considered are by no means the only lenses available. They are just the ones that I have found to be most useful and with which I am most familiar at this time. Interestingly, as I reflect on this material, I am aware that given the incredible array of factors that invite consideration when working with families, it is perhaps remarkable that therapy is ever successful. However, it certainly is, especially as we remain as conscious of what we don't know as of what we do. For me, the operative words in this regard include *sensitivity, respect, curiosity,* and *humility,* coupled with a recognition of the degree to which we are the recipients of a sacred trust (Becvar, 1997) when clients come to us for assistance. Also important to the success of our endeavors is awareness of what it means to be a family that is flourishing, the topic to which we now turn our attention.

CHAPTER THREE

Flourishing

Although the object of speculation as much as any other institution in our society (Frankel, 1963), the family as a focus of serious, methodologically consistent study is a relatively recent phenomenon (Hareven, 1971). Sociologist Reuben Hill is considered the father of family studies (Boss, 2006), and it was his work on stress and coping in families, which emerged toward the middle of the 20th century, that provided much of the foundation for a focus on strengths rather than pathology. In the field of family therapy, an emphasis on normal family processes and resilience (Kaslow, 1982; Walsh, 1982, 1998, 2003a, 2003b) has been built on this foundation. With the concept of flourishing, we continue the tradition of focusing on the positive and extend it to an understanding of health and success in families as comprising a distinct set of characteristics and processes that enable them to be successful, in general, and resilient in response to specific challenges.

Some of the synonyms for the verb *flourish* include *grow, thrive, prosper, blossom,* and *flower.* We could think of families that flourish as comparable to well-tended, lush perennial gardens. Although these gardens may be created in distinct configurations or designs, in each the differing requirements for sun and shade, for water and other nutrients, are accommodated appropriately, enabling the various plants within the garden to mature and bloom according to their individual timetables. The health of each plant adds to the beauty of the whole, with assorted types complementing or providing unique contrasts of color and form. Some of the plants may tend to spread and invite more closeness, whereas others need more space and therefore might be thought of as rather solitary. Such a garden is hardy, with both the individual plants and the unit as a whole growing and evolving through successive cycles involving the natural patterns of birth, death, and rebirth. Throughout the life course of the garden the various seasons, including those that are predictable as well as the unexpected or harsh storms and extremes of heat or cold, are weathered successfully. And even in its dormant stages, each garden provides beauty to the larger landscape of which it is a part.

Similar in many ways to such gardens, families that flourish can be understood as those that are effective in terms of the manner in which they are organized and cared for, and thus are able to achieve the goals that are important to them as well as to the larger society. Flourishing families are able to fulfill the four core functions in relation to (1) family formation and membership, (2) economic support, (3) nurturance, education, and socialization, and (4) the protection of vulnerable members (Patterson, 2002b), as described in the previous chapter. However, this does not mean that such families are perfect or never have problems. Rather, they certainly have their ups and downs, but they continue to provide contexts in which the healthy growth of their members, as well as of the family as a whole, is supported. Such support is manifest as all evolve, face, and successfully come to terms with both expected and unexpected developmental challenges. The unique needs of each individual are acknowledged and accommodated, with differences celebrated and seen as resources rather than liabilities.

In families that flourish roles and responsibilities are apportioned and handled in a reliable manner, and attention to the need for the accomplishment of tasks is balanced by appropriate attention to emotional wishes and requirements. Thus these families provide a safe haven for their members in times of stress as well as during periods of tranquility and are able to interact effectively with other systems. They have boundaries that are maintained in a manner that allows for more openness when in need of new information, and more closedness when too much new information would threaten the viability of the unit. In other words, order and stability are maintained by means of adaptability and flexibility: the ability to change, as appropriate. When a crisis occurs, these families evidence resilience, even becoming stronger in response to circumstances that are potentially debilitating—circumstances that for other families might be experienced as overwhelming.

As is apparent from the above description, the ability of a family to flourish is not dependent on a specific form or structure. Rather, it is a function of the presence of various *process dimensions* that underpin the ability to flourish. Accordingly, we recognize that the various changes over time in families in our society, as previously noted, are not the issue. Nor is there a fixed set of goals that is required, other than those associated with living successfully within the norms and standards deemed acceptable by the particular society of which the family is a part. Therefore, in contrast to the concern expressed by many regarding, for example, the increase in single-parent families or the decrease in the size of families, the perspective I am espousing is primarily focused on the patterns that characterize successful families, the ways in which each particular type of family operates to achieve its goals in a manner that is synergistic with the larger society. Each of the many different types and configurations of family now appearing in our society may have representatives whom I would describe as flourishing.

As we turn our attention to the various patterns or process dimensions by which families that flourish may be distinguished, it also is important to be aware of a critical proviso: Such processes may occur in many different combinations, with a majority, rather than all, of them being present in any one family. Indeed, as reported by one of the first groups of researchers to focus on the characteristics of well-functioning families, "health at the level of the family was not a single thread, and . . . competence must be considered as a tapestry, reflecting differences in degree along many dimensions" (Lewis, Beavers, Gosset, & Phillips, 1976, p. 206).

Dimensions of Flourishing

Certainly there are many threads to be identified and considered as we seek to understand the tapestry of a given family. The following discussion brings together various perspectives on the weaving of successful, well-functioning families, those to whom I refer as families that flourish. The specific threads, or processes, identified can be grouped into 11 categories or dimensions of flourishing: the atmosphere of the family, including the style of interaction utilized by family members both inside and outside the family; the approach of family members to problems and challenges; the orientation of the family to the larger context of which it is a part; the ways in which individual support is provided; the communication skills evidenced by family members; the family's approach to the enrichment and nurturance of both individuals and the family as a whole; the structure of the family; the family's mythology or story about itself; the family's awareness of itself as a system; the family's attention to rituals; and the orientation of family members to a transcendent dimension.

Family Atmosphere

We can think of the atmosphere of a family as its internal temperature, one that in families that flourish would tend to fall predominantly in the warm range. One of the many processes that successful families tend to demonstrate is a caring, affiliative attitude that is expressed between members as well as with others in their world (Lewis et al., 1976). That is, rather than taking an oppositional approach to human encounters, there is an awareness among family members of interdependence and connection, and a feeling of optimism tends to prevail. There is thus a sense that family members are concerned about, and seek to enhance, the well-being of each other, an attitude that also permeates their interactions outside of the family. Whereas they are not necessarily unrealistic about the shortcomings of others, they look for the best rather than the worst in human nature.

Indeed, although conflict certainly can and does arise, families that flourish tend to demonstrate respect for the subjective worldviews, opinions, differences, and values held by individual members (Lewis et al., 1976). The ability to agree to disagree, rather than an authoritarian stance, is thus preferred by family members. There is no one belief system to which all must adhere, no set way of thinking that is the rule or a requirement. Rather, opinions can be debated without fear of intimidation or repudiation because of them. Consistent with one of the basic principles of communication from a systemic perspective, there seems to be an understanding, however implicit, that "the meaning of a given behavior is not the *true* meaning of the behavior; it is, however, the personal truth for the person who has given it a particular meaning" (Becvar & Becvar, 2006, p. 72). Accordingly, there is respect for each person's perspective as valid for that person, despite the existence of differences in perceptions.

As the validity of each person's perspective is acknowledged and respected, an atmosphere is created that allows for the prevention of a conflict-ridden context. Rather than debating the rightness or wrongness of a particular view, the focus shifts to a search for ways to work together in spite of differences of opinion. Implementation of such an approach, in turn, adds to an atmosphere of affiliation and warmth.

Approach to Problems and Challenges

When the time comes to deal with life's larger problems and challenges, successful families generally are able to identify the various stressors, options, and constraints impinging on a particular situation (Walsh, 1998). In other words, they are able to include in their deliberations a consideration of the larger picture. They also tend to demonstrate resourcefulness as they engage in creative brainstorming and shared decision making. Instead of getting bogged down in a rehash of the details of a disagreement, they are able to articulate goals and formulate concrete steps aimed at achieving their desired solutions. Furthermore, they are able to recognize and learn from failure as well as to build on success. Theirs is a proactive stance that seeks to prevent problems, avoid crisis, and be prepared to deal with whatever challenges may arise in the future.

Consistent with the above skills and processes, negotiation tends to be the preferred method for resolving conflict in well-functioning families (Kaslow, 1982). Rather than choosing either a compromise that involves a tradeoff and a need to make concessions or conciliation that involves placating or pacifying one another, family members seem to have a belief in their ability to work things out together. And such give-and-take interactions prioritize the creation of win–win rather than win–lose situations.

As can be seen, the processes characterizing successful families tend to overlap and support the presence of each other. For example, a warm atmosphere is encouraged by a context of support, respect, and flexibility, and a context of support, respect, and flexibility allows for relationships that are able to minimize conflict and deal effectively with problems. Further, these dimensions tend to facilitate the fit of a family with others in its world.

Orientation to the Larger Context

The ability to avoid rigidity and opt for flexibility with one another tends to be reflected in the approach of well-functioning families to the larger context of which they are a part (Lewis et al., 1976). That is, such families are likely to share a recognition of the complex motivations guiding the behavior of others. They thus have moved beyond the simple dichotomies of black-and-white, either/or, us-versus-them thinking. They are able to demonstrate a willingness to change both form and structure as they interact in, impact, and respond to, an exceedingly complex environment. Not surprisingly, they also are likely to have a natural network of relationships outside the family from which they draw support and to which they devote some of their energy (Becvar & Becvar, 2006).

As mentioned previously, families that flourish tend to achieve a healthy balance between openness and closedness: the degree to which inputs from the larger context are, or are not, accepted by the system. They are able to recognize, adapt to, and assimilate relevant new information, thereby accommodating the need for change in appropriate ways. At the same time, they also are successful in maintaining the integrity of their own system, screening out information that is not useful or meaningful. They have rules and values that define a boundary, which distinguishes and maintains their uniqueness, as well as a rule that allows for the change in their rules when appropriate or necessary. And they understand the significance of responding well to the world in which they live.

Not surprisingly, well-functioning families generally are characterized by high levels of initiative, which is manifested in significant degrees of community involvement (Lewis et al., 1976). Their stance is one of active engagement, care, and concern for individuals and systems beyond the boundaries of their own family. For example, family members may become involved in activities at their children's schools, in their places of worship, in political advocacy, in neighborhood events, or just by being neighborly. Whatever their choice, they avoid the pitfall of social isolation, which can manifest in low levels of social skills and limited resources for handling adversity if and when it occurs.

Individual Support

In addition to initiative relative to the larger community, in families that are flourishing, initiative and autonomy in individual members also are encouraged and supported. These families tend to create a context that nurtures and fosters connection even as it facilitates emancipation and independence (Kaslow, 1982). There is implicit recognition of the ways in which independence and interdependence complement each other and enhance the well-being of the family and its members. High levels of personal autonomy are acceptable and may be expressed in several ways. For example, spouses or partners each engage in activities and have relationships separate from what occurs as a couple. Similarly, each child is encouraged to express his or her own talents or pursue interests that may be vastly different.

The varying developmental trajectories of individual family members also are acknowledged and accommodated. In other words, like the flowers in the perennial garden described in the introduction to this chapter, in families that flourish there is respect for the maturation processes of each member and an awareness that each has different needs. Not only is the growth of the garden, or family thus supported, but the individual members also are able to thrive.

Accordingly, family members have the ability to acknowledge what others feel and think and receive strong encouragement to assume individual responsibility for their own feelings, thoughts, and actions (Walsh, 1998). In other words, not only is effective communication the rule (Lewis et al., 1976; Kaslow, 1982), it is also the means by which healthy processes are modeled as well as encouraged.

Communication Skills

Certainly the ability to communicate effectively is an essential aspect of families that flourish. Individual members speak clearly and congruently so that both verbal and nonverbal levels match (Walsh, 1998). They thereby avoid sending double messages, which tend to encourage attempts at mind-reading. Further, as individuals participate in conversations, they seek clarification of any information that they experience as ambiguous or confusing. When interacting together, family members give each other direct attention and acknowledge the messages they are receiving. Discussions tend to occur in an orderly manner, and there is flexibility regarding the positions taken on various issues. In other words, a parallel relationship style (Harper, Scoresby, & Boyce, 1977) is likely to prevail.

To explain, in complementary relationships, there is a high frequency of interactions characterized by opposite kinds of behavior. For example, one person may be dominant while the other person is submissive, or when one person yells, the other withdraws. Symmetrical relationships are those in which interactions involve exchanges of similar kinds of behavior, such as both individuals yelling at each other or both individuals withdrawing. Although neither of these styles is necessarily good or bad, parallel relationships tend to be of a higher logical order (Harper et al., 1977). That is, not only do both complementary and symmetrical interactions occur in parallel relationships, but the positions taken by individuals shift from situation to situation. There is thus greater variation in behavioral style, with perhaps implicit awareness of the mutuality and bilateral nature of relationships (Becvar & Becvar, 2006).

At the same time, although they are able to assert themselves in a variety of ways, family members tend to agree more than disagree. And all of this takes place in an environment of friendliness, good will, and tolerance for difference, as noted above. What is more, the uniqueness of each individual is encouraged, and successes are acknowledged appropriately (Becvar & Becvar, 1997a, 2006; Riskin, 1982; Satir, 1982). For example, compliments are common, and accomplishments are recognized. Family members are able to express a wide variety of emotions, with permission to be angry with one another as well as to play well together (Kaslow, 1982). Over all, there thus tends to be openness in the expression of affect (Lewis et al., 1976).

Enrichment and Nurturance

Not surprisingly, members of families that flourish generally enjoy each other and are able to have fun together. They are able to be serious with, as well as to celebrate, one another (Becvar & Becvar, 2006). Playtime may occur informally in terms of such activities as joke telling, tossing a football, going for a bike ride, or taking a walk. It also may occur more formally, with regular planned outings, daily routines, or family vacations. Although possibilities abound, what is most important is that an accent on enrichment and the generation of positive energy is woven into the fabric of the family.

Similarly, families that are successful tend to engage in stable and consistent shares of nurturing behavior (Becvar & Becvar, 1999). Family members make time to be together in various one-on-one combinations and as a group. They seem to have an awareness that in order to thrive and grow, both the individuals and the relationships they create need to be tended in loving and thoughtful ways. For example, parents remember to honor and care for their spousal/partner relationship in addition to focusing on the care of their children. They get pleasure and energy from time spent together, balancing interactions and activities with each other alone with opportunities to be with other adults. In addition, they are able to meet their needs for intimacy and sexual expression in a context of relatively equal power (Walsh, 1998). They thus strengthen the foundation of their relationship and a commitment to one another in acknowledgment, however implicit, of the fact that they were a couple first and need to have more than their children to bind them together. In doing so, they model for their children a healthy, mature partnership. At the same time, they also avoid the dangers associated with living virtually separate lives that are joined only by their roles as parents, which may lead to the choice by one or both to go their separate ways once the children are grown.

Time spent as a group is also an important aspect of enrichment and nurturance. Thus, despite the hectic schedules so prevalent in today's society, families that flourish make an effort to bring all members together for at least some of their meals, even if it is only Sunday dinner, for example. In addition to going on outings, they also may attend religious services together, have family meetings, or just "hang out" with one another from time to time. In general, family members take pleasure from being in each other's company. Furthermore, as they enjoy opportunities to experience themselves as a unit, their sense of belonging is enhanced.

Indeed, as noted at the outset, the prevailing mood, or temperature, in flourishing families is one of warmth and affection, an attitude that is supported by a well-developed capacity for empathy. Accordingly, there is a lack of lingering conflict or resentment, and high degrees of spontaneity and humor are in evidence (Lewis et al., 1976; Kaslow, 1982). A sense of lightheartedness emerges from time to time, with expressions of humor that include good-natured teasing, storytelling, and permission to laugh at oneself as well as with each other. The ability to avoid taking oneself too seriously fosters flexibility and enables individuals to handle life's vicissitudes more easily than might be the case with a toosolemn approach. In addition, family members tend to go out of their way to do nice things for each other without the need for recognition or reward. Consistent with the notion that a happy family is one in which happy things happen, positive interactions are far more frequent than those that are negative, and they become a source of strength and revitalization rather than a drain on the energy and resources of family members.

Family Structure

Another important process dimension in successful families is the presence of a legitimate source of authority, one that is established and supported over time (Becvar & Becvar, 1999). Whereas authority generally is located in one or more parents, it also may be vested in grandparents, aunts, uncles, or other parental figures who may, or may not, be related by blood. Indeed, one of the more recent characteristics of family change is the increasing number of grandparents who are rearing their grandchildren (Casper & Bianchi, 2002). As with families in general, more important than the particular configuration are the processes present. In this case, it means that there is a person or persons who are in charge, that there is an appropriate hierarchy that is defined and respected.

Also important is the presence of a stable rule system that is consistently acted upon (Becvar & Becvar, 1999). Although flexibility rather than rigidity is the desired stance, those in charge are characterized by a strong alliance, presenting a united front with the children even though they may not entirely agree. When differences occur, as they surely will, they are debated in private. Thus, neither parent nor parental figure undermines the authority or the ability of the other parent or parental figure to be effective. In addition, there are clear individual and generational boundaries, so that both individual and relationship privacy are respected, with children able to be children, and parents assuming the responsibility that rightfully belongs to them. Clear boundaries also are evident as the rule of only two to a relationship, particularly relative to conflict, is observed.

Thus, for example, there is an absence of inappropriate internal or external coalitions such as triangulation. Parents don't involve a child in their conflicts, nor, during times of conflict with one another, do they seek support for a particular position from a friend or relative. Rather, they work out their difficulties and seek solutions for their problems together. Similarly, siblings in conflict are encouraged to resolve their own issues without parental interference as long as they abide by the family's rules (e.g., no hitting). Reciprocity, cooperation, and negotiation (Lewis et al., 1976) thus tend to characterize interactions, described above as one aspect of effective communication.

Whereas power issues relative to parent–child interactions initially are handled hierarchically, strong parental leadership slowly gives way over time to greater freedom for children in relation to their age and stage of development (Kaslow, 1982). When children are young, it is appropriate for parents to have all of the power and to function as the primary decision-makers. However, as children grow, it is appropriate that they gradually receive both additional responsibilities and increased privileges consistent with their level of maturity. Although parents take steps to relinquish some (perhaps most) of their control, they remain in charge until the time comes for the creation of new rules and the establishment of new relationships with their adult children. Given such practices, the need for rebellion on the part of adolescents is reduced or avoided, as young people are provided with opportunities to experience and learn how to handle greater freedom appropriately.

Family Mythology

In addition to the structural dimensions just described, successful families also tend to have a congruent mythology. That is, family members perceive, or have stories about, themselves that are consistent with the ways in which others perceive them (Lewis et al., 1976). What is more, the story they and others have match what is actually going on. For example, there is no pretense about being one big, happy family in which all is well when, in fact, there is a serious issue in need of attention. The reality of a family member dealing with chemical dependency, for example, is a problem to be solved rather than a situation to be ignored. Similarly, family members seek outside help when a challenging situation seems to require such intervention. Members of families that are flourishing, therefore, generally are able to recognize both their weaknesses and their strengths and thus are realistic in their capacity for self-appraisal.

In successful families the mythology often speaks to a vision of the family as a whole that can be an important source of strength. For example, in some families recognition of a tradition of strong women may enable female members to rise to the occasion when seriously challenged. Similarly, the idea that the family of which one is a member has always stuck together may enable members to bridge relationship gaps that otherwise might prove insurmountable. Such stories provide an interpretive framework, or lens, that encourages a focus on possibilities and potentials rather than limitations and liabilities.

Systemic Orientation

Although not necessarily explicit, a systemic orientation is another process dimension often found in flourishing families. These families have a sense of their mutuality, or shared influence and responsibility (Kaslow, 1982) that is consistent with the idea of recursion and circular causality. Family members can see that they are "in it" together, and they are able to acknowledge their "we-ness," their sense of family nationality. They recognize that all members participate in creating whatever is going on in the family. Such an awareness precludes the tendency to find fault and place blame in a manner that logically follows from a more traditional, linear view of causality.

Family members are likely to have a set of goals toward which both the family and each individual works. Some families may hold the goal that the children be successful in school, perhaps surpassing the level of education achieved by the parents. In other families the goal may involve traveling and experiencing other cultures. Whatever the family goals might be, individual goals also are supported and encouraged, and not everyone has to be good at the same thing. Consistent with research (Jones, 1995) regarding the importance of meaning and purpose in life for psychological well-being and the ability to evidence resilience, what seems most important is that successful families tend to do well in terms of supporting both individual and family goals.

Attention to Rituals

The observance of shared rituals and traditions (Becvar, 1985; Sawin, 1979, 1982; Walsh, 1998) is another important aspect of well-functioning families. Indeed, rituals play many important roles; they tend to enhance relationship identity and allow family members to accept growth, change, and loss while, at the same time, also helping to maintain their basic sense of continuity through time. Through participation in rituals, family members are able to acknowledge tangible as well as intangible realities, given the inclusion of both content and process. Further, rituals may help to strengthen the whole family and/or relationships within it. They may encourage or acknowledge role performance, and they may influence structures, rules, and boundaries. For example, I have often found it helpful to encourage families who have just experienced a divorce to continue to celebrate holidays but to do so in a way that recognizes and affirms the reality of their situation—that is, different configuration of family members, different ideas about how the celebration should occur. Rituals imply action, moving individuals from feelings of power-lessness to those of effectiveness, helping to recreate joy, structure grief, and enhance a sense of control, thereby alleviating anxiety (LaFarge, 1982). An important illustration of the significant role that rituals can play is the finding that their use in families with an alcoholic member may decrease intergenerational recurrence of the problem of addiction (Wolin & Bennett, 1984).

Rituals may include formal celebrations of holidays such as Christmas or Chanukah; life cycle transitions such as graduations, bar or bat mitz-vahs, weddings and funerals; and family traditions such as birthdays and anniversaries. They also may include the less formal but equally important traditions regarding mealtimes, bedtimes, and playtimes. In-deed, it is in the form of regular rituals that many of a family's nurtur-ing behaviors often are expressed. For example, couples may allot regu-lar time on a daily basis to do something fun together, or they may have a weekly or monthly date night. Similarly, there may be a weekly kid's menu night when, by turns, one of the children is allowed to choose what the family will have for dinner that evening.

Another of my favorite rituals, often shared with clients, is the use of a red plate to acknowledge and celebrate some sort of achievement by a member of the family, be it a good grade, a promotion at work, or a suc-cess relative to a family goal. The dinner of the person to be recognized is served on a red plate, which can be either ceramic or plastic. Further, the occasion, including date and details, is noted in a notebook (prefer-ably red) that is reserved for this purpose and kept with the red plate. For those who wish to embellish this ritual, accompanying pictures may be taken and added to the notebook.

Orientation to the Transcendent

In addition to ritual observance, another important process dimension often characterizing well-functioning families is the presence of a tran-scendent value system (Kaslow, 1982). Such a value system embodies a sense of relatedness and continuity in terms of both time and space, and may or may not include acceptance of, or adherence to, some kind of re-ligious belief system. It generally includes either a perception of har-mony in the universe, a belief in a supreme being, force, or spirit, or a system of values that is ethical and humanistic in nature. In other words,

successful families are characterized by the presence of a spiritual awareness that may be expressed either within or outside traditional religious
institutions, and that is characterized by specific values. For example, according to Elkins (1990), in addition to acceptance of a transcendent dimension, spiritual persons seek to understand the meaning and purpose
of their lives while also having a sense of mission or destiny. They tend
to see all of life as sacred, but seek ultimate satisfaction in the spiritual
rather than the material realm. They are likely to be altruistic, idealistic,
as well as realistic, and they feel called to help better their world. As their
efforts bear fruit, their relationships with self, others, and their world are
positively impacted, as is their commitment to and belief in a transcendent dimension. Thus awareness of a transcendent level is often a primary source of meaning and purpose—both of which, as noted above,
have been described as "critical for mental and physical health and for
psychological strength and coping" (Jones, 1995, p. 20). Once again, we
also note the ways in which the various aspects of the dimensions of
flourishing tend to support and reinforce one another, which brings us to
a consideration of the relationship between flourishing and resilience.

Flourishing and Resilience

As noted throughout this and other chapters, families that flourish are
not defined by a particular configuration or structure; rather, they come
in many different shapes and sizes. They are said to be flourishing as a
function of the particular processes that describe the ways in which the
families operate and individual members interact with one another.
However, they rarely are characterized by all of the process dimensions
outlined above. To reiterate, these families are not perfect; their members
are human and they have problems. However, they go for therapy or
seek other outside assistance if that seems an appropriate response.
What is most important, they tend to be distinguished by an essential
spirit, or have an aura about them, that speaks of strength, competence,
and confidence. Derived from many sources, the members of these families tend to believe in themselves. It is this spirit that seems to shine
through and enable them to cope effectively, even in the midst of the
most difficult situations.

In short, families that flourish manifest *resilience*, the capacity to respond effectively to crises and to grow from the experience (Walsh, 1998). Accordingly, family members are able to make meaning in the face of adversity. They succeed in creating a story about events or finding a purpose in the midst of tragedy by means of which they are able to regain a foothold on life. They thus are successful in retaining or reclaiming a positive outlook following a crisis. In addition, they find solace in a sense of transcendence or derive support from the spiritual realm, even when doing so requires additional exploration. They also evidence flexibility as well as a feeling of connectedness. Their communication is characterized by clarity, open emotional expression, and the ability to solve problems collaboratively. Finally, they have both social and economic resources, although this does not necessarily mean they are wealthy in a monetary sense. Rather, they use what they have well, and they do so in unique ways that speak to their ability to be flexible and adaptable, as is described in the following chapter.

Conclusion

If we were to sum up the distinctive aspects of families that flourish, we would need to note such characteristics as a sense of comfort and good will in relationships within the family and the outside world. The members of these families experience a goodness of fit between each other and the larger context. Their orientation toward life-affirming beliefs and behaviors enables them to prosper physically, mentally, emotionally, and spiritually, even if not economically. Armed with a healthy combination of the dimensions of flourishing, they are able to deal well with the tasks and responsibilities of normal life. Most importantly, when life presents challenges and crises, they are resilient: They are able to stretch, rebound, and return to more normal functioning strengthened by the experience.

Some families seem to have been "born" with the capacity for resilience. For other families, it is a dimension that requires education and encouragement. In either case, since I have yet to experience a perfect family, I suspect that all families would be enriched by attention in this domain. And I certainly believe that in therapy, we as professionals can facilitate resilience as we remain cognizant of the various process dimensions characteristic of families that flourish. Accordingly, we can include in our interventions strategies that support the emergence of, or enhance, those relevant processes already in place. Clients thereby not only achieve solutions for the problems with which they presented, but (ideally) they leave therapy having learned from the experience and better equipped to cope with whatever challenges life may bring in the future. However, in order to be successful in helping clients achieve such outcomes, a complete understanding requires more than an awareness of the general processes of flourishing. In addition, we must be knowledgeable of the many specific ways in which resilience may be manifested, a consideration of which we turn to next.

CHAPTER FOUR

Resilience

In the United States the predominant orientation at all levels, from policy makers to practitioners, has been to operate as error-activated systems, responding to crises when they occur and being concerned primarily with problems and pathology rather than with prevention and health (Becvar, 1984a). Thus, as Patterson has noted, "we have a long history of focusing on the causes of disease, deficits, and behavioral problems" (2002b, p. 233). Despite this mainstream position, however, since the 1930s a group of social scientists has taken an alternate path, choosing to examine and describe the traits of families who are able to deal with various difficulties successfully. In the 1960s and 1970s particular emphasis consistent with this more positive focus was given to two areas: (1) family stress, coping, and adaptation, and (2) family strengths (De Haan, Hawley, & Deal, 2002; Hawley & De Haan, 1996; Walsh, 2003a). More recently, the concept of resilience has emerged as an important area of study for researchers as well as a significant focus for clinicians (Haggan, 2002). Whereas initial research efforts on the concept of resilience were concerned primarily with the health and successful functioning of individuals (Patterson, 2002b), there is now a growing body of literature whose focus is resilience in families.

In the family-oriented literature there is widespread agreement about the need to understand resilience as involving processes that are fluid, evolve over time, and as being influenced by context, rather than as describing a phenomenon that can be defined by static traits and characteristics (Conger & Conger, 2002; De Haan et al., 2002; Hawley & De Haan,

1996; Kragh & Huber, 2002; Oswald, 2002; Patterson, 2002a, 2002b; Sandau-Beckler, Devall, & de La Rosa, 2002; Schwartz, 2002; Walsh, 1998, 2003a). Also generally captured by the concept of family resilience is recognition of its importance in enabling resistance to change-induced disruption as well as in fostering the ability to adapt when faced with a crisis. In addition, resilience typically refers to a quality of buoyancy that translates into the capacity of families to repair themselves and rebound from difficult situations even stronger than they were before such situations were encountered. Most researchers, theoreticians, and practitioners who focus on resilience probably would be comfortable with the following definition offered by Hawley and de Haan (1996):

> Family resilience describes the path a family follows as it adapts and prospers in the face of stress, both in the present and over time. Resilient families positively respond to these conditions in unique ways, depending on the context, developmental level, the interactive combination of risk and protective factors, and the family's shared outlook. (p. 293)

At the same time, there seems to be some disagreement between clinicians and researchers regarding whether a family must experience and successfully withstand a crisis—for example, some kind of hardship or exposure to significant risk—before use of the term *resilience* becomes appropriate. According to Patterson (2002a, 2002b), clinicians have tended to equate family strengths, competence, and the ability to deal with life's challenges with resilience if and when such challenges arise. By contrast, researchers, "have been more interested in outcomes to explain unexpected competent functioning among families (and individuals) who have been exposed to significant risk(s)" (Patterson, 2002a, p. 349). Patterson therefore advocates for the use of the term *resiliency* to describe a capacity that would be available should a crisis occur, and the term *resilience* to describe specific processes that emerge in response to significant stress.

Such a distinction may or may not be useful, depending on one's perspective and orientation. In either case, there are several important dimensions of resilience that are worthy of emphasis. First, the paths followed by families as they negotiate challenges and regain their balance vary widely (De Haan et al, 2002; Walsh, 2003a). How these paths are forged by each family is a function of the particular set of protective factors, risk factors, contextual factors, and circumstances characterizing each unique situation (Hawley & DeHaan, 1996). What is more, the ability to evidence resilience in one situation does not guarantee its presence in another situation, or in response to other stessors (Patterson, 2002a; Walsh, 2003a), nor is there one single coping strategy that is necessarily effective in all situations. Further, a both/and perspective that acknowledges deficits and problems as well as strengths and skills is inherent in a resilience orientation (Roberts & Escoto, 2002; Schwartz, 2002). Indeed, "family resilience further shifts the tendency to perceive family health or normality as residing in mythologized, problem-free families to seeking understanding how families can and do survive and regenerate even in the midst of overwhelming stress and crises" (Kragh & Huber, 2002, pp. 294–295). The utility of such an orientation has been summarized as follows:

> A family resilience framework offers several advantages. By definition, it focuses on strengths under stress, in the midst of crisis and in overcoming adversity. . . . Second, it is assumed that no single model fits all families or their situations. Functioning is assessed in context, i.e., relative to each family's values, structure, resources, and life challenges. Third, processes for optimal functioning and the well-being of members are seen to vary over time, as challenges unfold and families evolve across the life-cycle. While no single model of family health fits all, a family resilience perspective is grounded in a deep conviction in the potential for family recovery and growth out of adversity. (Walsh, 2003a, pp. 5–6)

As with other forms of diversity, it is important to keep in mind the proviso that each family is unique and therefore will evidence resilience in a manner logical to its particular context. At the same time, however, general patterns or trends have been found to characterize various groups of families, with each group varying in terms of what is experienced as supportive or helpful in dealing with particular kinds of challenges. We move now to a consideration of resilience factors related to sources of significant stress for families such as chronic illness, children with disabilities, severe mental illness, economic adversity, death of a parent, murder of a child, substance abuse, domestic violence, work–family conflict, and parenting problems. We also consider resilience factors related to effective functioning in gay and lesbian families and to the phenomenon of religious intensification. Finally, we conclude with a brief consideration of factors that may foster resilience in various cultural groups.

Resilience in Context

Although resilience continually emerges in small ways throughout the daily lives of families and their members, the situations and circumstances that are out of the ordinary, or fall outside the norm of the expected, are those that tend to be the focus of study for researchers. These are the more unusual or dramatic occurrences or circumstances that tend to push people to their limits and therefore also may call forth more heroic and more remarkable responses. The specific illustrations of resilience described in this section are derived from a review of the professional literature on the subject. However, it should be remembered that they are but a sampling of the types of situations in which resilience may emerge, and certainly many other examples are likely to become the subject of comprehensive study in the future.

Chronic Illness

Chronic illness in a family member brings with it a variety of challenges that extend far beyond whatever physical limitations are involved (Shapiro, 2002). For example, this particular stressor may be accompanied by mental health issues such as anxiety or depression, both for the patient and for others in the family. It may be accompanied by economic issues associated with the high cost of medical care or decreased income as the ability of various family members to work is impaired. And it may be accompanied by such relationship issues as lack of availability to other family members as well as irritability and vulnerability related to caregiving and care receiving. Nevertheless, families in this category certainly may evidence resilience in response to appropriate support, as the following review indicates:

> Consistently, researchers, providers, and policy makers recognize the efficacy of collaborative treatment approaches that involve patients and their families in health education and self-care, use linguistically and culturally appropriate communication to respectfully assess the patient and family's experience of the chronic illness, use cultural strengths and recognize stressors in treatment

planning; rely on collaborative, interdisciplinary treatment teams within the health system; provide culturally appropriate community services that support patient and family coping; and encourage patient, family, and community advocacy for improved services needed by the chronically ill. (Shapiro, 2002, p. 1376)

Specific suggestions for implementing such collaborative approaches include helping family members to create an illness narrative that is coherent for everyone involved (Shapiro, 2002). This step is consistent with a general recognition of the significance of meaning-making in enabling a family to withstand stress (Patterson, 2002a). Also consistent are suggestions to support accurate understanding of what is happening, help the family members communicate with one another effectively, enhance skills related to dealing well with larger systems, as well as explore, identify, and access resources within the individuals, the family, and the community (Patterson, 2002b; Shapiro, 2002). When such suggestions, which are consistent with several of the dimensions of flourishing, are attended to, family members often are able not only to withstand the impact of chronic illness but also to grow from the experience.

Children with Disabilities

Similar to those dealing with a situation of chronic illness, many families have successfully accommodated the challenges involved with the birth of a child with a disability, often scoring higher on standardized measures of individual and family functioning than would be anticipated given the circumstances (Patterson, 2002a). In this case, the specific stresses to which such families may be vulnerable include anxiety and depression, reductions in self-esteem, high levels of frustration, decreases in both marital and personal satisfaction, feelings of guilt and confusion related to others' reactions to the child with the disability, and significant grief and loss issues. Parents and other family members also may feel overwhelmed by the need to process a great deal of new information, often in short periods of time (Hartshorne, 2002).

Hartshorne (2002) suggests that one of the most important ways families who have children with disabilities may be supported is through the use of encouragement and a focus on strengths, rather than a focus on deficits or assuming that the tremendous potential for problems makes them inevitable. Along these same lines, it is further recommended that coping behaviors should not be pathologized; for example, mistaking courage for denial. Rather, courage should be recognized for what it is and understood as a significant resource facilitative of resilience. In addition, the following protective processes have been found in families in which there is a child with disabilities:

> (a) balancing the illness with other family needs, (b) maintaining clear family boundaries, (c) developing communication competence, (d) attributing positive meaning to the situation, (e) maintaining family flexibility, (f) maintaining a commitment to the family as a unit, (g) engaging in active coping efforts, (h) maintaining social integration, and (i) developing collaborative relationships with professionals. (Patterson, 2002b, p. 357)

Enhancing the emergence of such protective processes is again recommended as an important way in which therapists can promote resilience.

Severe Mental Illness

The risk factors, or subjective burden, experienced by families dealing with severe mental illness in one of their members (Marsh & Johnson, 1997) are many: grief for the member afflicted as well as for personal losses; sadness in response to symbolic losses related to hopes, dreams, and expectations; chronic sorrow as a function of ongoing experiences and challenges; life on an emotional roller-coaster as a function of repeated intervals of relapse and remission in the person with the mental illness; empathic pain for the afflicted person's situation; energy drain related to coping with symptomatic behavior and to caregiving responsibilities; disruption in family routines; obstacles in the service delivery system; and stigmatization. The significance of such factors is heightened by the fact that families tend to be the primary source of support for persons with severe mental illness.

Despite the pain involved, however, many families and their members are able to acknowledge an enhancement in various areas of their lives as a result of their involvement with mental illness. For example, in a study conducted in 1996, the following reactions were reported:

> [S]urvey participants told us about their family bonds and commitments, their expanded knowledge and skills, their advocacy activities, and their role in their relative's recovery. Our participants also affirmed their potential for personal resilience, noting

that they had become better, stronger, and more compassionate people. They cited their contributions to their family, their enhanced coping effectiveness, and their healthier perspectives and priorities. (Marsh & Johnson, 1997, p. 231)

The potential for such resilience may be enhanced through sensitive understanding of what the family is experiencing and an emphasis on normalizing typical reactions (Marsh & Johnson, 1997). A focus on the strengths and skills of everyone involved also is important, as is the need to offer education regarding the illness, the mental health system, and available resources. Enhancing skills in the areas of effective communication, problem solving, and stress management, in addition to resolving feelings of grief and loss are all crucial. Furthermore, it is important to be aware that family members fare better when they understand how to deal with the symptoms of mental illness and are able to respond appropriately when a relapse appears to be imminent. Indeed, a supportive family environment in which expectations are realistic and the needs of all members are recognized and accommodated bodes well for the emergence of resilience in the face of serious mental illness.

Economic Adversity

Whereas the experiences of chronic illness, children with disabilities, and severe mental illness share many similarities in terms of both risk factors and processes protective for resilience, very different behaviors and resources may be relevant when a family is faced with economic adversity. For example, a longitudinal study of families living in rural Iowa during a period of a severe downturn in the economy provides interesting insights about resilience. The results of the study are informative relative not only to financial strains but also to life-cycle issues as adolescents transition to early adulthood (Conger & Conger, 2002).

In this study the processes that enabled couples to deal well with their financial situation included high levels of social support toward one another as well as the ability to solve problems effectively (Conger & Conger, 2002). In addition, a high degree of mastery, or success in coping with various life challenges, ameliorated depressive symptoms at the same time that it also increased the capacity for handling economic difficulties. The latter effect, in turn, lessened the long-term experience of economic pressure for family members.

Regarding the relationships between parents and children in the context of economic hardship, school performance, peer interactions, and self-confidence were all found to be supported by "nurturant-involved parenting." Parents operating in this mode "demonstrate affection, warmth, and low levels of hostility toward their children and also monitor child activities, provide appropriate contingencies for desired and undesired behaviors, and set reasonable behavioral standards" (Conger & Conger, 2002, p. 371). Adolescents who were the recipients of nurturant-involved, as opposed to hostile, parenting also had fewer conduct problems than their peers, were able to achieve more satisfactory relationships with a romantic partner as young adults, and were more competent as parents. They also were protected from the negative influence of older siblings who had become involved with alcohol.

Death of a Parent

By contrast with economic adversity, once again an entirely different set of circumstances and potential resources surround family members' experiences of the death of a parent. On the one hand, such an event is likely to be extremely significant and to represent an intensely meaningful milestone in the life of the family. On the other hand,

> there is perhaps no other loss with greater diversity of meaning for survivors depending upon factors such as age, individual development, gender, and family life cycle stage. That is, for a young child the loss of a parent is both unthinkable and life-changing whereas for a mature, older adult it is highly predictable and often assumed to be less disturbing. Similarly, the ability to understand the meaning of the death of a parent varies considerably as a function of one's level of cognitive and emotional maturation. What is more, the death of a mother tends to have a very different impact than does the death of a father, and this impact may differ for sons as opposed to daughters. And when the last parent dies and orphanhood becomes one's reality, it, too, has widely varying ramifications depending upon the ages and developmental stages of the surviving children. (Becvar, 2001, p. 146)

Despite such potential variations, a study of 39 families who were surveyed regarding their perception of the factors and strengths they considered to be significant when dealing with this type of loss provides interesting information in terms of understanding how to facilitate resilience following the death of a parent (Greeff & Human, 2004). For example, support within the family for emotional issues and the completion of practical tasks was found to be most helpful in coping with the loss. Internal strengths and a sense of the durability of the family unit—hardiness characteristics—also contributed to resilience within the family. In addition, an optimistic attitude among individual members as well as support from extended family and friends were experienced as very important. Finally, successful adjustment to the loss was facilitated by religious/spiritual beliefs and activities. In addition to these findings, Walsh (1998) also identifies open, honest communication and economic resources as facilitative of the resilience of a family in the aftermath of the death of a parent.

Murder of a Child

Described as an event capable of pushing parents "beyond endurance" (Knapp, 1986), the death of a child understandably is looked upon as one of life's greatest tragedies. Lost are parents' hopes and dreams for that child, in addition to the special and unique bond, as well as the related roles that tend to characterize the parent–child relationship (Klass, 1988). In addition, parents tend to grieve the loss of the child as well as to lament and feel guilty about the lack in their ability to care appropriately for him or her. And because no part of the experience makes sense, parents are likely not only be shocked and numbed, but also may lose the belief systems that formerly gave meaning to their lives (Becvar, 2001). When the death of a child occurs under violent circumstances, the trauma experienced by parents is likely to be even more devastating and debilitating.

In recognition of research indicating that some trauma survivors are able to grow and thrive following a traumatic experience, Parappully (2002) sought to learn whether this might ever be the case with parents of murdered children. Sixteen parents who had been through such an experience and who responded to a questionnaire in a manner that indicated they had achieved a positive outcome, or signs of transformation in thinking, feeling, and behaving, were selected for the study. In the realm of thinking, such signs included the following:

> finding a new meaning/purpose in life; reappraisal and reconstruction of fundamental assumptions about self, others, and the

world; profound changes in ideologies, beliefs, attitudes, and values; increased openness to new ideas and to people, stronger religious faith, increased self-awareness, and positive self-regard; increased sense of coherence; and valuable lessons learned. (p. 37)

In the realm of feeling, such signs included "increased feeling of satisfaction and fulfillment, increased ability to experience pleasure and gratification, increased capacity for joy, increased optimism and hopefulness about the future, feeling more compassionate, and feeling called to a mission" (p. 37). And in the realm of behavior, such signs included:

more active involvement in the family and world outside, increased ability to deal effectively with the problems and challenges of life, more healthy interpersonal relationships, deepening of existing attachments and/or forming new emotionally satisfying attachments, becoming more caring toward others, striving to accomplish new goals, increased capacity for artistic and productive work, and having a quality of life exceeding the pretrauma period. (pp. 37–38)

Parappully (2002) identified various processes and resources that were facilitative of resilience for the parents of murdered children who participated in this study. Cognitive–emotional processes that mutually influenced and enabled the trauma to be transformed in a positive manner included acceptance of the reality of what had occurred, searching for and finding some meaning in the events, and making a personal decision to avoid letting the experience ruin the lives of the survivors. An additional process that proved to be very helpful was the decision to reach out to others in compassion, thus enhancing a sense of meaning and purpose in their lives.

There were also six categories of resources that were particularly helpful to participants in overcoming the tragedy in a positive manner. Such personal qualities as independence, determination, self-confidence, self-reliance, and optimism were all in evidence. Also important was spirituality, which included faith in God and religious belief, belief in life after death, thankfulness or gratitude for what they did have, and prayers and ritual. A third resource was the sense of a continuing bond with the victim, and social support, derived from spouses, family members, the community, support groups, or therapy experiences, comprised the fourth

category. Knowledge and skills from having previously coped successfully was the fifth resource category, and the importance of self-care was
the sixth.

Much useful information is available from this study. Despite seemingly overwhelming circumstances, the parents of murdered children
can be helped. What is more, their ability to be resilient may be enhanced
as therapists utilize the knowledge and experience of those who have
successfully survived such a tragedy.

Substance Abuse

When the challenges being experienced are related to substance abuse—
one of the most significant issues facing American families today—a variety of problematic patterns may emerge, including rigid roles, an indi-
vidualistic perspective, and poor communication (Sandau-Beckler et al.,
2002). Lack of understanding of life-cycle developmental processes and
issues also may be apparent, with a predominant focus on the present
at the expense of both past connections and future directions. Given the
chaos of daily life and a sense of being overwhelmed, family members
may feel that there is little energy available to search for order or meaning. Blaming and scapegoating tend to be common, and a fatalistic rather
than an optimistic outlook is likely to prevail. A sense of transcendence
or belief in a higher power, or God, often is undermined by the lack of
coherence in the values and behaviors of family members. To complicate
things further, families in which substance abuse is a problem tend to lack
the important qualities of flexibility and connectedness and to under-
utilize social and economic resources.

In an attempt to facilitate resilience in families dealing with substance
abuse, one clinical research study focused on the implementation of programs for at-risk youth at churches in various rural, suburban, and inner-
city communities (Johnson, Bryant, Collins, Noe, Strader, & Berbaum,
1998). According to the researchers, positive outcomes were achieved
by means of "an integrative parent–youth training model consisting of
information, affective education, and social skill development" (p. 306).
Early intervention and follow-up case management services also enhanced this process. The specific areas addressed by the program included increasing parents' knowledge about substance abuse as well as
improving their family management skills; enhancing family relationships

and bonding among members; supporting parent–child involvement in community activities; encouraging the use of community resources; and creating safe, supportive contexts.

The authors of another study gained insight into the importance of rituals in alcoholic families, reporting that "extreme ritual disruption was significantly related to greater intergenerational recurrence of alcoholism, whereas ritual protection was associated with less transmission" (Wolin & Bennett, 1984, p. 403). The importance of rituals (e.g., holiday celebrations and birthdays) was attributed to their ability to help the family maintain its sense of identity even in the midst of chaos. Indeed, as both studies indicate, despite circumstances of tremendous disruption and great confusion, resilience often can be facilitated when substance abuse is a problem.

Domestic Violence

An issue whose significance and challenges are equal to that of substance abuse is domestic violence, perhaps "the most common yet least reported crime in this nation" (Kragh & Huber, 2002, p. 290). In the United States more than 2 million women are victims of spousal/partner abuse each year. What is more, it is likely that a large percentage of cases of domestic violence are never documented.

Crimes in this category most often involve attacks on wives by their husbands or ex-husbands. Therefore, although domestic violence certainly can occur in reverse, the woman generally is seen as the victim, and the man is perceived as the victimizer. With the necessity for assuring the victim's safety, the standard response typically involves separating and treating the two parties individually.

Taking a family resilience perspective, Kragh and Huber (2002) suggest an alternative approach that assumes that people have inherent abilities and acknowledges the various attempts made by couples to solve their problems. Couples in which domestic violence has occurred are understood to be stuck in a destructive pattern and unable to find appropriate solutions. Rather than focusing only on deficits, it is recommended that therapists search for assets; the underlying assumption is that somewhere in the behavioral repertoires of such couples reside both the skills and the evidence of previous success needed to prevent further destructive interactions. As successes or exceptions to dysfunctional behavior, however small, are identified, skills can be recognized as available and able to be further developed. This empowering orientation in turn, may enable more appropriate behaviors in the present and future. None of these suggestions is intended to replace the need to recognize the significance of the violence or the necessity for an appropriate safety plan to prevent further abuse. However, these clinicians focus on accessing information related to both the abuse and to the potential for solutions. They thus offer an additional, more positive way to work with the problem of domestic violence.

Work–Family Conflict

Perhaps less challenging but more universal in its implications is conflict between work and family. Indeed, the relationship between work life and family life is certainly significant, as each impacts the other in terms of the ability of an individual to function in both spheres. Although this work–family dynamic has been present in families for centuries, today the issue probably is even more salient. Families in the 21st century are characterized by a high percentage of dual-earner couples. Possibly as a function of this reality, workers are demanding more time to spend with their families. At the same time, however, businesses often are requiring greater flexibility from their employees in order that they may compete effectively in the ever-broadening global marketplace (Grzywacz & Bass, 2003). It thus makes sense that the work–family interface may be challenging, and that when a reasonable fit between the responsibilities related to work and those related to the family cannot be found, various problems are likely to arise.

Grzywacz and Bass (2003) used family resiliency theory in an effort to identify factors that affected the mental health of employees as a function of work–family conflict and work–family fit. The results of their study indicate that the mental health of employees was negatively impacted by high levels of conflict, both work to family and family to work. By contrast, and although not found to be true in reverse, the more that the family was able to accommodate the demands of the workplace, the better the psychological well-being of the employee. In other words, "the magnitude of the effects suggests that family interfering with work is more detrimental to mental health than was work interfering with family" (p. 257). Given this finding, therapists who may be seeking to facilitate resilience relative to work–family conflict are advised to focus on ways in which the family can accommodate the requirements of the workplace rather than requesting changes in the employee to accommodate his or her family.

Parenting Problems

Rearing children is a serious and challenging undertaking, one for which parents generally are poorly prepared, at least in terms of formal education. Even when they have good instincts and are doing a fine job, parents often doubt their effectiveness, or question whether what they are doing is correct. It is not surprising, therefore, that one of the most common reasons for which clients come to therapy is to gain assistance in dealing with a problem, or "out-of-control," child. Similarly, other systems such as schools and juvenile courts also regularly refer families regarding parenting issues and problems.

As a means of facilitating resilience relative to the often tough job of parenting effectively, Roberts and Escoto (2002) as well as Schwartz (2002) advocate a primary focus on parental expertise and the identification of times when the children were parented successfully. From their perspectives, such moments represent ways to affirm past efforts in addition to offering models that may be used to enhance effectiveness now and in the future. Thus the focus shifts from the remediation of problem behavior to a consideration of what has worked. Having completed this initial step, it is then recommended that parents be encouraged to use "their strengths and talents more often to reduce stress, enhance family communications, and engage in problem-solving with their children" (Schwartz, 2002, p. 253). Such a collaborative approach is aimed at enabling families to utilize their inherent abilities and thus to overcome whatever deficits and problems they have been experiencing.

Gay and Lesbian Families

Although becoming more prevalent in our society, the family networks of lesbians and gay men continue to be challenged in many ways. Some of the issues with which these families are likely to be confronted include rejection by families of origin, stigmatization by the heterosexual majority, lack of legal sanction for committed relationships, and disputes over parental rights. Further complicating factors may include racism and economic inequality (Oswald, 2002). Nevertheless, many gay and lesbian families are able to function well, to thrive and grow, despite the inevitable hardships they face. Two important processes, described as *intentionality* and *redefinition* have been identified as crucial to such resilience:

> Intentionality includes conscious actions that gay and lesbian people and their heterosexual loved ones use to validate themselves as family members and strengthen their ties to supportive others. Redefinition includes the ongoing development of a belief system that affirms gay and lesbian people. The multiple and recursive processes included within these two categories promote the existence and success of gay and lesbian family networks. (Oswald, 2002, p. 375)

Within the category of intentionality, actions taken in support of a sense of family in a generally hostile context may involve the practice of choosing kin, including perceiving friends as members of the family; becoming parents either by natural means or by adoption; and integrating heterosexual individuals, including biological family members, into their lives. Such a sense of family may be further created and enhanced as disclosure is managed carefully, a community that provides social and material supports is developed, rituals are designed to foster identity and solidify relationships, and innovative strategies to achieve legalization (e.g., filing a power of attorney or mingling finances) are implemented (Oswald, 2002).

Politicizing is a major aspect of redefinition as members of gay and lesbian families become activists or educate their children regarding the management of stigma. Another important part of the redefinition process involves naming, which may include the creation of labels for parents and other non-kin family members, as well as the formulation of a common surname. Integrating homosexuality with other aspects of identity shared by all regardless of sexual orientation, for example, religion or ethnicity, further assists with the process of redefinition. Finally, envisioning family, "the process of redefining family to be an ongoing construction that affirms human differences, rather than an inevitable set of biolegal relationships that punishes those who resist or subvert social norms" (Oswald, 2002, p. 380), also is crucial to resilience.

Religious Intensification

Another interesting view of resilience factors is provided by a study of religious intensification, in this case, "the reactions and adaptations of mothers to their adult daughters' change from relatively moderate to fervent ('Ultra-Orthodox') observance of Judaism" (Roer-Strier & Sands, 2001, p. 868). The results of a qualitative study of 15 mothers and 15 daughters, which was conducted in South Africa, validated the importance of a shared family outlook, of a supportive context, and of specific protective factors in helping families to adapt, grow, and thrive despite the stressors involved. Stressors associated with religious intensification include the destabilization that often occurs when young adults make a choice to become more religious. For example, and particularly relevant to this study, among Jewish families religious intensification may involve distancing as the younger generation moves to a more religious neighborhood or refuses to eat at parental homes because of differences in dietary requirements. The latter behavior, in turn, challenges "the family's sense of cohesion and impedes family celebrations, which usually involve food" (Roer-Strier & Sands, 2001, p. 869).

Found to be particularly helpful in facilitating resilience among the families involved in this study was the view shared by the participants regarding the importance of maintaining the Jewish family. This view was especially significant in the South African context, where not only is being a member of the Jewish community a crucial aspect of cultural identity, but also, in the face of political and social upheaval, family relationships are highly valued. Finally, the daughters' rabbis also represented a protective factor by virtue of their reinforcement of the above views and values.

Cultural Diversity

As with religious intensification, the role of context also must be considered when the challenge involves understanding and facilitating resilience among diverse cultural groups. Difference generally is denigrated in our society, with cultural groups who represent a minority often suffering from racism, prejudice, the undermining of basic values, and concomitant negative influences on health status. Nowhere is this more the case than with native Hawaiians (Thompson, McCubbin, Thompson, & Elver, 1998). Despite their high-risk status, however, many families in this group have been able to demonstrate resilience, with community support found to be crucial to the process. Also important, not only to native Hawaiians but also to native Americans, is a family schema, or "generalized structure of shared values, beliefs, goals, expectations and priorities" (McCubbin, McCubbin, Thompson, & Thompson, 1998, p. 23), according to which adversity is accepted as part of the will of a higher power. Other protective factors for both of these cultural groups include their present-time orientation, as well as the significance of the land, of spirituality, and of thinking in terms of the group as a whole rather than of the individual. Thus many of the characteristics previously described that serve to distinguish one cultural group from another also may be understood as factors that play an important part in the ability of each group to evidence resilience. Keeping these factors in mind may enhance our cultural competence as well as our effectiveness as therapists.

Resilience and Flourishing

As illustrated above, resilience tends to be evident in families that (1) possess skills for effective communication, (2) demonstrate relational competence, and (3) engage in family enrichment practices, which may include spontaneity and humor. In these families effective parenting strategies are utilized, and attention is given to creating meaningful rituals and traditions. The presence of goals, values, and activities that encourage a sense of meaning and purpose, as well as an orientation toward, or awareness of, a religious or spiritual dimension are all in evidence. These families and their members demonstrate, through various combinations of processes, proficiency in the domains of functioning significant for resilience, including communication, organization, and belief systems (Walsh, 1998, 2003a).

Resilience is essential if families are to remain hardy and to flourish. Many families can be considered strong when life is going smoothly; they are characterized by a variety of the dimensions of flourishing and appear quite capable. However, not all of the families who otherwise seem to be functioning well are able to cope with, and overcome, serious challenges. They thus tend to collapse, never to recover. For example, a rather frequent story heard in my clinical practice speaks to the aftermath of the death of a parent, often the mother. Whereas the family members previously worked well together, enjoyed each other's company, were successful in school and at work, following the death of the mother, both the parent and the family that everyone had known and loved were lost

in the minds of the survivors. The resources of the family were not sufficient, and while a family remained, it was diminished by the crisis.
Quite the opposite is the case when resilience is present, and families
are able to respond to problems in ways that eventually enable them to
be even stronger, as described by Greeff and Human (2004) in their study
of families who had experienced the death of a parent.

Conclusion

As the specific illustrations of resilience hopefully make clear, the ability to assume an optimistic, positive attitude when working with families is likely to enhance one's effectiveness as a therapist. Although attempts to understand both the circumstances and challenges with which
particular families may be faced, as well the pain they may be experiencing, certainly are appropriate, a search for and an emphasis on the skills,
abilities, courage, and creativity they also possess are essential. Indeed,
resilience has been described as "a viewpoint to be used as a guide by
helping professionals to know where to look for resources and strengths
in family's stories that are too often laden with problems and seemingly
insurmountable obstacles" (Haggan, 2002, p. 279).

Here again we recognize the importance of a both–and perspective.
We understand that families may not be perfect, but that they still can
evidence resilience. We know that they have problems and pain, but that
they also have resources and abilities that can be discerned and encouraged. And we attempt always to remain cognizant that things perceived
as real are real in their consequences (Thomas & Thomas, 1928), and that
what we believe will influence what we see. The following exercise,
which I designed for use when teaching, helps to illustrate this idea.

First, I prepare two sets of directions that are randomly distributed to
students in the class, half of the group receiving one set and half receiving the other set. The first instruction reads: "The following is a video
clip of a healthy family. Please write down on your sheet of paper all of
the behaviors that are evidence of family strengths." The second instruction reads: "The following is a video clip of a dysfunctional family. Please
write down on your sheet of paper all of the behaviors that are evidence
of family dysfunction." I then show the final scenes from the video
Moonstruck, which is particularly usefully in highlighting the dynamics

of an Italian-American family. Not surprisingly, each group sees the same video clip very differently and in a manner consistent with the instructions they received. The discussion then focuses on the degree to which what each believes is likely to influence what each will see.

Indeed, for me, believing is seeing. And as I believe in and look for strengths, I am more likely to find them. Armed with such an attitude, as well as all of the information just distilled in this first section of the book, I can then proceed to the pragmatics, to the practice of therapy, with a focus on helping families to flourish through the facilitation of resilience.

PART II

Practices

CHAPTER FIVE

Putting Principles Into Practice

One of the great benefits of a systemic/cybernetic epistemology is that it provides a metaperspective according to which theoretical relativity is the rule. In other words, there is both awareness and acceptance of the potential utility to be found in *all* perspectives. Rather than having to operate solely according to the tenets of one model or rely on only one framework, the clinician is free to pick and choose among many theories and approaches, deciding in the moment which concepts or interventions would seem to be appropriate. In therapy, the relevant question thus becomes, what would be most useful with this client at this time? Of course, just as with theories of development or knowledge about cultural and structural variations in families, in order to take full advantage of such a position, as well as the question that follows from it, it is necessary to have an understanding of a broad range of approaches and therefore many options from which to choose. In this chapter I provide a brief review of the main theoretical schools of thought in family therapy as well as the particular interventions within each that I have found to be particularly helpful. In the final section, a case example offers a description of the way in which some of these approaches and related interventions may be integrated and utilized in practice, recognizing as well that other choices also might have been made.

As described previously, although mine is a postmodern orientation, I continue to make recourse to both the more modernist, so-called first-order approaches to family therapy and the various second-order approaches that have been created in an effort to be consistent with a post-modern stance. Those in the first-order category considered in the following sections include the contextual approach of Ivan Boszormenyi-Nagy, the natural systems theory of Murray Bowen, the experiential approach of Carl Whitaker, the structural approach of Salvador Minuchin, the communications approach of Virginia Satir, the strategic approach of Jay Haley, and behavioral/cognitive approaches in general.

First-Order Approaches and Interventions

First-order approaches are those primarily created by the seminal thinkers and therapists who began in the mid-1950s to focus on families. As described in Chapter 1, a major change occurred as these early pioneers shifted from a focus on individuals and intrapsychic dynamics to a consideration of families and interactional processes. Although the introduction of systems theory at the level of first-order cybernetics was quite revolutionary in its implications, the orientation of these early family therapists remained consistent in many ways with the modernist tradition of which they were a part. Accordingly, they generally saw themselves outside the system as they sought to understand and work with those inside the system. Therapists thus continued to operate more as experts who had specific models in mind about how families should function, as they intervened and worked in a manner that reflected these models.

Contextual Family Therapy

Consistent with his psychodynamic roots, Ivan Boszormenyi-Nagy (Boszormenyi-Nagy & Spark, 1973; Boszormenyi-Nagy & Ulrich, 1981) created a therapy that integrates both intrapsychic and interpersonal dynamics. The primary focus of this approach is on morality and contextualized judgments. Crucial to its implementation is awareness of the invisible loyalties to families of origin that spouses or partners bring to the family that they create together. The *context* referred to in contextual family therapy is that of the balance of fairness, or reliability and trustworthiness, that each person has previously experienced and thus subsequently participates in creating in relationships with others.

Basic Concepts and Constructs

Nagy believes that all people have a concern for fairness in relationships, what he terms "relational ethics," which he views as a fundamental force in society as well as in families. That is, an expectation to be treated fairly and to have one's welfare be considered and respected is everyone's right, according to this theory. The degree to which such behaviors did or did not occur in a person's family of origin determines whether that person's ledger of entitlements and indebtedness is balanced. The more that it is balanced—the more the person previously experienced equitability and fairness—the better able the person is to treat others in a similar manner. Further, as issues of entitlement and indebtedness are dealt with effectively by the people involved, their relationships become trustworthy.

Each member of a family is understood to have a ledger of entitlement and indebtedness. Debts are incurred through merit; as one gives consideration to the welfare of another, the other person incurs a debt. Such debts can be repaid only by the persons to whom they are owed. In other words, if you do something nice for me, you have earned merit and I have incurred a debt. Only by doing something nice for you can I repay this debt. When this rule is not followed—when one who has acquired merit seeks to collect from someone other than the person who owes the debt, or when a person seeks to pay off a debt owed by another—problems are likely to arise. For example, a wife may come into a relationship with a debt around affection owed to her by her parents. Her husband decides to try to repay this debt with frequent displays of affection toward his wife. However, despite very good intentions, not only will the debt not be repaid, but the husband is likely to feel that he has earned merit to which his wife does not feel that he is entitled.

Salient Practices

I have found that keeping in mind this particular dynamic referred to by Nagy as a ledger of entitlement and indebtedness can be very helpful in understanding some of the tensions the members of a relationship may be experiencing as well as in assisting them with resolution of their difficulties. Further, the concept of invisible loyalties (i.e., ties to one's family of origin that often exist out of conscious awareness) may offer a way to understand the logic of behavior in context.

An additional aspect of Nagy's approach that I have found useful to keep in mind is his consideration of the role of children. Nagy assumes a natural, unavoidable imbalance, or asymmetry, in the relationships between parents and children. That is, young children are not to be held responsible for debts incurred through acts of merit on the part of their parents. Rather, they are entitled, as a function of their age, to the care their parents give them. Inappropriate parental expectations for repayment by their children for such acts of perceived merit are likely to create problems, depleting children's trust resources and leading to symptomatic behavior. It is only as children grow and mature that a more equal balance in the ledger of entitlements and indebtedness slowly evolves and replaces the initial asymmetry.

Children also are seen as vulnerable to inappropriate claims for loyalty by one parent at the expense of loyalty to the other parent. Labeled by Nagy as "split filial loyalty," such behavior puts a child in a bind that violates the filial loyalty that is central to family dynamics and relational ethics. I certainly have found this way of understanding the creation of inappropriate triangles to be very useful. Indeed, the focus of this approach on relational integrity, trustworthiness, balances in commitments, and a multilateral perspective that encourages accountability for both self and others is very consistent with some of the significant processes characteristic of families that flourish, as described in Chapter 3.

Natural Systems Theory

Murray Bowen (1976, 1978) was the preeminent theorist among the seminal thinkers in family therapy. It was his belief that techniques without theoretical grounding were likely to be ineffective, and he often was severe in his criticism of family therapists, in general, for their fascination with clinical wizardry and their lack of emphasis on the creation of carefully conceptualized theory. It was Bowen's particular position that with theory as a guide to therapeutic action, the personal issues of the therapist would be less likely to influence therapy inappropriately.

Basic Concepts and Constructs

For Bowen, differentiation of self, including both the ability to separate feeling processes from intellectual processes and self from others, is an ongoing goal toward which all need to aim. Lack of differentiation leads to emotional fusion, termed by Bowen as an "undifferentiated family ego mass." Such fusion inhibits the ability of family members to be flexible, adaptable, and self-sufficient. Unresolved emotional attachments may lead to cutoffs from the family, expressed by means of either denial or isolation. There also is a tendency for parents to project their lack of differentiation onto their children, thereby creating a multigenerational transmission of emotionality leading to continually decreasing levels of differentiation.

Salient Practices

Natural systems theory has been much criticized as evidencing a male bias because of its preference for intellect over emotion and separation over inclusion. Although this may be a valid criticism, one that is consistent with an attempt to avoid making recourse to general ways in which all people should be, I nevertheless find that Bowenian concepts can be useful in some situations, depending on the clients and their circumstances. Indeed, helping family members to be flexible, adaptable, and self-sufficient is crucial to the process of facilitating resilience, and Bowen's model certainly speaks to this dimension.

At the same time, I am much more likely to utilize the Bowenian tool for understanding the larger family context. Like Nagy, Bowen (1976, 1978) was very concerned with the impact of past generations on present families. He believed that the nuclear family emotional system includes not only all of those currently living in the household but also all of the extended family members, whether living or dead, absent, or present. That is, the emotional systems of past generations are said to influence what is happening in the here and now. In order to capture and examine the intergenerational context of a family, his theory gave birth to the genogram. Whether literally drawn or only verbally related, I have found that asking family members to describe and get in touch with the characteristics, behaviors, and relationship patterns of a minimum of three generations can provide valuable information about, and insight into, the larger context within which problems have emerged. It also provides an opportunity for clients to learn more about and gain different views of themselves and their own family members.

Bowen was also similar to Nagy in his concerns related to triangles and triangulation. He believed that two-person relationships that are free of stress have little difficulty remaining stable. However, when the level of anxiety or conflict increases beyond what the relationship is able to handle on its own, a third person may be turned to or brought in by one member of the relationship as a means of support against the other member of the relationship. Children, in particular, may be vulnerable to having a problem projected onto them in this way. Regardless of the person chosen, such behavior may evolve into a series of escalating triangles as still others are drawn into and take one side or the other in the conflict. Resolution of triangles thus becomes a very important process in therapy and certainly is consistent with the rule to which I subscribe: only two to a relationship when dealing with conflict.

In addition, the idea of going home again, armed with an understanding of the dynamics of relationships, as suggested by Bowen, can be very helpful in various therapeutic situations. When appropriate, clients can be encouraged to renew previously abandoned or even just strained relationships through phone calls, letters or visits. As part of this intervention the therapist also may coach clients regarding behaviors that may enable them to avoid getting caught up in old patterns while, at the same time, having an opportunity to increase their understanding of the processes characteristic of their families of origin.

Finally, several provisos regarding therapist behavior also resonate for me. Bowen felt it was imperative to focus on patterns and process rather than getting caught up in specific emotional issues or content. What is more, he emphasized the importance of recognizing mutual influence and shared responsibility. And above all, he advised therapists to avoid being triangulated by taking sides with one member of a relationship. This caution, while always important in my mind, is particularly crucial when working with couples.

Experiential Approach

Despite his atheoretical stance and the creation of an approach that one would be hard-pressed to replicate, Carl Whitaker (1975, 1976a, 1976b; Whitaker & Keith, 1981; Whitaker & Malone, 1953) left a significant legacy that underscores the importance of creativity, spontaneity, and the utilization of humor. For Whitaker, therapy provides a context for growth on the part of the therapist as well as of the client. Indeed, he described it as involving an intimate parallel process in which everyone becomes equally vulnerable. He considered therapy to be an art and recommended that therapists follow their intuition and have faith in their own experience and ability in order to allow the process to unfold in genuine and authentically responsive ways. This is not unlike the postmodern stance according to which professionals are advised to avoid a set agenda or cookbook approach to therapy.

Basic Concepts and Constructs

Whitaker's view of families and their functioning is very consistent with the orientation described in this book. He considered healthy families to be those characterized by processes that enable them to grow as individuals and as a group, despite whatever problems they might encounter. Synchronous with the ideas of flourishing and resilience, he recognized the need for both separateness or autonomy and togetherness or cohesiveness. He also emphasized the importance in families of appropriate awareness of time and space, and of the need for boundaries between the generations at the same time that there is role flexibility, avoiding rigid patterns of triangulation, enmeshment, or disengagement. Furthermore, sex, passion, and playfulness were considered to be essential ingredients. Such a focus on healthy processes was reflective of Whitaker's emphasis on the importance of respecting the family's integrity and allowing the members to create their own destiny, rather than attempting to have them fit a mold advocated by the therapist.

Salient Practices

Some of the strategies suggested by Whitaker included redefining symptoms as efforts at growth and augmenting the despair of a family member (Keith & Whitaker, 1982). He thus utilized reframes and paradoxical interventions, both of which I also consider to be important therapeutic tools. He believed in "going crazy" so that the client could become sane. Although I suspect that few therapists would feel comfortable doing some of the things Whitaker did with clients (e.g., unexpectedly tossing a Frisbee, wrestling, falling asleep), I am not averse to giving out bottles of bubbles in order to help relieve tensions in a relationship. In addition, the inclusion of extended family members in the therapy process was a requirement for Whitaker. He also was one of the primary proponents of the use of a cotherapist. Although I wouldn't require it, I certainly have found that inviting grandparents or other relatives to join the therapy process can, at certain times, enhance the effectiveness of my work with clients. Similarly, inviting in a cotherapist also can be a very useful move, perhaps allowing for a different view when the process seems to be stuck, or facilitating the management of tensions that are in danger of inappropriate escalation.

Structural Family Therapy

In contrast to Whitaker's idiosyncratic style, Salvador Minuchin created one of the approaches that best lends itself to both replication and study. Provided by this approach are concrete conceptual maps about functional and dysfunctional families as well as specific guidelines for therapy. Furthermore, there is a great deal of research that supports the efficacy of this approach with families experiencing such problems as juvenile delinquency, anorexia, chemical addiction, alcohol, and the impact of low socioeconomic status. There is thus much in structural family therapy that can be relevant to the process of facilitating resilience.

Basic Concepts and Constructs

In the delineation of his approach Minuchin (1974, 1984; Minuchin & Fishman, 1981; Minuchin, Rosman, & Baker, 1978) describes three key concepts: structure, subsystems, and boundaries. Once again, utilization of these concepts may prove very beneficial, without having to adopt the entire theory. For example, according to Minuchin, *structure* refers to the patterns of interaction, or the consistent, predictable ways, in which the family organizes itself and thus functions. Attention to these patterns can provide important information that helps the therapist both to understand the context of the family and to identify specific areas in which change may be appropriate. Indeed, Minuchin believes that finding solutions to problems involves facilitation of appropriate changes in the family's structure.

Minuchin also views the family as comprised of a spousal subsystem, a parental subsystem, and a sibling subsystem. Thus he emphasizes the importance of a differentiation between the role of parent and that of partner for the members of the couple. He also emphasizes the importance of distinctions between the generations in the family. Such distinctions are maintained through the creation of appropriate boundaries, or rules for each relationship, that define the amount and kind of contact permissible within each subsystem. Ideally, boundaries are clear, meaning that they are both firm and flexible and that there is access between systems, with the possibility for communication and accommodation of change balanced by a degree of autonomy for the members of each subsystem.

Salient Practices

Relative to family dynamics, Minuchin believes in the importance of an effective hierarchical structure, with parents or parental figures forming an executive coalition that provides a united front to the children. This united front, in turn, enables the formation of an appropriate sibling subsystem. There also must be an appropriate balance between separateness and togetherness that avoids both disengagement and enmeshment. At the same time, there is great respect for the different forms or types of families that are able to provide contexts that foster healthy development for their members.

Therapy for Minuchin includes three phases: The therapist first joins with the family, assuming a leadership position, then evaluates the structure of the family, and finally helps to transform this structure. After completing the first step, which involves tuning into and respecting the family's natural hierarchy, the process unfolds through either spontaneous behavioral sequences or enactments requested by the therapist of relationship dynamics around a problem. Having thus ascertained a sense of the structure, the therapist can facilitate change in a variety of ways. Intensity is created through the use of voice tone, pacing, volume, and repetition. "Shaping competence," comparable to the idea of facilitating resilience, refers to a practice of emphasizing functional alternatives already available within the behavioral repertoires of family members and thus encouraging confidence. Structural alterations can be facilitated by suggesting changes in seating arrangements, meeting separately with various subsystems, or using paradoxical injunctions to create confusion. Although not necessarily in the service of creating the ideal family structure described by Minuchin, I have found that his concepts and interventions can be extremely useful in facilitating meaningful change as I seek to help families flourish.

Communications Approach

Virginia Satir (1964, 1972, 1982; Bandler, Grinder, & Satir, 1976; Satir, Stachowiak, Taschman, 1975) created what she called a process model. While very experiential in its expression, this approach emphasizes the importance of effective communication and its relationship to self-esteem. Hers was a very positive, humanistic view according to which all individuals were understood as having a natural inclination toward, and the resources necessary for, positive growth and development. Satir had a profound influence on many, both professionals and laypeople, and the work she began continues today through the Avanta network she created toward the end of her career.

Basic Concepts and Constructs

Satir believed in mutual influence and shared responsibility and saw therapy as a process involving interaction among all participants that provided a context for facilitating the development of whole persons. When working with clients she emphasized the importance of first making contact with each family member, demonstrating and modeling her feelings of self-worth while also affirming the value of every other person. She believed in both the ability of families to change and the possibility of finding solutions for all problems, regardless of their severity. She advocated spontaneity, a willingness to experiment, and flexibility regarding time, place, and style. Included in her therapeutic repertoire were metaphors, games, and humor, responding in the moment in whatever way seemed most appropriate to achieve change.

Salient Practices

Not surprisingly, given her orientation, there is much in Satir's theory and practice that I find meaningful. Indeed, as the leading female among the seminal family therapy theorists, she became a significant role model for me during my early training and subsequent professional development. Although Satir did not use the term, certainly one can discern a focus on resilience as an essential aspect of her perspective. Her emphasis on growth, development, and potentials has provided an important counterpoint to the field's tendency to focus on dysfunction.

Satir had an extremely powerful presence at the same time that she was very respectful and gentle with her clients. She did a great deal of supporting and affirming, both through touch and with her words. She moved people around, literally, and utilized the technique of sculpting: having people express their feelings about family dynamics through positioning and body posture. For example, consistent with her belief that various styles of communicating include both verbal and nonverbal behavior, she might encourage demonstrations of the stances of placating, blaming, being super-reasonable, or being irrelevant. Above all, however, she wished to encourage clients to communicate in a congruent manner. The goal, as she saw it, was consistency between words, feelings, and context, and she focused on skill development in this area as an important aspect of therapy. Indeed, it was her belief that the ability to communicate effectively was crucial to fulfillment of a family's potential to support the healthy development of its members. She might point out problematic patterns, help clients get in touch with their feelings, or demonstrate functional interactions. This she did through the creation of a trusting context in which clients felt safe enough to reveal themselves fully and experiment with new behaviors.

Satir also devised the "family life fact chronology" to help clients depict important events in the life of their families, beginning with the birth of the oldest grandparents. Similar in many ways to the genogram, this tool can provide useful information about intergenerational family patterns characteristic of a particular family. It also may facilitate understanding of the larger context within which symptoms have emerged and within which they may be understood as logical responses. Accordingly, there is much about her approach that can be utilized as the therapist seeks to help families flourish.

Strategic Approach

Although not trained as a therapist, Jay Haley generally is acknowledged as the primary exemplar of the strategic approach to family therapy. Influenced by his involvement in Gregory Bateson's early research on communication, including his study of the work of Milton Erickson, by the theorizing that subsequently took place in the initial development of the Mental Research Institute (MRI) in Palo Alto, and by several years of association with Salvador Minuchin, Haley (1963, 1973, 1976, 1980, 1984) created an approach that not only is unique and often effective but also frequently the object of criticism. Although certainly more modernist than postmodernist, the approach nevertheless provides useful information for therapists seeking to help clients solve their problems while, at the same time, facilitating resilience.

Basic Concepts and Constructs

In strategic therapy the focus is on resolution of the symptom, with clear definitions of the problem as well as the goal to be achieved. The therapist makes an effort to engage with clients, and each member of the family is expected to participate actively in the process. The therapist also assigns tasks to be completed outside of therapy, although he or she gives no explanations either about what is going on or what the clients are to do. Indeed, Haley does not believe that insight facilitates change; rather he believes that feelings change as a function of behavioral change. And many of the therapist's efforts to facilitate change, either during therapy or as homework assignments, are paradoxical in nature.

In the effort to create solutions to problems, Haley recommends attention to sequences of behavior, or communication patterns, as they reveal themselves in the present. He believes strongly in the concept of power, viewing symptoms as efforts to influence or control relationships at the same time that they also are a denial of control, given that they generally are understood as behaviors one cannot help doing. Haley also understands symptoms as clues to problematic coalitions or triangles, particularly those that represent a violation of boundaries across generations. The goal of therapy is thus to intervene in such a way that the problematic, covert patterns are interrupted and new, healthier behavioral sequences can emerge.

Salient Practices

The paradoxical interventions utilized by Haley generally involve either prescribing the symptom or prescribing resistance to change. In both cases, the therapist remains in control by anticipating client responses. However, whereas the paradoxical intervention may represent a very effective strategy in the hands of the ethical therapist, it also can be misused. It is primarily in this realm that criticism of the strategic approach has arisen. Indeed, there are some symptoms that should never be treated in a paradoxical manner (e.g., suicidal ideation). What is more, in order to be effective and ethically utilized, there needs to be awareness that such an intervention only looks paradoxical from one perspective but actually make sense from another perspective (Dell, 1986).

To illustrate, let us consider a person who has come seeking help because of symptoms of depression. The therapist realizes that telling a depressed client to cheer up not only is unlikely to help, but also may exacerbate the problem, because now the client also is likely to feel bad or guilty about not being able to cheer up. Further, given his or her systemic perspective, the therapist views all behaviors as making sense in context. In order for change to occur, there must be a change in context. The therapist therefore recommends what may appear paradoxical to an observer but is logical given this perspective. The therapist suggests that it may be important for the client to keep feeling depressed for a time in order to understand where the feelings are coming from and what information they may be providing. At the same time that this suggestion is consistent with the therapist's perspective (i.e., not paradoxical), it also represents a change in context as the client is given permission to feel what he or she is feeling, and thus he or she is likely to experience a reduction in symptoms.

The appropriate utilization of paradoxical interventions, particularly in the form of reframes, certainly has proved useful to me over the years. And the focus on solutions, articulated by Haley as well as by other strategic therapists, has always been a crucial guideline. Indeed, it just seems to make sense that if you want to help families flourish, one of the best way to do so is to assist them in getting where they want to go. This proviso also represents a foundational assumption for the newer, postmodern solution-focused and solution-oriented approaches, which are discussed later in this chapter.

Behavioral/Cognitive Approaches

Although no one theorist or therapist in the realm of behavioral/cognitive therapy stands out for me, there are several aspects of this approach that often provide rich resources. For example, it is the client who defines the goal, which in this case involves replacing undesirable behaviors with those that are more desired. Therapy is action-oriented, homework assignments are typical, and the entire process is focused on facilitating change. Education of clients may be involved, and efforts at cognitive restructuring (i.e., alterations in clients' beliefs and attitudes) may be of particular importance.

Basic Concepts and Constructs

Behavioral/cognitive approaches are based on such foundational notions as classic and operant conditioning, positive and negative reinforcement and punishment, social learning theory, shaping, contingency contracting, and cognitive restructuring. The focus is on the here and now, with an attempt to help clients achieve their desired solutions, articulated in clear and concrete terms. Baselines of current functioning are created, and progress toward goals is measurable in a manner consistent with the quantitative research paradigm.

In the realm of cognition, individuals are understood to operate according to mental schema that may be inhibiting their ability to achieve resolution to problems. Accordingly, cognitive restructuring may assist clients to replace unhelpful automatic thoughts and negative attributions with viewpoints and attitudes that are more helpful and more positive. The creation of new behavioral options thus is facilitated as therapists utilize self-report questionnaires and a conversational approach to the process of helping clients change their belief systems.

Salient Practices

Behavioral parent training (Chamberlain, Patterson, Reid, Kavanaugh, & Forgatch, 1984; Patterson, Reid, Jones, & Conger, 1975) is aimed at helping parents learn how to take charge of, and retain control over, their children. Rules and realistic expectations in the home are to be precisely defined and consistently maintained. Parents are taught how to reward appropriate behaviors as well as to create logical consequences for inappropriate behaviors. They may be given oral instructions or written material to read; they may be prompted to engage in role-plays or behavioral rehearsal; and they may learn how to create contingency contracts with their children. Such contracts specify who will do what in return for what. In addition, the contracts may provide a useful means of negotiation between the generations, which thus may open lines of communication.

Contingency contracting also may be a useful strategy when working with couples (Stuart, 1969, 1980); for example, creating caring days in which each spouse or partner agrees to do a behavior for which the other spouse or partner has indicated a desire. Two other important aspects of behavioral marital therapy include communication skills training and enhancement of the ability to solve problems. In addition, behavioral rehearsal may be utilized, and homework assignments may be given. Thus, couples might be invited to notice and record the pleasing things that each did for the other during a week (Azrin, Nastor, & Jones, 1973). Overall, therapists are concerned with facilitating both an increase in the frequency of positive behaviors and a reduction in the frequency of negative behaviors.

In conjoint sex therapy, the focus again is on helping couples to achieve their goals, this time relative to creating a healthy sexual relationship. Although health in this realm may be defined differently by different couples, the general focus is on facilitating flexibility, openness, involvement, trust, commitment, love, erotic attraction, and individual autonomy and responsibility (Heiman, LoPiccolo, & LoPiccolo, 1981). The therapist may educate clients about sexual physiology and techniques, help them overcome problematic patterns and behaviors, and facilitate the reduction of anxiety. The therapist also attempts to assess the degree to which psychological and relationship or physical factors may be playing a role in the problems with which clients are dealing (Kaplan, 1974), sending them to physicians or referring to specialists in the area of sex therapy as appropriate.

Two strategies that I have found very helpful when working with clients around sexual issues are (1) precluding sex for a specific length of time, and (2) performance of a sensate focus exercise based on the work of Masters and Johnson (1970; see the Appendix). The former recommendation is made when issues of control seem to be playing themselves out in the bedroom. In the latter case, suggesting a nongenital pleasuring activity can help clients learn more about each other as well as connect and feel intimate in a manner that allows for a reduction of anxiety and inhibitions.

Effective functioning as parents as well as as a couple or marital partners, including a satisfying intimate relationship, have been described previously as crucial aspects of families that flourish. Behavioral/cognitive approaches, like all of the approaches discussed in this section, provide information, however modernist or first-order the basic assumptions, that may be useful as one seeks to facilitate resilience. Ideas drawn from these approaches can be particularly effective when combined with the orientation and suggestions gleaned from various second-order approaches, considered next.

Second-Order Approaches and Interventions

Second-order approaches began to emerge as therapists became aware of the various biases inherent in the classical approaches to family therapy. The creators of these newer approaches were particularly responsive to the ideas promulgated by postmodernists working in a variety of different disciplines. Accordingly, therapists sought to recognize and to practice with an awareness of the inevitability of subjectivity—that is, the degree to which they influence what they perceive in therapy as well as what occurs in their work with clients. They attempted to be more respectful of their clients by acknowledging the expertise of everyone involved, as well as the ethical aspects of the therapy process as a whole. As described in Chapter 1, these second-order approaches are consistent with the perspective of second-order cybernetics, with its emphasis on autopoeisis, structural determinism, an epistemology of participation, and perturbations from within rather than interventions from without. The second-order approaches to family therapy considered in the following sections include the reflecting team approach of Tom Andersen, the solution-focused therapy of William (Bill) O'Hanlon, the solution-oriented approach of Steve de Shazer, the narrative approaches of Michael White and David Epston, and the collaborative language systems approach of Harlene Anderson and Harry Goolishian.

Reflecting Team

Tom Andersen has created an approach that very much embraces a postmodern perspective. For example, Andersen (1987, 1991, 1992, 1993) believes it is extremely important to have clients articulate how they would like to use their time together in therapy. Viewing himself as a participant–observer, he also advocates exploring the history or background for the idea of coming to therapy, with conversation and dialogue the primary therapeutic intervention. Andersen believes that as each of these areas is addressed, a context of safety, support, and mutual respect may be created. Also addressed at this point may be his style of doing therapy.

Basic Concepts and Constructs

For Andersen, a crucial milestone in the evolution of his approach was the acknowledgment of his concerns about the fact that therapists tend to avoid sharing their deliberations with clients. Advocating for much greater transparency, which he feels is a reflection of ethical, respectful behavior, he developed the idea of using a reflecting team in therapy. The therapist/interviewer and the family/client system are observed, silently, by a team of colleagues, either in the therapy room or behind a one-way mirror. At some point in the process, attention shifts to the team, and each member is invited to share reflections regarding what he or she saw or felt, always communicating with uncertainty and offering thoughts and ideas tentatively. While speaking only in terms of positives, these reflections are directed toward the other members of the team rather than toward the therapist and client. When the focus shifts back to the conversation between the therapist and the client, therapy then may continue with an incorporation of whatever emerged from the process of the team's reflections.

Even when a team is not available, which is highly likely given the logistics and costs involved, Andersen suggests that the therapist have what he calls inner and outer conversations. Clients may be asked for their reflections on what other family members have said, with subsequent encouragement of reflections on the reflections. The therapist also may take part in this process, sharing inner reflections and then inviting clients to reflect on what they heard. All of these behaviors are consistent with Andersen's belief that it is important to be aware of the many different ways in which situations can be understood. This openminded perspective, in turn, may facilitate the creation of new descriptions and new meanings, leading to new definitions of the self—all of which, ideally, supports achievement of the clients' goals.

Salient Practices

While I have not had the opportunity to participate in a reflecting team process very frequently, and then only in a training context, I believe there is much of value in Andersen's approach. Assuming an ethical, respectful stance certainly is predominant in this regard. Similarly, I believe that being sensitive to what one is telling oneself about the process is crucial, given the awareness that what one believes inevitably influences what one sees and how one behaves. Furthermore, the idea of offering ideas and suggestions in a tentative manner is consistent with my belief that the therapist does not have all the answers and that the expertise of the family must be acknowledged, just as is that of the therapist. Indeed, in order for families to flourish, it is important that their members experience themselves as competent. The reflecting team approach seems to offer much in this regard.

Solution-Oriented Therapy

The roots of the solution-oriented approach created by William O'Hanlon (1993a, 1993b; O'Hanlon & Wiener-Davis, 1989; O'Hanlon & Wilk, 1987) can be traced back to his studies with psychiatrist Milton H. Erickson, best known for his innovations in the realm of hypnotherapy. This influence is apparent in the pragmatic orientation of O'Hanlon's approach, which includes an emphasis on language and the framework of meanings according to which problems are defined and more of the same solutions generally are attempted. The therapy process involves articulating and questioning assumptions in order that problems can be redefined and the achievement of solutions may be facilitated.

Basic Concepts and Constructs

O'Hanlon accepts the concept of a multiverse, which involves a recognition of the multiple views that people may hold and the many and varied ways in which they may live. Reality thus is understood as subjective, based on each person's perceptions and the meanings attributed to them, which are expressed in language. Given the preeminent role of language, it is in this area that the therapist focuses to facilitate change in accordance with the two guiding principles of acknowledgment and possibility: That is, clients are respected and validated, and an attitude that solution and change are possible prevails.

Through therapeutic interactions (i.e., talking together), O'Hanlon helps clients behave differently in relation to a problem and to view it differently, as he also encourages the utilization of client strengths and resources, all with a focus on achieving solutions to problems. He joins with clients, using some of the same words or metaphors that they have used and encouraging descriptions of the problem as well as of exceptions to it (i.e., times when the problem did not occur). He validates clients' experiences, normalizes perceived problems, and guides the conversation in a goal-oriented direction. He also offers hope and encouragement, assuming that positive outcomes will be forthcoming. And always he recognizes the expertise that clients have relative to their own lives.

Salient Practices

Like O'Hanlon, I have found that paying close attention to language may be extremely beneficial. For example, I often encourage clients to speak in terms of what they would like rather than what they don't like. I may point out some ways in which their negative self-talk might usefully be replaced by positive, self-affirming statements. I also may help them to think in terms of *when* what they desire will occur rather than *if* it will occur. Affirming as well as normalizing rather than pathologizing are behaviors that are second nature to me, and I have found that searching for and exploring times when clients have been successful can prove extremely useful in my efforts to facilitate resilience. And all of this takes place in the course of conversations that in many instances, as O'Hanlon notes, represent therapy only as they are defined as such.

Solution-Focused Therapy

In the creation of his brief, solution-focused approach, Steve de Shazer (1985, 1988, 1991, 1994) was much influenced by the orientation of the MRI, where he worked early in his career. Assuming a social constructionist perspective, he, like O'Hanlon, was primarily focused on the role of language in the creation of reality. By contrast, however, he suggested that the therapist does not need to know what the problem is in order to find a solution, or even that problem and solution are necessarily related. More crucial, according to de Shazer, is an examination of the story the client is telling him- or herself about what is going on, and then finding ways to help him or her restory, or reconstruct, that story so that the desired changes occur.

Basic Concepts and Constructs

Once again similar to O'Hanlon, de Shazer emphasized a search for exceptions—those times when things were going well. He believed that doing so encourages clients to participate in solution talk that not only helps to deconstruct the complaint, or problem, but also provides suggestions for future behaviors. Clients also may be asked to predict when such exceptions might occur in the future, thereby planting seeds for their occurrence.

During the course of conversation, de Shazer might do what he called creatively misunderstanding what the client is saying in order to induce confusion and thus facilitate the evolution of a more comfortable reality. He also advised participation in progressive narratives that indicate movement toward the desired goal. He believed that goals agreed upon with clients should be workable, meaning small rather than large; meaningful, concrete and specific; achievable; require what is perceived to be hard work; focus on the beginning of something new rather than the end of something old; and involve new behaviors. And in the effort to help clients articulate their desired goal, he generally utilized the "miracle question":

> Suppose that one night there is a miracle and while you were sleeping the problem that brought you to therapy is solved: How would you know? What would be different?
> What will you notice different the next morning that will tell you that there has been a miracle? What will your spouse notice? (de Shazer, 1991, p. 113)

Other questions employed by de Shazer might focus on what clients like about their lives that they would like to retain. He also used scaling questions to help define the intensity of a problem, the degree of change desired, movement from one time to another, or what might be required in order for change to occur. Finally, as clients achieve the change they desired, therapy is considered to be over.

Salient Practices
As one who espouses a postmodernist orientation to helping families flourish, there is much in this approach that makes sense to me. As with O'Hanlon, I agree with the focus on language. I also find the types of questions utilized by de Shazer to be very helpful, particularly some version of the miracle question. That is, without a clear idea of the clients' goals, efforts to be helpful and to facilitate resilience are likely to be less than effective. In addition, focusing on the positive and emphasizing what may be possible can enable clients to realize their strengths and potentials. What is more, to the degree that this approach encourages awareness of each person's participation in the creation of his or her reality, including the problems being experienced as well as any experiences of self as flourishing, it seems to offer very useful ideas.

Narrative Approaches
Two of the leading proponents of narrative therapy are Michael White and David Epston (Epston, 1994; White, 1991, 1995; White & Epston, 1990). Their approach involves helping clients create and live according to their own stories, as opposed to their being lived by universal principles, or ultimate truth stories, regarding how they are supposed to be. White and Epston believe that such ultimate truth stories, created by mental health professionals and social scientists, deny or subjugate the

personal experiences of clients. Two important aspects of their approach in therapy include "externalization" and "reauthoring lives."

Basic Concepts and Constructs

Externalization involves using carefully crafted questions that enable clients to see themselves as separate from the problems they are experiencing. For example, the therapist may ask how long the client *has been affected by* anxiety. The client can then begin to see anxiety as something to be dealt with rather than defining him- or herself as an *anxious person*. By asking how the client has been affected by anxiety, both the therapist and the client also may get a sense of its relative influence. And asking how the client has been able to influence the impact of anxiety on his or her life may emphasize a degree of control not previously recognized. Furthermore, by searching for exceptions, or what White and Epston call unique outcomes, clients can get in touch with times when the problem-saturated story did not fit the circumstances.

As clients experience a separation between themselves and their problems, they participate in a process of reauthoring their lives. That is, they take part in the cocreation of alternative stories about themselves—stories that can then be performed, repeated, or expanded as new experiences lead to new meanings. This process of reauthoring lives also may be aided by the use of questions that either situate unique outcomes in the context of a sequence of events, the upshot of which was positive, or that encourage reflection on, and the development of, meanings relative to this sequence of events. Clients thus may be asked how they were able to prepare for participation in the unique outcome event, as well as what such participation says about the person involved. Finally, the entire process can be enhanced by the use of letter writing.

Epston, in particular, believes in the utility of writing letters to his clients following a session. Such letters serve as reminders about the conversation and the new story that has evolved. Serving as case notes, they also allow the therapist to be transparent about his or her thoughts and feelings. The storied nature of reality is thus further emphasized, awareness of which is implicit in this approach.

Salient Practices

Although Epston's position certainly is one with which I agree, I generally don't utilize letterwriting. However, I am very much an advocate of a narrative approach, in general, and often make use of the questions and other perturbations associated with this approach. The search for exceptions and unique outcomes helps clients recognize/remember their strengths. Similarly, the externalization of problems enables them to see themselves far more broadly, as much more than persons only with problems. Perhaps most important to me is the emphasis on an ethical, respectful stance toward clients, one that I believe is most supportive of, and consistent with, a desire to facilitate resilience.

Therapeutic Conversations

Harry Goolishian and Harlene Anderson (Anderson & Goolishian, 1986, 1988, 1990), who also fall into the narrative camp, created an approach that emphasizes the importance of conversation and refuses to be formulaic in any way. Accordingly, no specific set of techniques is advocated. Even more than is the case with O'Hanlon, the conversations of Anderson and Goolishian with clients bear little resemblance to therapy in a more traditional sense.

Basic Concepts and Constructs

Anderson and Goolishian believe that problems create systems or conversations organized around the problem, and therapy consists simply of caring, empathic conversations that provide a context for the creation of new meanings. Therapists take a nonexpert, not-knowing position, valuing multiple perspectives and seeking to "dis-solve" problems. The focus is thus on stories, which evolve and change in the process of being told and retold. Consistent with one of the basic concepts of a second-order cybernetics perspective, therapists participate with their clients in a process of nonpurposeful drift, meaning that they get wherever they go, and therapists do not strategize about, or design, the form of the outcome.

Salient Practices

In theory I believe that this approach makes a great deal of sense, and I certainly agree with its assumptions. However, I find that in order to help clients get where they want to go, I usually need to be somewhat more directive. I recognize the extent to which this may not be consistent with a postmodern stance, but I also am aware that doing therapy at all is really not consistent with such a stance. Thus, I attempt to find a balance between the ethical, respectful attitude and behavior it advocates and the responsibility I feel when I agree to do therapy to help clients achieve their goals in the best way I know how.

Selecting Perturbations

The process of selecting perturbations, or choosing how to be with and respond to the members of a particular client system as we interact together, is grounded in all of the clusters of knowledge and information about individuals and families discussed in Part I of this book. This process is further informed by my awareness of the various approaches and practices described in this chapter. The specifics are guided by the goals that clients articulate for themselves, as I seek to help them get where they want to go. Although my orientation is definitely postmodern, I feel free to utilize ideas and practices from both first-order and second-order approaches. And always I keep in mind the processes that are characteristic of families that flourish, and of the importance of facilitating resilience. Although much of this work occurs in an almost intuitive way based on years of experience, I constantly remain aware that my stories about clients and what they might perceive as helpful are always open to revision. What is more, although there may be some ways of proceeding, or perturbing the system, that are consistent with most of my clients, rarely does the process repeat in exactly the same way. The following case example thus provides an illustration of what one of my first sessions might look like as it evolved in a manner that seemed most appropriate for this client system.

Case Example

Barbara Warner called to request therapy for her family. She said that she and her husband were having problems with the older of their two sons, and that differences of opinion about what to do with him were causing a great deal of conflict and tension in their marriage. In response to my questions, Barbara told me that her husband's name was Stan, and that their sons, David and Mark, were ages 20 and 15, respectively. I suggested that all four family members come to the first session. After consulting with Stan, Barbara made an appointment for the following week.

At the appointed time, I greeted each of the family members and showed them into my office. Mark seated himself on the couch next to his mother, Stan took the chair closest to them, and David sat two chairs removed from his father. We chit-chatted a bit about my directions to the office, the traffic they encountered, and their efforts to get to the session on time. Without further ado, I then asked the following question, directed at no one in particular: "So, what are we doing here tonight?"

Barbara looked to Stan, who immediately replied in a vehement tone that he was fed up with David's laziness and frustrated that Barbara continued to coddle him rather than pushing him to get out and find a job. He said that at David's age, *he* already had been working for several years, and he couldn't understand his son's behavior. He also said that having to deal with David's behavior was making him so upset that he was having trouble concentrating at work. What is more, he was worried about the example David was setting for his younger brother.

I then asked Barbara to give me her perspective. Barbara was soft-spoken but able to express clearly her concerns about the fact that her son was having problems that she felt her husband was refusing to acknowledge. She did not see David as lazy because she could understand how being as shy as he was would make finding a job extremely difficult. She said that he had always been a good kid, had done well in school, and had graduated from college more quickly than his peers. She felt that David and Mark were very different, but that they had a good relationship. What is more, she said that she didn't believe that David was a negative influence on Mark.

Next I turned to David, who I was aware had been observing and listening intently to his parents. I asked him how he felt about coming to therapy and what his perspective "on things" was. He replied that he thought therapy was a good idea, that he knew he should be able to work, and that he would like to stop being such a burden to his parents. He said that he had always been shy, had difficulty making friends, and preferred to spend time at home with his family. He helped around the house as much as he could, but he really wasn't ready to go looking for a job.

Finally, I asked Mark for his perspective. He smiled and shrugged his shoulders, saying he didn't know what the big deal was. He said he didn't really know why he needed to be here, but that he was willing to come if it would help his brother. I thanked him for coming and said I thought it was important for him to be present, because the family members were all in the situation together and that everybody's perspective was important. I asked him if he wanted to add anything else, and he said that he was tired of the constant arguing between his mother and his father.

I summed up what I thought I had heard from each person, checked it out with them, and then said that I had another question that I would like everyone to answer, and that it didn't matter who went first. I said, "If I were able to help you, what would we have accomplished by the end of the time of our working together?" Once again, Stan replied first, stating that all he wanted was for David to get a job and get on with his life so that he, Stan, could get on with his. Barbara, speaking next, said that she also wanted David to be able to get a job, but that she wanted help for him so that this could happen. David said he would like to be able to do what his parents wanted him to do, but that he needed to be able to do it in his own time. Mark said he hoped therapy would help his mother feel happier and that his parents would quit fighting.

I acknowledged my sense that all of their goals seemed realistic and then said that I would see what I could do to help them achieve these goals. However, I said that my guess was that they had gotten where they were now over a period of time, that miracles were not likely, and that it probably would take some more time to get where they wanted to go. In order for me to help them do that, I said I would like to have a bit more information about the history of their family. I then requested that each person tell me, in 10 minutes or less, about the family in which he or she grew up, responding along the way to my queries about where that person was born, how his or her parents got along, how he or she got along with each of his or her parents, how each did in school, and what kinds of jobs his or her parents had. For Barbara, Stan, and David, I also asked what each did after graduating from high school and requested that any serious relationships each might have had be noted. And for Barbara and Stan, I asked how they had met, how each had experienced the first year of marriage, reactions to the birth of each of their sons, and when each felt that they had begun to experience problems.

Stan reported that he had been born to a poor, working-class couple who had fought constantly for as long as he could remember. Neither of his parents had finished high school, his father had been a heavy drinker, and he had mostly tried to steer clear of him. He had gotten along well with his mother, who became a widow with three children while he was still in high school. His father had died as the result of an accident in the factory where he worked, and that as the oldest, he then had felt a responsibility to help his mother. He immediately found a part-time job in a supermarket, where he continued to work throughout high school and while going to college on a part-time basis at night. Once he had his degree, he was able to advance in the food industry, and now had an important administrative position with a well known chain of grocery stores. He said that he had never had time to do much dating, but that when he was introduced to Barbara by a friend, he was immediately attracted to her, that they had known each other for 2 years and had married when she was 25 and he was 27. The first year of marriage had been challenging, given their different backgrounds, but he thought basically they had been pretty happy. He was extremely proud when David was born and doubly pleased when Mark came along 5 years later. He said that he and Mark got along well but that he had always been a bit puzzled by David. However, he said that David's strange behaviors hadn't really become an issue until about a year ago, when he had finished college and failed to move on.

Barbara reported that she was the second of two children, and that the family in which she and her older brother grew up was very close-knit and loving. Her parents were very gentle people who rarely fought, and she had gotten along well with both of them. She and her brother had had some typical sibling rivalry while growing up, but outside of the home he had always been very protective of her. She had done well in high school, had dated a fair amount, and had had one prior serious relationship, which continued until she was a junior in college. Following the end of this relationship, she had dated several men but had not been seriously interested in anyone before meeting Stan. She had been working as a teacher for 2 years when she happened to go with some friends to the supermarket where Stan was working. She wasn't immediately attracted to him but had agreed to go out with him when he called. Over time she had come to appreciate his maturity and sense of responsibility, and eventually she fell in love with him. Like Stan, she also felt that the first year of their marriage had been difficult, particularly because she had been on her own for 4 years and had a hard time adjusting to Stan's need to be in charge. She had never seen her parents fight, so was confused and shaken by some of their more heated arguments. Over time, however, she felt that they had adjusted to each other fairly well.

She, too, was thrilled when David was born and immediately wanted more children. Although saddened by how long it took to get pregnant again, she was overjoyed with Mark's birth. She had given up her teaching job willingly in order to stay home with the children, but had intended to go back to work once both boys were in school full time. Because Stan was opposed to this idea, she had not yet done so. She said that although the two boys certainly were different, she had not experienced problems with either of them, always encouraging them to pursue their particular interests. She felt that her husband had never really understood David, and that she had often had to intervene on his behalf. She acknowledged that things had escalated in the past year, but believed that David, although shy, would get a job when he was ready.

Both boys had listened in fascination as their parents told their stories, sometimes showing surprise at learning some new detail about their family. When I asked David how he would describe the family in which he grew up, he said that he knew that both of his parents loved him but that he never felt that he quite fit. He believed his father was disappointed in him because he preferred the computer to sports. He remembered being excited when Mark was born, and he really liked having a younger brother. He was grateful that his mother was always willing to go to bat for him, but sometimes felt that she interfered rather than helped. He said that he had never dated, but that once he figured out what he wanted to do with his life, dating probably would follow.

Mark said that it was hard following in David's footmarks academically, but he didn't blame his brother for that. He reported that he got along well with both parents but wished that his father had had more time to do things with him when he was younger. Now that he was playing high school sports, however, that wasn't such a big deal, and he was grateful when either one or both parents came to his games. He said he and his mother got along well despite the fact that she was overprotective and worried about him too much.

Throughout their narratives I was able to offer affirmation to each person. For example, I complimented Stan on his ability to rise to the challenges presented when his father died, and Barbara for her devotion to her family. I also attempted to affirm the family as a whole, saying that I felt that they had expressed a great deal of love and affection for one another, and that I believed they had what was needed to solve their problems. I said that I was going to give them all a homework assignment but first had one more request to make. I then asked each to state what he or she felt was the best thing about being a part of this family. Mark said, "We take great family vacations!" David's reply was, "I feel a great deal of security." Barbara stated, "I know that everybody cares about everybody." Stan said, "I am really proud of being able to provide for and take care of my family in ways that my father did not."

I asked that they all reflect, without comment, on what each person had said. Then I noted that what I was going to suggest for homework wasn't going to solve their problems. However, since there had been so much focus on problems recently, I thought it would be good to generate some energy to help them achieve their desired solutions. I therefore suggested that they do something fun together as a family sometime during the interval before our next meeting. After ascertaining that they understood my request, felt comfortable with the process, and wanted to proceed with therapy, we scheduled an appointment for the following week.

Summary and Reflections

As I reflect on this session, I am aware of the various theoretical stories that came to mind and informed the process while I was working with the Warner family. Overall, I attempted to maintain a respectful stance with my clients, establishing a connection with each person and taking my cues from each regarding how best to proceed. I also introduced the systemic notion that the involvement of everyone was important. From a structural perspective, I certainly was tuned into the seating arrangements as well as the ways in which both the marital and the parental subsystems seemed to be having difficulties, whereas the sibling subsystem appeared to be functioning to the satisfaction of the two brothers. I asked that each person share his or her perspective of both the problem and solutions desired, using my version of the miracle question to facilitate the latter. Along the way, I attempted to model effective communication and to offer an optimistic view regarding my ability to help them achieve their goals.

My introduction of the homework assignment included a somewhat paradoxical injunction when I suggested that the family's problems probably would not disappear overnight. Although I believed this to be true, I also was aware that making this idea explicit might free them of unrealistic expectations, which actually might speed up the process. The homework assignment was aimed at generating good will and positive energy between Stan and Barbara, consistent with my belief in the importance of a well-functioning marital subsystem as well as an effective parental coalition. The articulation of a verbal genogram provided me with a context for understanding and normalizing what was going on, while it also enabled each person to tell his or her own story as well as hear old stories in new ways. Affirmations of family members' strengths certainly is an important way to facilitate resilience, and encouraging each member to describe something positive about the family was aimed at helping all members recognize the ways in which they already are flourishing.

Although not consciously aware in the moment of all of the stories to which I was making recourse, this retrospective look at the process of therapy with the Warner family illustrates the kind of theoretical integration that is possible with a second-order cybernetics, postmodern orientation. Even more importantly, it also provides a view of the way that such an orientation can be utilized to help families flourish through a process that focuses on facilitating resilience. In the latter regard, it certainly is not the whole story, and thus further reflections on this case example are provided in the next chapter.

CHAPTER SIX

Assessing, Analyzing, and Perturbing to Achieve Solutions

From a modernist perspective, according to which the therapist generally perceives him- or herself as outside of, and separate from, the client system, he or she engages in the processes of assessing, diagnosing, and treating families and their problems by utilizing concepts, instruments, and interventions that are consistent with his or her model or approach of choice. For example, a contextual family therapist working with the Warners, the family introduced at the end of the previous chapter, might see an imbalance in the ledger of entitlements and indebtedness between Stan and David, and/or split filial loyalty between Barbara, Stan, and David as causing their problems and thus as issues in need of attention. Working from a natural family systems framework, it is likely that the therapist would seek more information about the grandparent generation, doing a full-fledged, three-generational genogram, and then focusing on issues around differentiation of self as the source of the problems the family is experiencing.

A structural family therapist might tailor his or her interventions to deal with the hypothesized ineffective executive coalition between Barbara and Stan and the need for clearer boundaries between the parental and the sibling subsystems, emphasizing a change in structure as the path to problem resolution. From the communications perspective of Virginia Satir, a likely assumption would be that low self-esteem on the part of both Stan and Barbara has played a role in the triangulation of David into their marital relationship, leading to the problems their older son is experiencing and the inability to communicate effectively with one another.

As a strategic therapist, the goal would be to find ways to solve the problem as presented, hypothesizing that David's reluctance to leave home perhaps reflects fears about what would happen between his parents if he did. The therapist might suggest, paradoxically, that the parents work together to encourage David to stay at home, at least for the present. If a cognitive–behavioral approach were more the therapist's style, he or she might see the need for behavioral parent training, helping Barbara and Stan work together to create realistic rules and expectations for David, encouraging them to reward appropriate behaviors and to create logical consequences for inappropriate behaviors, as defined by them.

None of the above approaches is necessarily wrong or bad, and certainly some of the ideas from several of them entered my mind as I reflected on the session in retrospect. However, most of these approaches involve a search for the causes of problems, with a model of how a family *should* function guiding the process of therapy, and with the therapist understood as the expert. By contrast, I drew upon various models as sources of information about the context that might be useful as the Warners and I worked together to achieve the solutions they desired. Consistent with the perspective espoused in this book, the therapist is encouraged to understand him- or herself as a part of the therapist–client system, including the role he or she is playing relative to either overlooking or facilitating resilience. What is more, the process of analysis, assessment, and perturbation to achieve solutions is understood to be more akin to storytelling, with new narratives constantly evolving and being recreated in a process shared between therapist and client, both of whom have expertise. Interventions from without are replaced by perturbations from within as questions are asked and responded to, ideas are suggested and tested, and an epistemology of participation replaces the concept of treatment. The focus shifts from problems and their causes to helping clients achieve the solutions they desire in whatever ways seem most appropriate to and for them. Further, assessment primarily involves monitoring throughout the process the degree to which the clients' desired outcomes are being achieved and the extent to which the family is flourishing.

As therapists sit with families, they certainly may be aware of the many ways of understanding family dynamics and the areas of focus suggested by various schools of family therapy. However, they are free to make recourse to more than one of them. More importantly, they also remain cognizant of the fact that none of these perspectives necessarily describes the way the family really is. Rather, they recognize that each participant in the process has his or her stories and expertise; that together they comprise a multiverse of equally valid realities. Therapists therefore keep in mind that whatever they believe may be happening, or whatever theoretical lens they may be using to view the family, it is just *their* story, and their story is no truer than those of the family members.

As therapists proceed in a manner consistent with a concern for facilitating resilience, they are aware that the practices of assessment, analysis, and perturbation do not represent discrete categories or distinct phases of therapy, nor are they understood in the traditional, problem-focused manner. Rather, they refer to ongoing and overlapping processes whose primary orientation is the achievement of solutions. Although therapists acknowledge the presence of the problems that led clients to seek professional assistance, they are more concerned with uncovering and supporting clients' strengths and potentials. And they encourage the processes within the family that will enable them to achieve their goals and to flourish.

When assessing, analyzing, and perturbing to achieve solutions, it is recommended that therapists keep in mind several guiding principles and practices regarding process. Like the concepts of flourishing and resilience, which are characterized by particular process dimensions, effective practice is more about the way therapists think and behave with clients than it is about the specific models or interventions chosen. The guiding principles and practices to be considered include suspending judgment, becoming sensitive to language, exploring the client's context, cocreating realities, supporting and validating, and reflecting on the process of assessing, analyzing, and perturbing to achieve solutions. Aspects of my work with the Warner family are used to illustrate these various principles and practices in the following sections.

Suspending Judgment

Typically, when therapists assess a client system, they are making a judgment, describing their conclusions about what they believe is happening in that system. Such assessments generally precede intervention, and more often than not the primary focus is on problems, or what is not going well, as defined by both the client and the therapist. Generally, there is little recognition or acknowledgment by therapists of the role of their own perceptions in the process of assessment. By contrast, avoiding assessments that are judgmental in the sense of describing conclusions about good / bad, right / wrong behaviors and waiting to come to conclusions are two important aspects of my position relative to suspending judgment (Becvar, 1997).

To the extent that assessments are made, they are done so in a way that highlights strengths, resources, and skills in addition to describing the problems perceived by the clients. Although therapists may add their views by describing what they see, they recognize that all they can do is infer and make tentative hypotheses about what may or may not be going on. Further, they seek to avoid evaluating clients in a condemning or blaming manner when they (i.e., clients) behave in ways that may be considered inappropriate or unacceptable. Indeed, when thinking about making a judgment, it is conceived of as a process to be implemented in a manner consistent with the Greek term for judgment, *shatot,* meaning to discriminate or shed light on a situation so that it can be seen and understood more clearly. What is more, this understanding evolves over time, as the process of therapy unfolds and new information emerges.

Consistent with the systemic view that all behaviors fit, or are logical to context, the challenge is to try to understand how a given behavior somehow makes sense relative to the dynamics of the family. For example, therapists might ask themselves how the reactions and perceptions of each member of the Warner family could be understood as logical. Certainly Stan's anger toward, and frustration with, his older son is understandable, especially given Stan's history and experience in his family of origin. Similarly, Barbara's sensitivity to David could be seen as a reflection both of her nature and as an empathic response, given previous unsuccessful attempts to have her own wishes acknowledged by her husband. David's behavior might be understood as a developmental issue related to both his natural shyness and to his completion of college ahead of his peers and without much experience in the social realm. And Mark's relative lack of concern surely is typical of a teenager who is absorbed in his own world and is more aware of his parents' conflict than he is of problems with his brother.

In terms of the family as a whole, therapists might also be intrigued by a consideration of the logic of what is going on through the lens of birth order. Describing a systemic perspective on sibling position, Hoopes and

Harper (1987) posit that the structural characteristics of a family create the context into which children are born and according to which sibling positions develop. They suggest that the interface between individual and family needs influences the evolution of issues around belonging, intimacy, identity and dependency. Children are said to be influenced particularly by unresolved emotional issues their parents may be experiencing, and may assume responsibility for them, either implicitly or explicitly, trying in some way to achieve resolution. The particular roles assumed by each child emerge as a function of the unique environment that exists at the time of that child's birth.

The entry of the first child into the system increases the complexity of the communication network as well as the likelihood of coalitions and the need for productivity. At the same time, parents generally are more uncertain and inexperienced with their first children than with those that follow, and they tend to place greater pressure on these children to achieve. The first child is inclined to respond to overt levels of communication and to the explicit demands of a situation for stability, feeling an implicit duty to reflect the family's publicly affirmed values. The first child's role is similar to that of the parent who represents achievement of the family's goals, which in traditional families typically is the father. And the first child may be particularly sensitive to what is going on with the father.

The second child's birth not only adds complexity but increases the possibility of isolation for one as the other three create a triangle. Both maintenance and productivity needs also increase. Parents, however, generally have moved past their initial anxieties around childrearing and are able to be more consistent with discipline and better able to provide warm, supportive care. The second child is likely to detect and express unmet or unresolved feelings experienced by other family members, and is particularly receptive to implicit elements in relationships. This child tends to be especially tuned into the parent who assumes social and emotional leadership, which in traditional families typically is the mother.

The arrival of the third child creates more possibilities for instability in the system as well as more maintenance needs as the unmet goals of individual family members accumulate. This child often finds it difficult to find a place in the family, given that upon entry into the system he or she is faced with the existence of a parent–child dyad, a sibling dyad, and dyads between each parent and a child. Although the parents are now outnumbered by their children, they tend to be more comfortable in their roles. The third child is inclined to identify and support existing dyadic relationships, but also has great disruptive powers and thus learns the importance of balance in relationships. This child tends to be particularly sensitive to what is going on in the primary dyad, that of the marital pair.

The birth of the fourth child once again increases the complexity of the family, although this is balanced by the well-established roles of the older siblings. Although more demands are put on the parents in terms of stability and productivity requirements, the first and second children may help out a great deal in this regard. The primary role of the fourth child relates to the preservation of the system as a whole, responding to needs for unity and harmony and helping to keep the family goal-oriented. The fourth child is the family troubleshooter, signaling when an aspect of the total system is breaking or has broken down.

This birth order theory is descriptive rather than prescriptive, and was derived from clinical work with traditional families. It thus may or may not fit, and it does not claim to offer "the truth." However, it may prove useful in the attempt to understand the logic of a system. In the case of the Warners, the therapist is alerted to consider the possibility that David's behavior somehow is a reflection of the pain that Stan may be experiencing, and that the son provides a distraction for the father as the latter focuses on the problems that the former is experiencing. Similarly, Mark's concern with the marital conflict and his desire for his mother to be happier may reflect his sensitivity to what Barbara is experiencing but has not voiced. Accordingly, the therapist's awareness also might be directed to a need for sensitivity regarding marital issues.

In addition to the process of searching to understand the ways in which various behaviors may make sense, suspending judgment also means assuming the basic goodness of each individual, as illustrated above. Although the therapist certainly may recognize socially undesirable and/or unacceptable behaviors and definitely does not condone them, particularly in the case of instances of abuse or injustice of any kind, he or she attempts to avoid labeling people in a pejorative manner. For example, it would not be appropriate to call Stan overbearing, Barbara passive–aggressive, David lazy, or Mark uncaring, despite the fact that they and their behaviors could possibly be construed in this manner. Rather, the assumption is that each person is doing the best he or she can, given his or her personal frame of reference and background of experience. Such a stance is consistent with an orientation toward acceptance and detachment. That is, the therapist aims to accept people "where they are" while detaching from "shoulds"—ideas about how they are supposed to behave. Accordingly, the therapist may search for the ways in which people have learned to behave in a manner deemed problematic by others or unacceptable by society. The intent is to participate with them in such a way that new, more socially accepted behaviors emerge, believing such behaviors to be more consistent with their basic nature. Rather than criticizing or condemning, the intent is to practice compassion, an orientation that is more in keeping with the goal of facilitating resilience.

Furthermore, the therapist believes in the importance of postponing evaluations about behaviors and situations, recognizing that with time and perspective, meanings may evolve and change, not only for him or her but also for clients. Thus, Stan's behavior toward David might be construed as a form of love and concern coupled with a lack of knowledge about how to have a meaningful relationship with his son. Indeed, he did not experience such a relationship with his own father, and he has had very little experience relating to someone who, on the surface at least, seems to be very different. Similarly, it is possible to create an alternative story about Barbara, who in her efforts to be sensitive to and protect David, may unwittingly have participated in preventing the formation of a closer relationship between father and son. What is more, she and Stan acknowledge coming from very different worlds and having struggled through the years to find a way of working together as partners and parents, and thus their current conflict is understandable.

As some or all of the thoughts just noted are running through the therapist's head, the therapist needs to remain cognizant of the reality that he or she wishes to participate in creating with the family. Accordingly, the therapist recognizes that the more he or she is able to be respectful of people and their problems, rather than judging or blaming them, the more likely he or she is to be participating in the creation of an atmosphere of safety and trust. Such an atmosphere or context is essential to the establishment of meaningful relationships and productive conversations. Indeed, these are understood as requirements for the therapy process to proceed as well as for positive change to occur.

Becoming Sensitive to Language

As therapists participate in conversations with clients aimed at achieving solutions and facilitating resilience, they also strive for sensitivity to language—the clients' words and phrases as well as their own. Such a sensitivity involves both awareness and behavior. Given the belief that reality is socially constructed through language, listening to the ways in which clients express themselves can open a window into their worlds, enabling therapists to understand clients more fully and connect with them in effective and more meaningful ways. For example, Stan Warner's narratives about his views and experiences consistently were characterized by expressions about the importance of being responsible, providing for his family, working hard and being successful, and getting on with his life. My story is that this is how he believes a good father and husband behaves, and that such expressions are illustrative of his ways of showing the love he feels for his family. This story also helps to make sense of Stan's opposition to Barbara working outside the home, which he may believe would reflect negatively on his ability to take care of his family. Similarly, his choice to work rather than take time off to spend time with his young sons also is understandable from such a perspective. As I later reflected on Stan's language (i.e., the way he told his story), I also sensed a need for order, for things to occur in a logical progression, with interruptions or intrusions experienced as undermining the secure world he had been working so hard to create for his family. Thus, in future conversations it would seem important for me to acknowledge both dimensions, either implicitly or explicitly, in whatever efforts I might make to facilitate change.

How therapists language situations and behaviors is crucial in another important way. Consistent with a belief in the importance of mindfulness in relation to what someone or something is called, formal diagnoses are avoided whenever possible. Should a diagnosis seem to be necessary or appropriate, however, therapists might engage clients in a conversation about what having such a diagnosis may mean or how it might be perceived by others. Therapists also might express their belief that although clients may be experiencing a diagnosable problem, they are not themselves a diagnostic category. Rather, therapists might explain, such categories were created to facilitate the process of therapy rather than to pigeonhole people.

In general, however, postmodern, second-order therapists prefer to view specific behaviors as problematic rather than grouping them into a category that then becomes the focus of treatment. Furthermore, therapists do not treat. Rather, they see themselves as interacting and working with others, perturbing and being perturbed, in an ongoing, recursive process of mutual influence and shared reality construction. Accordingly, they are aware that each of their questions or statements represents a perturbation. Therefore, they are careful about what they ask, what they say, and how they frame questions and responses, always being sensitive to the fact that their words may be given more weight or be construed differently than they intended. Although miscommunications still may occur—that is, the message sent is different from the message received—therapists attempt to seek clarification as often as possible.

In acknowledgment of the idea that things that are perceived as real are real in their consequences (Thomas & Thomas, 1928), therapists are aware of the importance of belief systems and the ways in which perceptions can be influenced through language. At this point in my professional (and personal) life, I engage in this process almost instinctively, as I reframe behaviors in a more positive light than the one currently being used to describe such behaviors. I am aware, however, that in doing so it is important to avoid minimizing what clients may be experiencing and running the risk of being perceived as a "Pollyanna" who really doesn't understand. At the same time, in order to be effective, I believe that therapists must think creatively and from the perspective of the other, using language and metaphors that are likely to resonate with, or be meaningful to, that person. Thus, for example, in conversations with Barbara Warner, I may choose to relate to her through the languages of mothering and teaching, both of which I share with her. And throughout this process I am continually on the lookout for ways to achieve greater understanding of each member and the family as a whole.

Exploring the Client's Context

In one sense, I always am exploring clients' contexts as we converse with one another and I seek to understand each person's problems and desired solutions, the logic of various behaviors, and the languages different individuals use to describe their world. At the same time, I also may make use of specific tools to help with this process, and many of my explorations tend to have a particular focus. My request that each member of the Warner family describe the family in which he or she grew up, guided by questions from me, illustrates my use of a verbal genogram, something I do fairly regularly. The stories that are narrated by each family member enable me to learn specifics about such system characteristics and issues as ages, marriages, divorces, deaths, education, ethnicity, geographic locations, health and illness patterns, occupations, and religion/spirituality. Along the way I also am able to tune into developmental information and to infer patterns of interaction within the family and between the generations. Such inferences may include my story about system rules and boundaries, various interpretive frameworks, and the ways in which communication occurs. And throughout, I am searching for evidence of resilience, for strengths that can be highlighted, and for resources that can be called upon as needed or appropriate. I also am aware that family members may be learning new information or hearing old information in new ways as each person tells his or her story.

Descriptions of the larger context provided by family members may be helpful, and I may assemble these into a mental "ecomap" (Hartman & Laird, 1983). Accordingly, other systems with which the family may be involved are noted along with the degree to which the energy exchange between them is experienced by family members as either positive or negative. Such considerations may inform the search for strengths and resources. For example, the role of Stan Warner's workplace may be perceived very differently by each family member. In addition, although I didn't ask in my first session with the Warners, I may wonder what role, if any, is played by Stan's mother and Barbara's parents. I also may wonder what the family's religious or spiritual beliefs are, if any; what their friendship circles look like; and to whom they turn in times of need. I am aware that the referral to me was made by one of Barbara's friends, so I know that there is at least one significant other in her world.

When the conversation with clients is focused on the problem that brought them to therapy, I find it useful, if possible, to hear all participants' perceptions. Not only is it common for family members to have different stories about the problem or what each experiences as problematic, but also paying attention to the reactions of various family members to one another's descriptions can provide useful topics for further discussion. Indeed, it is interesting to note that with the Warners, Stan, Barbara, and David were focused on David's problems around getting a job. By contrast, Mark did not have a problem with David, but was concerned about his mother's happiness and the conflict between his parents.

Similarly, it can be useful to ask each person to describe his or her desired solution so that everyone is clear about perceptions regarding where they have been and the direction in which each would like to head. If the goals of individual family members are too different or in conflict with each other, it may be important to provide opportunities for further discussion so that some kind of consensus is reached. As I go about this process, I prefer to ask clients to describe what would be going on if things were the way they would like them to be, or how things would look if I were effective in helping them get where they would like to go, as I did with the Warners.

In general, clients tend to be very articulate about their problems and what they don't like. However, it is not at all unusual for them to have difficulty describing what they would like. Therapists can ask clients to think about particular behaviors that they would desire to experience for themselves or receive from others to replace those behaviors or situations about which they have complaints. Sometimes this process occurs in session, and sometimes clients are asked to reflect on the questions at home and return with a list outlining what they would like to see happen. Sometimes the miracle question (de Shazer, 1991) is used. In any case, it is not likely that therapists will be able to help families until the clients have articulated their goals. Once they have done so, therapists then can focus on helping them attain these goals and ultimately flourish.

Cocreating Realities

As noted throughout this and other chapters, the main job of therapists is to help clients get where they want to go. This goal can be accomplished in whatever ways seem most appropriate, drawing on ideas from both modernist and postmodernist approaches. Throughout the course of therapy, therapists act in a manner that hopefully helps clients achieve their desired solutions and also facilitates resilience. As therapists engage in assessing, analyzing, and perturbing to achieve solutions, an important part of the process involves a consideration of how aware clients are of the degree to which each of them participates in the creation of the reality he or she is experiencing, as well as the extent to which they recognize that the family situation is a reality for whose creation all members share responsibility. When such recognition is lacking, it may be useful for therapists to encourage clients to understand the idea of recursion, or mutual influence and reciprocal responsibility—one of the key process dimensions in families that flourish. At the same time, while helping clients learn to understand the extent to which the behavior of each has an impact on and influences the behavior of others, therapists also recognize that this awareness applies to themselves as well. For example, resistance is seen as a relational concept. That is, if clients choose to ignore therapists' suggestions, perhaps regarding a homework assignment, it is important for therapists to accept their share of the responsibility for their clients' behavior. In doing so, they might acknowledge that the suggestion was inappropriate, or was made too soon, or that the client had every right to choose not to accept the suggestion. In this way clients are helped to see therapists as fallible as they demonstrate respect for what can be considered a healthy boundary mechanism on clients' part. This attitude in turn, validates the expertise and knowledge family members have about themselves and contributes to the creation of a reality that is supportive of both the therapy process, in general, and the achievement of the clients' goals, in particular.

It also can be useful for therapists to support a shift away from the tendency to place blame while also encouraging awareness of the importance of paying attention to one's own behavior in order for change to occur. In all of this, therapists attempt to model systemic awareness as well as ways to communicate effectively. Given the importance of effective communication in facilitating both resilience and flourishing, therapists also can teach clients various communication skills that are grounded in a systemic perspective (Becvar & Becvar, 1997a). For example, I believe it is important for clients to learn how to speak in terms of "I" messages, in which they take responsibility for the feelings they experienced in response to the actions of others. Similarly, I believe in the importance of learning the utility of paraphrasing (e.g., restating a message) and of being able to choose responses rather than merely reacting to one another (e.g., pausing before speaking). Sometimes it is appropriate to provide information about how to discuss difficult issues that tend to end in conflict. Accordingly, I might suggest that relationship pairs pick a spot where they can sit facing each other. Using a timer of some sort, each is allowed 5 minutes to speak his or her mind without interruption from the other. The pair then must separate and think about their responses for at least 30 minutes. Upon returning, they have another 5 minutes each, followed by a 30-minute break. This process is repeated as many times as it takes to resolve the disagreement. As clients engage in new, more useful behaviors, they also are participating in the creation of new realities—ideally those that are supportive of the achievement of their goals.

Some clients may find it helpful to become aware of the tendency to respond to each other on the basis of the stories they are telling themselves about the other, rather than on the basis of what the other is actually doing or saying. Indeed, having such an awareness can change how they respond to one another, which is certainly an important aspect of reality creation. Furthermore, speaking in terms of *stories* may encourage recognition of the role of beliefs and personal frameworks in creating reality—which perhaps brings with it awareness of clients' ability to change that reality.

Another potentially useful topic for therapists to discuss is the process of triangulation, a problem that can occur at an intergenerational level, but one that certainly also occurs in many other ways. For example, I generally suggest to clients that as long as they are in therapy with me, they avoid discussing their problems with well-meaning others such as friends, family members, or coworkers. I explain that such discussions are likely to muddy the waters, and that over the long term these outside discussions might work against the therapeutic process, despite whatever short-term relief they may seem to provide. At this point I am likely to introduce my idea regarding the rule of only two to a relationship and to suggest that when there is a problem, it is more appropriate to speak directly with the other person involved than to talk about him or her with a third party. For example, if I wished to encourage detriangulation as well as support the creation of clearer boundaries in the Warner family, I might suggest that each of the possible dyads—Stan–Barbara, Stan–David, Stan–Mark, Barbara–David, Barbara–Mark, David–Mark—spend time together on a regular basis so that they can feel more comfortable with each other and learn to experience each other in new and more meaningful ways. As such suggestions are followed through, hopefully they help to create realities that are more to the liking of everyone involved and thus are supportive of the family's ability to flourish.

As already indicated, I often give homework assignments. These, too, can be aimed at helping clients to experience new behaviors and situations (i.e., to create new realities). The assignments might be intended to help them (1) generate a feeling of greater energy, (2) encourage a sense of mutual commitment to the process, (3) shift the focus away from the problem and onto potential solutions, or (4) all of the above considerations. However, equally as significant as the assignments are the ways in which important information is gained from family members' responses to each assignment. Hence my suggestion to the Warner family to do something fun together during the period before our next meeting. On the one hand, I felt it might be useful for them to try to come together as a family with a focus on fun—certainly a new reality for them at the present time. On the other hand, whatever they do with the suggestion, I will receive it as information and validate it as a response that was appropriate for them. Their response to my suggestion will inform future perturbations aimed at achieving solutions, and my response to their behavior hopefully will participate in the creation of a reality that is supportive of the achievement of their goals.

Supporting and Validating

Indeed, when seeking to facilitate resilience, a great deal of emphasis is given to validating and affirming clients whenever there is an opportunity. Accordingly, an important aspect of the way in which postmodern therapists engage in assessing, analyzing, and perturbing to achieve solutions involves acknowledging and complimenting clients regarding various efforts they may have made to solve problems in the past. They may be commended both for efforts attempted as well as for achievements made. Therapists also can recognize and express understanding of whatever feelings of "stuckness" clients describe regarding their present situation. Therapists thus attempt to normalize when appropriate, helping clients to understand their responses to various situations as typical of others who have had similar experiences. Clients also can be commended for choosing to come to therapy, given an awareness that for many individuals and families, doing so may have been a difficult step. Further, therapists can praise clients' successes, however small, and suggest that they do likewise with each other whenever additional successes occur.

In an effort to be supportive of success, however, it is essential for therapists to explore what success means to each individual as well as what each individual would experience as encouragement or affirmation. Such information is important not only for the therapist but also for clients; it enables accomplishments to be acknowledged and validated in ways each person experiences as meaningful. For example, offering verbal praise to a spouse who would prefer a hug is not going to communicate to the recipient the message for which he or she was looking. Having learned each person's desires in this regard, therapists then might suggest that relevant "consequences" be provided for appropriate behaviors, noting that we are quick to do so when undesirable behaviors occur but usually somewhat lax in the reverse. And therapists certainly might seek out the causes of success; that is, what enabled a person to make a desired change or achieve a particular goal.

Similarly, therapists might engage in a search for talents, exploring hidden abilities and unique outcomes in an effort to help clients enlarge their stories about themselves and each other as well as to facilitate the expansion of their behavioral repertoires (White & Epston, 1990). In other words, therapists and clients can consider together instances in the past when the client was able to circumvent or overcome a problematic situation. For example, I might wish to explore with David Warner the times when he has been able to overcome his natural shyness and engage successfully in social situations. Even if he could find only one time, I might then ask how he was able to do so, what thoughts, feelings, or behaviors facilitated his ability to be successful. Such a focus might enable David to recognize previously unacknowledged resources and skills. And if such a conversation were to take place in the context of the whole family, new perceptions of him as a person, as well as of the situation that brought them to therapy, might emerge. Supporting and validating thus can be understood as behaviors consistent with assessing, analyzing, and perturbing to achieve solutions to the clients' goals in a manner that facilitates resilience and enables families to flourish.

Reflecting on the Process as a Whole

As mentioned in the introduction to this chapter, assessing, analyzing, and perturbing to achieve solutions involves ongoing, overlapping processes. An important and continuing aspect of therapy involves taking time to reflect on one's consistency with the guiding principles and practices relative to the processes in which he is engaged. It is essential that therapists remain cognizant of the story that they are telling themselves about clients, as well as about themselves, at each step along the way. It also is important to be sensitive to one's influence as a therapist on the way events have unfolded and how this influence might continue to impact what evolves in the future. In addition, it may be helpful to consider the impact that other stories the therapist could have told might have had on the unfolding of events, and to reflect on the ways in which additional stories might be helpful as the process of therapy continues. Similarly, it is important to be aware of any influence the therapist may have had on the selection of goals. For example, therapists might ask themselves questions about the therapy process that include the following: What other questions might I have asked? What issues or aspects did I privilege, and what issues might I have overlooked? They also might want to consider the meanings that clients may have inferred from the topics upon which therapists chose to focus. By engaging in such reflections, therapists attempt to remain conscious of their role as cocreators of the therapeutic realities being experienced during sessions.

In terms of specific perturbations chosen to facilitate achievement of clients' goals, it is crucial for therapists to be aware of how their thinking, language, and behavior may have influenced the outcome. For example, therapists may wish to consider the ways in which they did or did not go about obtaining agreement with, or "buy in," relative to specific suggestions or assignments. In this regard they might reflect on the degree to which they were able to provide meaningful noise (Keeney, 1983). In other words, did their perturbations offer new information in ways that acknowledged the requirements for both stability and change and also were meaningful and acceptable to the client? Therapists also may want to consider the kinds of negotiation skills that they employed or modeled. Likewise, they may reflect on the kinds of feedback they provided to clients along the way, and whether or not this feedback was helpful. It also may be important to reflect on the stories therapists were telling themselves about successes and failures.

Ultimately, of course, an evaluation, or an analysis and assessment, of the overall process also needs to occur. Of the utmost importance is a consideration of whether or not clients feel that they achieved their goals. They came to therapy for help, and if they feel that they received the help they desired, then I believe therapy was successful. To my mind, there is no better marketing strategy than a satisfied customer. That is, when clients feel that the therapy was helpful or successful, they tend to be free with their compliments, and they also are likely to be an important source of referrals.

Another important aspect of the evaluation process involves a consideration of how therapists feel about what was achieved *and* how it was achieved. Important questions to ask include the following:

Were clients' perceptions included throughout the course of therapy?
Did clients feel validated and supported?
Was I successful in helping clients achieve their goals?
Was I successful in facilitating resilience?
If similar problems were to arise in the future, would the clients be able to handle them successfully?
Is the family characterized by processes that would put them in the category of flourishing?

In these above reflections, therapists also would do well to be aware of such contextual issues as the impact of the setting in which the therapy occurred as well as any time constraints that may have affected the process. Therapist–client characteristics also may be important considerations. For example, how did such dimensions as class, ethnicity, gender, age, sexual orientation, or physical challenges of both therapist and client impact what occurred? And always there must be sensitivity to the value and ethical issues that are a part of every therapeutic encounter (e.g., therapists' biases, risks of change).

Indeed, from the purest second-order cybernetics / postmodern perspective, therapy is not appropriate. Whatever the system is doing, it is logical to that system and is neither right nor wrong, good nor bad—it just *is*. However, given that systems exist in a cultural context in which problems are experienced and behaviors are described as acceptable or not, therapy is an appropriate response. As therapists attempt to keep a foot in both worlds, with a focus on facilitating resilience and enabling families to flourish, they must make every effort to behave in as ethical and respectful a manner as possible.

The various process principles and processes just described are summarized in what I call the Systemic Analysis/Multidimensional Assessment (Becvar & Becvar, 2006). This instrument, which can be found in Appendix B, presents the basic ways in which I attempt to maintain my standards for the ethical and respectful practice of therapy. Another look at the manner in which the guiding principles and practices can be operationalized in relation to the processes of assessing, analyzing, and perturbing to achieve solutions is illustrated in the following case example, which is also the subject of further reflections in the next chapter.

Case Example

Carolyn Wells was 21 years old when her mother insisted that she come to therapy. Carolyn was described to me as a bright, talented young woman who had excelled in all areas during high school and had maintained a B average during her first 2½ years in college. However, she had been placed on academic probation at the end of the second semester of her junior year. Particularly distressing for Carolyn's mother, Marie, was the fact that Carolyn had lied not only about her grades but also about several other aspects of her life. Carolyn had told Marie that she was attending class regularly and seeking extra help, but Marie had since learned from conversations with Carolyn's academic advisor that not only was this not the case, but the main reason for Carolyn's poor grades was failure to attend class and complete assignments. Most important for Marie was to understand why Carolyn had lied to her and to prevent such behavior from occurring in the future.

Since Marie had called for the appointment, I asked that both she and Carolyn come together, at least to the first session. However, Carolyn wanted to come alone, and I said that would be fine, aware that at some time in the future a joint meeting might become possible, if appropriate. Carolyn was a tall, attractive, seemingly mature young woman who appeared to be quite comfortable with the idea of coming to therapy. I shared this latter perception with her, and she acknowledged that she was actually glad to have someone with whom to talk about what had been going on for her. When I asked her to say more, she quickly recounted the following series of events.

Carolyn said that her father had died before she was 3 years old and that she and her mother had always been close. She knew that her mother had worked very hard to support the two of them, and Carolyn also had worked hard to please her mother. Indeed, she had worried about her mother for as long as she could remember because she seemed so sad most of the time. Marie had never shown much interest in dating or other activities outside the home after becoming a widow, and had focused most of her time and attention on Carolyn. Carolyn felt that the only time her mother seemed to really cheer up was when Carolyn achieved success, either by doing well in school, excelling in sports, or having lots of friends. Therefore, the last thing in the world she wanted to be was a disappointment to her mother, which she had felt she would be if she told her mother what was happening with her grades. So, she had begun to lie, and once the lying started she didn't seem able to stop it. However, she really had thought she might be able to salvage her grades, although obviously that had not happened. And now she felt horrible because she had become an even greater disappointment to her mother.

As I listened to Carolyn tell her story, I felt sad for her as well as for her mother. I asked Carolyn how her mother had responded when the truth had come out. She said that at first her mother had been hurt and angry, and then she had become silent and withdrawn, remaining that way for several days. Her only response beyond that was to insist that Carolyn go to therapy. Next, I asked Carolyn about her desire to come to therapy alone. She replied that she thought it would be helpful to talk with someone who could be more objective, but that she hoped that at some point she could share more with her mother about what had been going on in her life.

In fact, Carolyn said that making the adjustment to college had been very difficult. She was attending on a scholarship and so had experienced pressure to maintain a B average from the beginning. In addition to her studies, she also had a part-time job (a requirement of her scholarship package) and thus had had little time to participate in extracurricular activities or to socialize with friends. She had not been very happy but didn't want to burden her mother, who had been so excited that Carolyn was going to an excellent school. Carolyn reported that she had had a brief relationship with a young man, who broke up with her in the middle of the last semester for reasons that she could not understand. At that point, she just seemed to lose interest in her studies. She had overslept and missed many of her classes and had failed to complete assignments, which added to the feelings of shame she already had been experiencing.

I asked Carolyn how she thought I might be able to help her in addition to being able to provide an objective sounding board. She said that she would really like to sort out her relationship with her mother, and that she would like to get back on track with school. She wanted to regain her scholarship and graduate as close to the schedule as possible. I assured her that I thought this might be doable.

I then said that many thoughts had been running around in my head as I listened to her, and with her permission I began to wonder aloud about some of these thoughts. I wondered how, if she were in her mother's shoes, she thought she might be feeling. I wondered if her mother might be sad about what had happened to Carolyn rather than disappointed in her. I wondered whether Marie might be feeling that somehow she had failed her daughter. About Carolyn, herself, I wondered how she had managed to do so much with so little support. I wondered if she was aware of the enormous load she had been attempting to carry all by herself.

By this point, Carolyn had begun to cry softly, acknowledging that she really hadn't thought about some of the things I mentioned in the ways that I was suggesting. She admitted that there had been times when she was angry with her mother and wished that she would get a life of her own. She also was angry that she had not had a father, but she never felt that she could share her feelings about his absence with her mother. She knew that her mother had done her best, but she wished that things could have been a little easier. She wished that she could have some of the freedoms enjoyed by her classmates at college. After talking about all of this for a while, I asked Carolyn if she would be willing to try to talk with her mother about some of these issues if I were present to help her. Without even a moment's hesitation, she said she would and that she would invite her to the next session.

The second session began with introductions and some small talk aimed at establishing a level of comfort, particularly for Marie, who seemed somewhat nervous but expressed her gratitude that Carolyn had wanted her to come with her. I then asked Carolyn to tell me what she had told her mother about coming to therapy. Carolyn replied that she had told her mother that there were things she really wanted to talk with her about, and that she thought it might be better if I were there to help both of them with the process. Marie added that she was relieved to know that Carolyn had felt good about her first session, and that if her daughter trusted me, that was good enough for her.

I then asked Carolyn where she would like to begin. Almost immediately dissolving into tears, she said she was so sorry that she had been a disappointment to her mother, and that she felt so badly that she was burdening her mother with her problems. She said she was sorry about the lying and felt awful about how angry she had made her mother. She also repeated many of the things that she had shared with me about how grateful she was for all her mother had done for her, and how hard she had always tried to do things to make her mother happy, and that now she felt like such a failure.

With tears in her eyes, Marie responded that, of course, she didn't like the lying but that she had been most angry that Carolyn had felt she couldn't come to her and tell her the truth. She had always been proud of how close they were, and of the fact that they had been able to share things with each other. She also said that from the moment she was born, Carolyn had been everything she could have wished for in a daughter, and that although she was sad about what had happened, Carolyn was neither a disappointment nor a failure. With that, she reached out and took her daughter's hand.

Although this was certainly an auspicious beginning, I remained aware that there was much more on Carolyn's mind, and that Marie's story also needed to be heard and taken into consideration. We therefore spent some time exploring what it had been like for Marie as a young widow with a small child. Marie described her anger at her husband's death as well as her struggles over the years to make a good home for her daughter. I asked if she had ever dated, and she said that she had had a few dates but that she had never had a desire to get involved seriously after her husband died. She said she didn't want to risk being hurt again, and that she preferred to devote as much time as possible to taking care of Carolyn. During this conversation I was able to compliment Marie on all that she had achieved, despite challenging circumstances and limited resources. I also expressed my understanding of how proud she must be of her daughter. I then asked Carolyn what it had been like for her growing up in her family.

Carolyn said that she had always been proud of her mother, too. A little more tentatively, she told her mother that she could remember worrying about her from the time she was a small child. When Marie asked her to explain, Carolyn shared her perception that her mother had always seemed so sad, and that she had just wished she could be happy. She also said that as she got older, she had really missed having a father but didn't want to tell her mother for fear of upsetting her. So, despite the fact that they were close, for quite a long time she had felt that there were some things she couldn't discuss with her mother. I then asked Carolyn if this was similar to what had happened with her grades, and she said that it was. She told her mother that she had been having some struggles of her own but that, once again, she didn't want to upset her mother and so hadn't said anything. Although originally she had felt that she could handle things, they had gone from bad to worse, and now she was in serious trouble.

Marie then said, "So all along you have been feeling that you needed to take care of me, just as I have been feeling that I needed to take care of you?" When Carolyn nodded in agreement, Marie asked Carolyn if there were other things she had wished she could tell her mother. When Carolyn said that there were, Marie assured her that she would like to hear about them now, and that she was strong enough to handle whatever her daughter had to say. With many pauses, Carolyn proceeded to tell her mother about the challenges she had experienced making the transition to college, her envy of other kids who seemed to have so much more freedom, and her sadness at the breakup of her relationship. Marie apologized to her daughter for not being sensitive enough to what Carolyn was going through and thanked her for being willing to share more now.

I complimented them both for their demonstrations of trust and caring and allowed us all to sit with this poignant exchange for a moment. I then asked if they would like to begin focusing on where they might go from here, saying that I thought they had many resources on which to build and achieve what they desired. With Carolyn's permission, I shared with Marie that Carolyn had expressed the desire to sort out her relationship with her mother and to get back on track academically. I then asked Marie what her desires were, and she said that both of Carolyn's goals sounded good to her, and that she was much more hopeful now than when we began. As I was concluding the session, I asked if they would like to continue to come together, and both replied that they would. I then suggested that each reflect on what had transpired during the session but that they not talk about either our conversation or the problems that brought them in until the next appointment. I also suggested that Carolyn go to see her academic advisor about her options and that she keep her mother posted regarding whatever she learned. Both agreed, and we shared our farewells until the next meeting.

Summary and Reflections

Assessing, analyzing, and perturbing to achieve solutions with Carolyn and Marie Wells was characterized throughout the first two sessions by a suspension of judgment. That is, I sought to understand the logic of the behaviors of both daughter and mother in context. Rather than being critical of Carolyn for lying or blaming Marie for a lack of sensitivity to what her daughter was experiencing, I could see that the actions of both made sense, given the nature of the relationship they had created together. Thus Carolyn constantly sought to avoid distressing her mother, and Marie trusted that her daughter was able to handle her new life, given her previous track record, and that Carolyn was being open and honest with her. Inviting both to share their personal stories further enabled me to understand the context they had created and in which they had lived since Marie was widowed. These narrations also allowed my clients to understand aspects of their world that previously had been unrecognized.

In regard to the use of language, I noticed particularly the clients' emphasis on achieving success, avoiding disappointment, and the burden of feeling shame. Accordingly, it seemed particularly important to support and validate both Carolyn and Marie, and to do so in a way that would be meaningful to them. I thus complimented Marie on her success as a mother, and I complimented both for their ability to trust and care for each other.

I also attempted to participate in the cocreation of new realities in several ways. With Carolyn, I used wondering, both about her mother's challenges as well as her own struggles, as a means of helping her to view both situations in a slightly different light. When both mother and daughter were present, I focused on the creation of a more open and honest conversation. Further, not only did I shift the focus to a consideration of solutions, I encouraged them to avoid talking about their problems outside of therapy.

As I reflect on the process as a whole, I am aware of many personal factors that may have influenced my behavior in these two sessions. Having been a single parent, I could relate to the challenges involved with parenting without a partner. I also was sensitive to the impact the loss of husband and father must have had on Marie and Carolyn, respectively. In many ways this family of two already had demonstrated resilience, a factor on which I was able to build. To my mind, it seemed clear that their ability to flourish had merely been sidetracked and soon would be restored. It thus made sense to offer hope to these clients, which I did in both sessions. Finally, my homework assignment represented a further perturbation aimed at helping them to achieve the solutions they desired.

CHAPTER SEVEN

Supporting a Positive Self-Concept

What and how we think about, or conceptualize, ourselves is extremely significant, guiding ideas and thoughts about what we can and cannot do or become and influencing beliefs about actions or behaviors that may or may not be seen as possible. The term *self-concept* refers to these perceptions, or the mental image, that each individual has of him- or herself. Emerging from the theorizing of René Descartes, perhaps best known for his dictum, "I think, therefore I am," as well as the work of Sigmund Freud (1900/1955) and Carl Rogers (1947), awareness of the importance of internal thought processes relative to self-perception and behavior has been an important aspect and area of study in the mental health professions for many years.

Although much about this construct and its impact continues to be debated by various theorists and researchers, generally the self-concept is believed to evolve over time as an individual interacts with others, constructing and taking on various roles and thereby gaining in self-awareness. The postmodern view of this process is that the self is negotiated and defined in the context and as a function of each individual's relationships and relational communities. Indeed, from such a perspective, we are called upon to recognize the degree to which the self one experiences is influenced by, and cocreated within, a culture that includes not only the larger society but also the various individuals who comprise each individual's personal world.

Regardless of orientation, there does tend to be agreement among professionals that the self-concept is learned, that it tends to be stable and organized, and thus that it is somewhat resistant to change. At the same time, the self-concept also generally is understood to be dynamic in that it is part of an ongoing developmental process, and various aspects can be influenced and altered in a matter of moments as the individual responds to specific situations. For example, although a person may have a fairly positive view of him- or herself, that person often is quick to call him- or herself stupid after making just the smallest mistake. Similarly, in the midst of strangers a person might suddenly feel shy despite the fact that this same person usually tends to be outgoing and confident with colleagues and friends. Each of these experiences, however brief, has the potential to alter one's self-concept.

Whether poor or positive, each person typically behaves in a manner that is consistent with his or her self-concept, or feelings, assumptions, beliefs, image, and knowledge about him- or herself. The creation of good self-esteem—that is, the ability to have one's self-worth affirmed and to gain self-assurance as one interacts with others—is facilitated by a self-concept that is positive, realistic, and includes confidence in one's ability to deal effectively with whatever problems may arise. In order to flourish, it is important for individuals to be able to assess their strengths realistically and to act with a sense of confidence in their own competence. It also is important that individuals' perceptions of themselves be shared by their family members.

Certainly in therapy the ability of clients to follow through on suggestions and attempt new behaviors is enhanced to the extent that they believe in themselves and their own abilities. More importantly, resilient individuals are those who evidence initiative and autonomy, given a positive sense of self at all levels—mental, emotional, physical, and spiritual. In this chapter the discussion provides more in-depth descriptions of various ways to support a positive self-concept, some of which already have been touched on briefly. Specific topics addressed include encouraging success, acknowledging accomplishments, searching for talents, changing negative self-talk, becoming sensitive to professional language, and considering the therapeutic relationship. Once again, these discussions include reflections on and illustrations of concepts drawn from the case example at the end of the previous chapter. This chapter then offers another case example and concludes with a brief summary and further reflections on the therapy processes described.

Encouraging Success

There is no question that experiences of success and failure impact and influence the creation of one's self-concept. The more that one is successful—that is, experiences oneself as competent—the more likely it is that one's self-concept will evolve in a positive direction, and thus the more likely that one will evidence resilience. By contrast, the more that one is unsuccessful—experiences oneself as incompetent—the more likely it is that one's self-concept will evolve in a negative direction, and thus the more one is likely to be overwhelmed when faced with serious challenges. Although this dynamic may be self-evident, often less acknowledged is the fact that what constitutes success for one person may be very different for another person. Also important is an awareness that the self-concept seems to be much more vulnerable to failure, which, as noted above, can undermine in an instant a longstanding and otherwise positive view of the self. Although certainly only one aspect of the therapy process and my thinking about it, the stories of Carolyn Wells and Marie, her mother, presented in the case example at the end of the previous chapter, provide an interesting look at both of these aspects of the self-concept.

When Carolyn came to therapy, she was defining herself as a "disappointment" and a "failure." This negative self-labeling occurred despite the fact that she had achieved multiple successes in a variety of situations throughout her life, was described by her mother as bright and talented, and most likely had had a very healthy, positive self-concept prior to her problems in college. Carolyn's entire view of herself was then altered in a negative fashion as a function of relationship and academic difficulties in one relatively short period in her life. As most of us tend to do in times of stress, she had lost the ability to look at the bigger picture and to assess realistically both herself and her situation. However, while I could and did attempt to normalize, or explain the logic of what had occurred, among other considerations I also felt it important to help her find ways to achieve a positive outcome by experiencing herself as competent in one of the areas in which she previously had been successful. Hence my suggestion at the end of the second session that she consult with her academic advisor about her options relative to improving her grades and regaining her scholarship. In addition, my recommendation that she keep Marie informed about whatever she learned was intended to help reestablish a relationship based on trust and reopen the lines of communication between mother and daughter.

Indeed, much of Marie's self-concept, also apparently generally positive prior to the current problems, seemed to be based on her perception of herself as a mother and the degree to which she was effective in that role. As revealed in the course of conversation, this effectiveness meant not only that her child was successful, but also, and perhaps more importantly, that she and her daughter share a very close and special relationship with each other. As Marie indicated, she was more upset that Carolyn had been unable to speak to her about what was happening, which prompted the lying, than she was about her daughter's academic problems. Furthermore, although Carolyn had stated at the outset that she wanted to sort out her relationship with her mother, doing so seemed to be an even higher priority for Marie. In suggesting that they avoid talking about the problem, including what had taken place in the session, and focus on solutions instead, I hoped to help them create healthier ways of interacting as they worked to achieve the goals articulated by both.

Throughout this process, I attempted to remain sensitive to what these clients might experience as success. That is, consistent with their desired goals, or the solutions to the problem that they had specified, it was important to help them feel competent and thus regain confidence in areas that were significant to them. To have complimented them on, or have suggested, behaviors in areas that they perceived as insignificant probably would not have been helpful. Worse, they might have felt that I had not listened well and that my understanding of their situation was lacking. Indeed, sensitivity to this aspect of therapy is useful for both professionals and clients in several ways. First, therapeutic interventions in general, and those relative to supporting a positive self-concept in particular, are likely to be more effective if they are tailored to fit the unique characteristics of the individuals and families with whom the therapist is working. In addition, as therapists model this behavior, clients may be helped to understand the importance of acting in a similar manner, making choices about what to compliment or encourage that are tailored to and thus are meaningful and appropriate for each family member. This is similar to the idea that when buying a gift for another, it is important that the gift be something that the other person would appreciate rather than selecting something that the buyer would like to receive. Finally, as part of this conversation, the importance of finding suitable ways to acknowledge success also may be addressed.

Acknowledging Accomplishments

As with the specifics regarding what a person might experience as a success, or conduct worthy of note, the ways in which various accomplishments and behaviors are acknowledged may be a very important consideration as therapists attempt to facilitate resilience. Although therapists may make some general recommendations to clients in this regard, a very useful exploration might focus on times when each person felt that he or she had received from others the desired or appropriate recognition for a goal achieved or for the demonstration of a particular skill. Indeed, although lack of recognition is a common complaint among spouses and relationship partners, they often also find that, despite the best of intentions, they have missed the mark when attempting to validate one another. The following brief scenarios may serve to illustrate this phenomenon.

Harry and Diane were both successful professionals with very high-powered, demanding careers. In terms of their relationship, however, Diane was frustrated by the fact that the only time Harry ever seemed to acknowledge her successes in the business world was when they were socializing with friends. She therefore felt that somehow she wasn't living up to Harry's standards, which for her was demoralizing. She said that what she really wished for was that her husband would send her some flowers at the office when something good happened for her professionally. Harry's explanation was that he expected nothing less than success from his wife, and that he thought buying and sending flowers not only was a waste of money but that her wanting them didn't fit his image of his wife, the successful professional.

By contrast, Jim sent flowers to his wife Nancy on every occasion, including birthdays as well as in recognition of accomplishments in her world as a busy homemaker and mother. Although Nancy thought the flowers were nice and she appreciated his efforts, she felt that Jim was taking the easy way out and that he wasn't really very appreciative of her accomplishments. This judgment added to her mixed feelings about herself, which were fed by many negative societal messages about being a stay-at-home mom. What she really wished for was that Jim would show some initiative and originality, picking out gifts such as a piece of jewelry or an article of clothing, which would demonstrate to her in a meaningful way that he appreciated what she had done. However, she had not wanted to say anything to Jim about this wish for fear of hurting his feelings.

Although many dynamics were undoubtedly at work in the relationships of the two couples just described, part of their respective conflicts emerged around lack of understanding regarding how each person would like to be affirmed; what each would experience as meaningful validation. Helping the members of each couple, or helping each person in a family, to articulate preferences in this realm is likely to prove fruitful both in easing tensions and in supporting the development of a positive self-concept. And such discussions regarding the acknowledgment of accomplishments also can include consideration of what might constitute either too much or too little. That is, although most of us probably are familiar with the adage that the punishment should fit the crime, in the same way it is also appropriate for the consequences of successful behavior to be logical, or fit the achievement.

As a strong advocate of the idea that no accomplishment is too small to celebrate, I certainly encourage clients in this regard. However, either giving too much or giving too much too soon, particularly for something that does not seem to warrant such a response, may not only encourage unrealistic expectations but also (paradoxically) lead to a devaluing of subsequent affirmations. Additional problematic ramifications also may ensue. This issue can be particularly salient in relationships between parents and children, as illustrated in the following two vignettes.

Bud and Ellen Stewart, both academicians, were strongly committed to educational achievement. They therefore began rewarding each of their three children with $1 for every "A" and $10 for all "A's," as soon as report cards started coming home from school in the first grade. As the children grew, these amounts were increased, and the children also were given expensive gifts for additional academic accomplishments. Although competition might have evolved had these children not been equally talented, fortunately this was not a problem in the Stewart family. However, eventually the children came to expect similar expensive gifts for other achievements, for example, in the realm of sports and music, and were disappointed when they were not forthcoming. Over time they also just took for granted the financial rewards they received for doing well in school—something they all believed they probably would have done anyway because of personal motivation. Indeed, they did not experience anything particularly special about the rewards they received for academic success.

Another example is provided by Peter, an only child who was doted upon by his parents and given pretty much anything he wanted as he was growing up. In fact, he was treated as so special that his self-concept was beyond positive; Peter certainly could be described as having an inflated sense of himself. Unfortunately, as an adolescent, his conceited behaviors led to alienation in most of his relationships with others, as well as frustration on his part that others did not seem to value or reward him as he felt he should be valued and rewarded. In adulthood Peter reported repeated frustrations in his efforts to create and maintain a long-term relationship.

There is thus a delicate balance that must be sought when desiring to support a positive self-concept, in this case through acknowledgment of accomplishments. Careful thought and sensitivity to each person is essential, as is consideration of appropriate responses relative to each situation. Behaving according to these rather simple provisos and helping clients to follow suit can both prevent problems and facilitate the ability to flourish. The same also can be said of efforts to identify the talents of clients, particularly those that may not be readily apparent.

Searching for Talents

A *talent* generally refers to an innate ability or gift that enables one to do easily what others may perceive as difficult. Thus we tend to think of a talented person as one who is naturally endowed with skills in a particular area. Actors, artists, athletes, musicians, child prodigies, and adult geniuses all come to mind in this regard. However, it is my belief that everyone has talents, however small or previously unrecognized they may be. And as they are uncovered and affirmed, therapists can help families, and family members can help each other, in ways that are (1) very supportive of a positive self-concept and (2) facilitative of the achievement of solutions and thus of the ability to flourish.

A primary mode of exploration in the search for talents may involve asking clients to describe some areas in which they believe they have strengths or in which they feel good about themselves. However, the first response to such a question is likely to be embarrassment, given that in this society we do not believe it is appropriate to "blow one's own horn." A corollary to this rule is that we must be humble regarding our own abilities. When embarrassment or reticence is a response to such a request, therapists can explain to clients their belief that they are the experts on themselves, and that they have a great deal more knowledge than does anyone else regarding times when they have experienced themselves as talented. If clients continue to struggle, therapists then might help them to search, encouraging them to pinpoint specific behaviors that enabled them to achieve something, and describing such behaviors as talents of which they rightfully may feel proud. Whereas this process is similar to the search for unique outcomes (White & Epston, 1990), or times when a problem was not experienced, the search for talents also may move into realms other than those associated with the problem as part of the process of facilitating resilience.

For example, when working with a client who is experiencing depression, the therapist certainly may ask whether there are ever times when that person is able to hold the depression at bay, or when depression has less influence. In addition, as part of a more general exploration to understand the larger context, the therapist might include questions about times when the client exhibited strengths or accomplished goals, however small, of which others weren't even aware. This search might include uncovering such accomplishments as completing an assignment despite the desire to quit or doing a chore when other more pleasant activities were beckoning. They might then discuss the skills and talents evident, at least to the therapist, that were demonstrated in these situations.

Family members also may provide an important source of information regarding individual talents. Asking each family member to describe the areas in which he or she perceives every other family member to have strengths and abilities can be extremely revealing and also may encourage the "observers" to view the "observed" in a very different light. In turn, the "observed" may begin to feel very differently about themselves, about the "observer," and about their relationships. What is more, questions in this realm may participate in shifting the conversation away from problems and deficits and onto potential resources that could be utilized both to attain the desired goal and to facilitate resilience.

In addition, helping individuals focus on the talents, skills, or assets of the family as a whole supports a positive self-concept for individual members. For example, at the end of a session I often ask each person to tell me what he or she believes is the best thing about being a part of this particular family. Even very young children can participate in this activity, which tends to affirm both individual and family strengths and may provide useful information to the members and the therapist.

Talents also can be discerned and highlighted by means of reframing (Watzlawick et al., 1974) or creatively misunderstanding (de Shazer, 1991). Both perturbations have the potential to change perceptions and shift the therapeutic process in a positive direction. To illustrate, a person described as manipulative might be complimented on his or her ability to negotiate or manage the world, behaving in such a way that others respond by doing his or her bidding. Further exploration might reveal the specific behaviors that have been successful for that person in his or her attempt to manage the world, and how these behaviors could be applied in other situations whereby such a talent would be commended rather than criticized.

Efforts to work with and help children experience greater success also can be supported by a similar process of relanguaging behaviors and thus changing the labels that tend to categorize them in a negative way. Accordingly, a child perceived to be stubborn or obstinate could also be understood as someone with an innate ability to stand up for what he or she believes, to persevere despite seemingly insurmountable barriers, to have a sticktoitiveness that potentially enables him or her to accomplish a great deal. Similarly, a child who has been described as having a short attention span and a tendency to jump around from one project to another might be portrayed as one who has a keen interest in many areas and is very creative in his or her use of time and talents.

As the therapist expands on such alternative stories with each child, both the children and the others in their world may begin to see and thus experience them differently. As noted many times previously, how we language people and their behavior is likely to have a direct and significant influence on the way that they and their behaviors are perceived and experienced. Certainly this influence is the case when the focus shifts to the ways in which clients both perceive and language, or tell stories about themselves. And just as people tend to focus primarily on problems, generally the conversations people have with themselves include a great deal of negativity.

Changing Negative Self-Talk

Although in general I am not inclined to recommend self-help books, for years I have been encouraging clients to read and follow the instructions provided in the book *What to Say When You Talk to Yourself* (Helmstetter, 1986). Helmstetter focuses on self-talk, particularly the negative messages people have internalized and then tend to repeat as part of a never-ending commentary on their abilities, their behaviors, and themselves in general. Not surprisingly, such negative self-talk, which tends to be a common phenomenon, has been found to lead to irrational thinking about the self as well as about others in one's world (McAdam, 1986; Ryan, Short, & Reed, 1986). It therefore is likely to undermine one's self-concept and thus the potential to be successful and to feel competent—in short, to be resilient.

Helmstetter (1986) encourages readers to reprogram their internal dialogue, replacing the negative self-talk with positive, self-affirming messages. Specific recommendations include creating an audiotape using one's own voice and playing it at least once or twice a day for several weeks. Scripts are provided that can be employed in this process; for example, there is one that specifically aims to enhance one's self-esteem. Although it is not necessary to use one of these scripts, Helmstetter emphasizes the importance of putting whatever messages are selected for the audiotape related to one's particular goals in the present tense (e.g., "I am a good person"; "I am accomplishing my goals"; "I am a person with many skills").

In order to facilitate this self-affirmation process, especially when clients seem reluctant or are unable to follow through on their own, despite having expressed interest in making a tape, I may track their language during a session and write down specific phrases related to the solutions they desire, translating negatives into positives as I go, and creating a beginning script that fits each person. For example, "I am so angry and I know it's not helping me" can be rephrased as "I am releasing my anger." The statement "I just wish that I could lose weight" might become "I am losing the weight I desire easily and comfortably while also staying healthy." The statement "I am a successful person with lots of talents and skills" can be substituted for "I am such a loser." At the end of the session I might offer these suggestions for a script to the client so that he or she can take them home and make a tape. On some occasions I have brought in a tape recorder and helped clients to make their tapes as part of our session.

Although this approach may seem extremely simplistic, I have seen remarkable results. Clients with a variety of complaints have achieved their desired goals, be those goals about weight loss, completion of a dissertation, forgiveness, relationship building, or general health. I also am a believer in the process because of my success with such a tape to facilitate my own physical healing.

Although the audiotape exercise may not be appropriate for young children, a very simple exercise can help them learn to speak about themselves positively and without undue embarrassment. Known as "brag time," during a family meal everyone might be invited to share one thing that happened during the day that helped that person to feel good about him- or herself. After each person has taken a turn and been affirmed, family members might consider when and how much of the information just shared it is permissible to tell others or if it should remain within the family. Accordingly, learning how to engage in appropriate self-talk, along with a consideration of boundaries, can begin at an early age.

I certainly know from both personal and professional experience the power of language to facilitate success and support the development of a positive self-concept. Indeed, I firmly believe that what we say and how we say it, either about ourselves or about others, will have a powerful impact. It thus logically follows that I am extremely wary of language that is negative.

Becoming Sensitive to Professional Language

As is no doubt obvious by this point, I am strongly opposed to the use of language or labels that are negative or that tend to pathologize in any way. Such opposition includes diagnostic categories, as noted in the previous chapter, and applies to conversations with clients as well as to

written notes and assessments—all of which raise issues of ethics and integrity (Becvar & Becvar, 2006). I believe it is inconsistent for me to use
an individual diagnosis when a basic tenet of my theoretical orientation
is that problems arise, or are created and defined, in the context of relationships. I also am concerned about the realities, as well as the self-
concepts, I might be participating in creating, both for my clients and
for the larger society, if I were to define those with whom I work and
the problems they are experiencing in individual rather than contextual
terms. Indeed, I am troubled about the degree to which the labels that we
have created about mental illness have become reified; generally they are
seen as the way things really are, rather than merely as stories authored
by professionals to assist them in their work.

At the same time, I also recognize the realities of today's managed care
world. Although I am fortunate to be able to see primarily private-pay
clients, reducing my fee when necessary or appropriate, I know that this
is not always possible for others, including therapists who have some
of the same misgivings about labeling that I have. I realize that a great
many professionals are dependent upon third-party payments and
therefore must abide by the rules of insurance companies, whose requirements for reimbursement include diagnosis according to such a
classification framework as that provided in the DSM–IV (American Psychiatric Association, 1994).

When diagnosis becomes essential or clients arrive with a diagnosis in
hand, one general strategy may be for therapists to share their views on
this topic. Indeed, doing so may afford therapists an opportunity to help
clients see their diagnosis as a professional story about the symptoms
and behaviors with which they are dealing rather than as a description of
themselves as individuals. Accordingly, therapists may be able to externalize the problem (White & Epston, 1990), helping clients to understand
that rather than being particular disorders, they are people who are dealing with specific challenges that are understandable, and that there are
ways to overcome these challenges. In so doing, clients may be freed to
see and experience themselves differently, that is, as persons who are
capable of dealing with their situations.

Therapists also may try to help clients understand how a diagnosis
may be detrimental in the future, for example, should they need to
switch to another insurance company. I have a client whom I saw many

years ago for couples therapy who calls me whenever her insurance provider changes in order to verify that therapy focused on the relationship rather than on a mental illness. Therapists might even have a conversation with clients about the particular diagnosis that seems the most appropriate and also is the most benign. Interestingly, such explicit acknowledgment of clients' opinions and expertise, as well as encouragement of their participation in the selection of a diagnosis, may support feelings of competence and help to create a more positive self-concept before the process of searching to achieve solutions even begins.

Finally, as therapists write their case notes or reports to insurance companies (in those instances in which clients choose to receive reimbursement from a third-party payer) they can choose to include strengths and skills from their perspective as well as from the perspective of the clients. Similarly, when referring clients to other professionals, for example, to obtain an educational evaluation, therapists can recommend only those who think systemically, who understand the importance of context, who are able to write reports that emphasize strengths and skills, and who are able to indicate what might be helpful for the client rather than only what may be perceived as problematic. These issues bring us to a further consideration of the therapeutic relationship, particularly in relation to supporting a positive self-concept and thereby facilitating resilience.

Considering the Therapeutic Relationship

Whether or not therapists focus explicitly on providing support for a positive self-concept, how they interact with clients inevitably will have an impact on clients' perceptions of themselves and the challenges with which they are dealing. Given my theoretical orientation as well as my clinical focus on helping families to flourish, I am particularly sensitive to the notion that both the self and problems are defined and have meaning only in the context of specific relationships. Such a notion was one of the prime motivators for the creation of postmodern, second-order therapeutic approaches that sought to "establish a symmetrical relationship characterized by a partnership of co-equals" (Becvar & Becvar, 1997b, p. 183).

Accordingly, the more therapists are able to behave in a manner that is respectful of, and sensitive to, clients' perceptions, goals, and knowledge about their lives and contexts, the more positive this impact will be. As therapists listen attentively to a client's story and as they seek clarification and solicit articulation of what the client would like to have happen, they are communicating an implicit belief in the client's competence. Ideally, they also are participating in family or relationship therapy that is understood as "a dialogue of living persons," a concept that offers "a perspective that makes it possible to capture something of the mutuality and shared activity of a therapeutic encounter in practice" (Rober, 2005, p. 385). In other words, as therapists, we are invited to recognize that each participant in the therapy process is a living, breathing, live person with his or her own stories about hopes, dreams, successes, and failures. And each person is constantly tuned into, and interacting with, all of the others as together they create a particular relational context.

Building on the work of Russian thinker Mikhail Bakhtin, Rober (2005) suggests that the therapeutic dialogue can be conceptualized as an ongoing, never-ending process that is unique to each situation. According to his position, it is essential that consideration be given to the social context in which particular words are spoken, given that the meaning of the words is dependent upon this context. However, rather than attempting to capture the specific meaning of the words, understanding becomes a practical issue regarding knowledge about how the therapist should proceed:

> This kind of understanding fits a view of language in which the function of language is not representing the world, but coordinating our actions together. . . . From this perspective, the therapist's focus is not aimed in the first place at the content of the client's story—it is not a question of data or information—but rather at the continuation of a sensible dialogue with the client. (Rober, 2005, p. 388)

Consistent with this perspective, as participants are able to anticipate and coordinate their interactions with one another, they are acting from within the context of the relationship. In the course of such a creative dialogue, in which true collaboration is experienced, the therapeutic relationship that is so essential for effectiveness is more likely to be established. So also is a positive self-concept, and thus resilience, likely to be supported.

Up to this point we have focused primarily on ways in which therapists and other individuals may participate in the creation of relationships that support a positive self-concept. At the same time, it also may be important to consider how the self-concept affects relationships. That is, according to Hinde, Finkenauer, and Auhagen (2001), "relationship processes occur in the heads of individuals, with the participants having their own idiosyncratic views of the relationship as well as a shared one" (p. 187). In other words, each person's self-concept influences the way that that person perceives a particular relationship, adding emphasis to the importance of cultivating understanding and sensitivity in this realm.

Certainly systems theorists and practitioners have long recognized the idea that the whole is greater than the sum of its parts. That is, each relationship is comprised of the individuals involved as well as their interactions, or $1 + 1 = 3$. We also know clinically that clients often experience both the therapeutic relationship and their therapists in ways that the latter may find surprising. This phenomenon certainly might be explained, to some extent, by the differing self-concepts of those involved, thus highlighting again the significance of this dimension.

Indeed, throughout the writing of this chapter, I have been wondering about the responses of readers to my choice to devote so much attention to supporting a positive self-concept. Certainly this is not a topic often found in books focused on ways to help families. However, as therapists seek to assist clients in the attainment of their goals and, in the process, greater resilience, supporting a positive self-concept appears to be an area worthy of attention. The following case example provides an illustration of these ideas.

Case Example

Therapy with Marina and Gale included several phases that took place over a number of years. The two women, both of whom were in their early 30s, first came to therapy seeking better ways to enhance their understanding of each other, resolve conflicts in their relationship in a more productive manner, and prevent problems in the future. At that time they had been together for a year and were in the final stages of planning a commitment ceremony that was scheduled to occur in 2 months. Both were certain that they wanted to spend the rest of their lives together, but they also realized that they needed to find ways to reconcile their very different problem-solving styles. Although they were fairly comfortable with the ways in which they had worked out the sharing of household tasks and responsibilities, when it came to personal and relationship issues, they often found themselves bogged down in a pattern that wasn't working. That is, whereas both were willing to address differences and problems as they arose, Gale felt that Marina not only wanted to process their dilemmas, she wanted to puree them. Marina, on the other hand, often felt frustrated because Gale usually ended their conversations before what she perceived as resolution or closure had been achieved. Both would go away from such interactions frustrated and angry.

During the course of this first phase of therapy, the focus was primarily on effective communication. I listened carefully as each young woman told her story, asking for examples and illustrations when appropriate. Once both had agreed that I had a clear understanding of their problematic pattern, I began to make suggestions. My intention, consistent with their wishes and goals, was to help them to find new, more effective ways to respond to one another. I first helped them to understand that they seemed to have very different strategies for handling information and making sense of it. Although I did not administer the Meyers–Briggs Type Indicator® (MBTI) instrument, I borrowed concepts from this inventory to help them alter the stories they had created about each other. That is, I explained my perception that Marina seemed to be a person for whom the conversation was the means of working out what she thought and felt. By contrast, Gale seemed to prefer internal reflection, after which she could share whatever conclusions she had reached.

These ideas seemed to resonate for both and proved to be very helpful in paving the way for the suggestions that followed. For example, I encouraged Gale to let Marina know when she was reaching her limit in a conversation and to offer to schedule a time at a later date when the topic could be revisited. I pointed out my belief that it wasn't that Gale didn't care, it was just that she needed a break. At the same time, I encouraged Marina to let Gale know when she needed to talk, but also to be sensitive to the fact that several brief conversations might work better than would a long, drawn-out dissection of their issues. They found tools such as these very useful and were able to terminate after only three sessions.

Phase two of the therapy occurred 5 years later as Marina and Gale were struggling to make decisions regarding how to bring a child into their lives. Gale wanted to adopt a child from another country, and Marina very much wanted to be artificially inseminated and give birth to a child. Each woman had valid concerns about the other's preference. Gale explained that her parents had finally come to terms with the fact that their daughter was a lesbian, and they seemed to have accepted Marina into the family as well. Although she felt that they probably would respond favorably to an adopted child, she feared that they would find the idea of Marina having a baby totally unacceptable and would go back to excluding them, as well as their child, from their lives. She also worried about her legal rights to a child born to her partner. Marina, on the other hand, worried that in order for them to adopt a child, they would have to lie about their relationship, knowing that same-sex couples often are denied the opportunity to adopt. She felt that they had worked too hard in the process of coming out and living openly to go back to denying their relationship. She also was concerned that she would not be able to love an adopted child in the same way that she would love a child of her own.

Although the obstacles that Marina and Gale had enumerated were serious, I did not believe them to be insurmountable and told them so. Given that their goal was to be able to make a decision with which both would feel comfortable, our conversation continued with a focus on finding ways to deal with the challenges each had enumerated. I asked Gale how she and Marina had been successful in managing to gain acceptance of their relationship from her family. She responded that letting her parents know how crucial their acceptance was to her happiness had been extremely important. I wondered if that also might be the case, should she and Marina decide that Marina would have a biological child. Regarding legal rights to a child born to Marina, I wondered if they had talked with other same-sex couples who had dealt with this issue. I also shared stories of couples I knew who had changed their names in order to enhance the legal rights of both parents. One couple had created a hyphenated name that was a combination of their separate names. The choice of the other couple was for the nonbiological parent to take the surname of the biological parent.

In response to Marina's concerns, I wondered if they had explored options or countries in which a same-sex relationship did not preclude the possibility of adoption. In addition, knowing her to be a doting aunt, I also asked her how she felt about her nieces and nephews. When she replied that she "loved them to death," I wondered how she could doubt her ability to love a child that she and Gale might adopt together. I then suggested that their decision-making process might be helped by further explorations on both of their parts, and I encouraged them to work together to see what they could learn.

Over the next several months, our discussions focused on the information they had gathered relative to their original concerns and on additional fears and issues that emerged along the way. For example, Gale was worried that she would not feel as much a parent as Marina if Marina were to have a biological child. Marina also acknowledged that she would feel unfulfilled and might resent Gale if she were denied the opportunity to give birth to a child. In addition to discovering more about themselves and each other, they also learned a great deal from the Internet, from conversations with friends, and from discussions with the personnel of various adoption agencies. At my suggestion, the two women also eventually decided to share their thoughts and ideas with Gale's parents. Surprisingly, not only did Gale's parents not have the negative reaction that Gale had anticipated, they were pleased to have been consulted and said they would welcome a grandchild, regardless of the process the couple selected.

This phase of the therapy process provided many opportunities for me to recognize and applaud how well Marina and Gale worked together, to acknowledge the resources that each brought to their explorations, and ultimately to compliment them on their ability to make a decision with which both could live comfortably. Their demeanor had changed visibly with each small step taken and each challenge successfully negotiated. They already had many strengths on which to draw, having successfully created a loving relationship against difficult odds, but now they also felt competent and confident enough to exercise both options for expanding their family. That is, they not only began the process of adopting a child, but Marina also set the wheels in motion to have a child by artificial insemination. They agreed that they were willing to accept whatever occurred in terms of the timing of the arrival of their two children.

Although I received announcements regarding the birth of their son Sam and the subsequent adoption of their daughter Natalie, it was several years before Gale and Marina called for another appointment. Sam was now 4 years old, Natalie was 3, and both parents were anticipating what might happen when the children started school. They were particularly concerned about helping Sam and Natalie deal with the reactions of teachers, other children, and the parents of other children, to the fact that they had two mothers. Up until this point the world that Sam and Natalie inhabited had been fairly protected and safe. Other than the members of their families of origin, they socialized primarily with members of the gay and lesbian community of which they were a part. And the heterosexual friends who also were included in their world were very accepting of same-sex relationships.

I asked Gale and Marina how the subject of their relationship had been handled thus far and learned that Sam and Natalie had been told from day one that sometimes children had two mommies, sometimes they had two daddies, sometimes they had one mommy and one daddy, and sometimes they only had either one mommy or one daddy. They had not talked about any one way of being a family as better than another, but had emphasized that what was important was that children have a parent or parents who love them. Acknowledging that their concerns about the future certainly were valid, I then suggested that because the children were getting older, perhaps the time had come to expand this story, noting that not everybody felt as they did, and that the children might hear different kinds of things from other people. They might even get teased about having two mommies, because other children might not know about all the shapes in which families can come. However, they could feel proud that they had parents who loved them very much, and this love would give them the ability to handle teasing as well as other challenges. In addition to incorporating these new parts of the story into what they told the children, I invited Gale and Marina to bring Sam and Natalie to the next session.

As I observed the interactions between the children and their mothers, I had a sense that this family really was thriving. They all seemed to enjoy the life they had created, and Gale and Marina appeared to be doing a great job of continuing to support each other and work well together. Although naturally curious and interested in exploring my office, the children were well-behaved and responded appropriately to parental requests, for example, to pick up a toy or share a game. At the same time, I was aware of the fact that children, as well as adults, can be very cruel to one another. I therefore chose to explore several additional strategies that Gale and Marina might employ that would enable Sam and Natalie to continue to evolve a positive self-concept.

First, I suggested that Gale and Marina initiate a "brag time" as part of their evening meal together. I also suggested the use of the red plate, as described previously. In addition, I recommended that a floor-length mirror be hung in their respective rooms so that both children could admire themselves as well as be shown and complimented on how wonderful each is, how special each looks.

Finally, I shared some of my ideas about encouraging success, acknowledging accomplishments, and searching for and emphasizing talents. During this part of the conversation, we once again revisited the ways in which Marina and Gale had been successful in overcoming obstacles in their life and creative in figuring out ways to handle problems before they became overwhelming. I shared my belief that these were resources about which they could now teach their children. At this point I also was able to compliment them on their ability to anticipate potential pitfalls and seek professional assistance, as they now had done three times. We then met for two more sessions just to be sure that things were on track. When phase three of the therapy ended, Gale and Marina both assured me that I would probably see them again some time in the future.

Summary and Reflections

Much of my work with Marina and Gale reflected an emphasis on supporting positive self-concepts in order that the couple might achieve their goals and ultimately the family might flourish. Success was encouraged through a focus on communication skills as well as by affirmation of the various ways in which Marina and Gale were able to handle a variety of challenges. Thus I complimented them on their resources and strengths during each phase of the therapy, noting how well they worked together, their talent for effective decision making, their ability to handle challenges, their skills as parents, and their knack for anticipating potential pitfalls in the effort to avoid problems before they occurred.

The role of professional language also was significant as I attempted to normalize, as appropriate, to suggest actions that supported achievement of their goals, and to offer an expansion of the story that Marina and Gale currently were telling their children about their family. The expanded story to be shared with Sam and Natalie was intended to prepare them to deal with whatever teasing or even stigmatization with which they might be faced as the children of a lesbian couple. With its emphasis on the strengths of their family, this story was intended to provide validation for Marina and Gale as well as to encourage strength and pride in the children.

Finally, I made explicit suggestions for additional ways in which Marina and Gale might support positive self-concepts for Sam and Natalie. These suggestions included brag time, use of the red plate, and installation of full-length mirrors. Various other ideas about how to encourage success, acknowledge accomplishment, and emphasize talents, as discussed earlier in this chapter, also were part of our conversations. As apparent from the case example, despite its nontraditional form and the need to overcome a variety of obstacles, by the end of therapy this family had exhibited a great deal of resilience and certainly could be said to be flourishing.

CHAPTER EIGHT

Encouraging Effective Parenting

As noted at the beginning of Chapter 2, one of the primary roles assigned by society to families is that of the socialization of children. Families thus are charged with the task of creating for their members a context that is supportive of the emotional well-being of each individual, one that fosters the formation of a healthy identity. Additionally, this role, which serves both families and society, includes the goal of rearing young people who will evolve into well-functioning, productive citizens who also are able to nurture successfully the next generation, transmitting to them, in turn, the norms and values of their society. At the same time, one of the basic process dimensions of families that flourish is the presence of a legitimate source of authority, with established rules and roles. In other words, resilience is supported by the presence of parents, or a parental unit, that is effective.

Despite the enormity and significance of the responsibilities associated with childrearing, those who assume them, however implicitly, by virtue of becoming parents rarely have any formal training for the job. What is more, probably even less often are parents conscious of all that is expected of them by society relative to the performance of this job. Certainly books on the subject of parenting abound, and some of the more fortunate may have had a class or two on parenting in either high school or college. For most, however, the family in which each person grew up generally represents the primary "classroom" within which he or she learned whatever he or she knows about parenting, with on-the-job training as the norm.

Accordingly, and for good or ill, parents tend to respond to and treat their children as they were treated by their parents. Even when they promise themselves as children that they will never do what their parents did with or to them, they may fall back on, and thus find themselves making recourse to, some of the same strategies they despised while growing up. In addition to frustration with their children, they then also are likely to feel angry with themselves. Whether or not this is the situation, parents often feel overwhelmed, may be confused by their children, and find themselves at a loss as to where to turn, especially when their best efforts don't seem to be working.

It is little wonder that issues around parenting frequently arise in the context of therapy. What is more, attention in this area certainly is likely to be an important aspect of helping families to flourish. It is my observation that many parents are unsure of themselves and prone to self-doubt, often despite the fact that they appear to be managing quite well. In this case, reassurance that they seem to be doing the right thing becomes very important and may be all that is needed. On the other hand, even when not presented as a problem, there are times when consideration of a need for guidance relative to parenting may be appropriate as part of the process of facilitating resilience. Although the therapist cannot be expected to provide a comprehensive course on the subject, it is important that he or she be conversant enough to be able to offer some assistance.

There are several general ideas and processes that I have found to be very useful as I seek to help clients become more effective in their roles as parents. The specific topics addressed in this chapter thus include expanding the meaning of discipline, choosing responses rather than reacting, respecting individual differences, utilizing natural/logical consequences, acknowledging children's wisdom, practicing feedforward, owning one's impotence, and modeling desired behaviors. Some of the illustrations for these concepts are drawn from the case example at the end of the previous chapter, and an additional case example, with summary and reflections, concludes this chapter.

Expanding the Meaning of Discipline

Discipline generally is thought of, and indeed is defined as, the practice of punishing an individual for the violation of rules or codes of behavior, or the means of enforcing obedience to such rules or codes (Oxford University Press, 2005). Although engaging in discipline in a manner consistent with such a definition may be appropriate at times, it can be useful for the therapist to expand the meaning so that it includes the concepts of disciples and discipleship. These terms refer to a process in which young people gain knowledge from a teacher, in this case a teacher who is also parenting his or her children. Indeed, all three words—*discipline*, *disciples*, and *discipleship*—as well as their Latin roots are similar and related in meaning. That is, *disciplina*, the root of *discipline*, means instruction or knowledge, and *discipulus*, the root of *disciple* and *discipleship*, means learner, from *discere*, to learn. Building on this awareness, the therapist can invite parents to think of discipline as a process of instructing and strengthening, of providing knowledge to their children, the disciples who learn from them no matter what they choose to say or do, or how conscious the parents are of this process.

From such a perspective, parents can view themselves as instructors, or mentors, whose responsibility is not only to create and enforce rules and limits but also to educate and to guide, with as much emphasis on the latter aspect as on the former. Accordingly, the job of parenting includes anticipating and meetings children's needs, providing both structure and nurture in equal amounts. That is, children need a firm, consistent environment, and they also need to be loved unconditionally (Lasch, 1979). They need to be prepared, to the extent possible, for all of life, including its vicissitudes. In families that flourish, such processes tend to be present.

Marina and Gale, whose evolving relationship and family life were presented in the case example at the end of Chapter 7, provide a wonderful illustration of this orientation. First and foremost, they took very seriously their roles and responsibilities as parents. They obviously adored their children, but they also understood the importance of setting limits and helping their children learn to behave appropriately. They did not seem to worry, as some parents do, about being the "bad guy"— fearing that their children wouldn't like them if they scolded or imposed consequences. They appeared to know instinctively that they should be in charge, that there is an inevitable and needed hierarchy between parents and children. Indeed, creating and maintaining such a hierarchy can be understood as one expression of parents' love for their children. When Marina and Gale came to therapy for the third time, their goal was specifically focused on finding ways to prepare their children for the challenges the children were likely to encounter as a function of having a lesbian couple for parents. The parents wanted to be sure that their children had sufficient knowledge and strength to be able to cope effectively as they moved out of their safe and protected world.

As the therapist considers with clients the idea of parenting as a process of instructing and strengthening, it is recommended that he or she also elicit and affirm the expertise of parents, particularly in terms of the knowledge and wisdom they possess regarding their children. Contrary to the tendency so prevalent in this society to look to professionals for guidance, parents need to recognize that they are often the best judges of what is appropriate for their children, and their insights, however intuitive, need to be considered. At the same time, it also may be important to offer a variety of behavioral strategies that they might consider adding to their parenting repertoires. The first such strategy focuses on responding as opposed to reacting.

Choosing Responses Rather Than Reacting

Although certainly not limited to relationships between parents and children, the idea of *choosing responses* rather than *reacting* can be extremely useful for those who would be guides and mentors for young people. It also is consistent with several of the processes characteristic of families that flourish. Conversations on this important topic often begin with a consideration of the way that children seem to be particularly adept at "pushing their parents' buttons"—the fact that children just seem to know how to get a rise out of their parents. For example, what mother has not had the experience of having her quietly playing child or children immediately start clamoring for attention the minute she picks up the phone? What parent has not suffered the embarrassment of an otherwise generally well-behaved child who decides to throw a temper tantrum in a public place such as the grocery store or while visiting friends? These are certainly common occurrences for many parents. Unfortunately, also common are reactions on the part of parents that leave much to be desired, which many clients freely admit.

As a way to help parents deal with such situations more effectively, they can be invited to consider several related issues. First, the therapist might feel free to point out that generally children are far wiser than adults give them credit for being. That is, they seem to have a built-in radar system that enables them to tune into and be aware of family dynamics from the moment they are born. Indeed, they seem to know their parents' strengths as well as the areas in which their parents are vulnerable; the creation of the kinds of disruptive scenarios described above is not accidental! If children perceive a crack in their parents' armor, they are likely to attempt to crawl through it.

The second issue involves the matter of control: who is in charge when one simply reacts rather than carefully choosing how to respond. As the therapist can explain, when a person has a knee-jerk reaction to having his or her button pushed, then the one who is pushing the button is in charge. However inadvertently, the "reactor" is thus giving away his or her power to the "pusher." At the same time, although it may appear otherwise, it is important to be aware that children generally really want their parents to be in charge. Indeed, a great deal of what children do seems to be as much about testing to be sure that their parents can handle them as it is about testing their limits and trying to get their own way. Thus, the parent who, rather than yelling at the child, excuses him- or herself from the phone call for a moment in order to enforce the rule about interruptions, maintains his or her authority, and the child is ensured that his or her limits are in place. Similarly, effective parenting of a misbehaving child when in a grocery store or while visiting friends involves being willing, despite the circumstances, to help the child learn that such behavior is unacceptable. This willingness requires that parents respond calmly and firmly, despite whatever inconvenience or embarrassment they may experience, knowing that in the long run they will gain the respect of their children as well as increase their own self-respect as they do so.

A third issue to be considered is that of avoiding power struggles whenever possible and understanding, just as systemic therapists do, that resistance is a relational concept. In other words, it is important for parents to understand that how they behave with their children will influence how the children behave with them. With young children this may mean asking a question in such a way that either answer is the right one. For example, the question "Would you like spinach or peas?" rather than the question "Would you like a vegetable?" gives the child a choice and thus a measure of control, *and* it communicates that avoiding vegetables is not an option. With older children, avoiding power struggles may involve choosing one's battles carefully. Indeed, I have had many conversations in therapy about the relative importance of messy rooms and funky hair as compared with academic success and respectful following of the family's rules. When teenagers are otherwise doing and behaving well, I suggest shutting the door to the messy room or allowing them to make decisions about their appearance (within reason), trusting that eventually they probably will make choices that are more consistent with their parents' values and desires relative to neatness and appearance.

The fourth issue in choosing responses rather than reacting focuses attention, once again, on language. That is, it is extremely important for parents to be sensitive to the impact their words may have on their children. As a general rule therapists would do well to advocate for people to treat each other kindly, gently, and with respect. This may mean encouraging parents to avoid using language that is shaming and helping them learn how to criticize inappropriate behaviors rather than demeaning the whole child—a process that is very similar to the one in which therapists engage as they externalize problems (White & Epston, 1990). It may mean suggesting that parents assure their children that they are very much loved despite having done something wrong. And it may mean helping parents to understand the extent to which they participate in creating relationships with their children as a function of how they choose to respond. This point also brings us to the next parenting strategy for consideration, that of respecting individual differences.

Respecting Individual Differences

Believing in a multiverse, as I do, when teaching I try always to emphasize the idea that not only is each family unique, but each child grows up in a *different* family despite having the same parents, the same residence, the same last name. Similarly, I often find it important to help parents understand this concept, recognizing that in families that flourish, a sense of connection is facilitated by support for individual autonomy, and vice versa. However, in my experience it is not at all unusual to learn that parents tend to think about and treat their children as a group, often failing to recognize the unique individual that is each child.

For example, even though differences in age, gender, and other personal traits are acknowledged, the young children in the family often all have the same bedtime. Although parents may feel that this is more convenient or fear that their children would resent and react negatively to new rules, amazing effects may be forthcoming from even the smallest of changes in bedtime routines. For example, the therapist might suggest that the parents put the youngest child to bed first, even if there is only a 15-minute wait before the next child's bedtime. In order to enhance this new routine, the parents can be encouraged to take turns being responsible for getting a particular child to bed each night, so that each child gets one-on-one time with each parent. This one-on-one-time, which may involve reading a story together or just talking about the day, establishes an opportunity for connection and the creation of meaningful memories for the parents as well as for the children.

Helping parents to respect individual differences relative to age also may be addressed through a consideration of privileges and chores. Just as it is appropriate for older children to have more freedom than their younger siblings, they also are likely to benefit, despite their groaning, from having to handle more responsibilities. As a way to implement this idea in a fun and equitable manner, the therapist might suggest that on each child's birthday, he or she be given a new privilege and a new chore commensurate with the age now attained. Such a ritual affirms the growing maturity of the child, as well as what that growth entails in terms of contributions to the family; it also affirms the distinctions between children.

It is equally important for parents to create expectations of each child that are realistic for that child in all aspects of his or her life, not just around chores and privileges. Different children have different talents and abilities, all of which need to be recognized and encouraged. Thus, although parents who are scholars may have a difficult time relating to athletic success, if this is the realm in which a child has interests or skills, this is the area to which support needs to be directed and in which talents need to be affirmed. By contrast, expecting academic achievement beyond a child's capabilities is likely to undermine whatever potential for success in this realm he or she may possess. Certainly parents generally have a variety of hopes, dreams, and expectations for their children. However, the role of parents is to nurture and support in ways that fit their children, rather than attempting to shape them according to the plans and aspirations they have for them. In order to emphasize this point, I often share with clients the poem "On Children" from *The Prophet* (Gibran, 1923/1983). The message of this poem is that although parents are the creators of their children, they do not own them. Although they are to house and to love their children, parents are not to try to program their children's thoughts or expect them to be replicas of themselves. Rather, parents are to act as stable bows who send forth arrows, or children, who are able to fly swift and far as they move into a future that will not include the parents.

There are many ways in which the "bows" may be stable. Respecting individual differences certainly is an important one. Another is the manner in which the aspect of discipline that involves enforcement of rules and codes of behavior is handled. From my perspective careful handling involves the use of natural or logical consequences.

Utilizing Natural/Logical Consequences

As noted above, effective parenting requires the provision of a firm and consistent context of expectations and limits. This context is created when parents are both very clear about their rules and follow through and enforce consequences for violations of the rules. As an advocate of Adlerian theory in this regard (Dinkmeyer & McKay, 1973/1996), I believe that the enforcement of rules is best handled by having the "punishment fit the crime." Rather than spanking a child, for example, or sending him or her to his or her room for all transgressions of the rules, the consequences of specific misbehaviors are tailored to follow naturally from the particular rule that was violated.

To illustrate, many parents complain about their children's invariable misbehavior when the family goes to a restaurant for a meal. Depending on the age of the child, I have several recommendations. These include having the acting-out child wait in the car until the family finishes eating, or having the whole family leave and getting take-out food for everyone who behaved appropriately. The one who misbehaved misses that meal. Although parents may be concerned about this tactic, I advise them that missing one meal is not likely to cause harm to the child. An additional option is to tell the child who misbehaved that he or she will stay home with a baby-sitter the next time the family goes out for a meal, and then following through with this consequence.

Another problem frequently mentioned by parents involves children who get into fights while riding in the car, particularly on family outings. In this case, the therapist might suggest that the parent who is driving pull over to the side of the road, turn off the engine, with the parents sitting quietly until the fighting subsides. This pattern should be repeated as many times as it takes for the children to get the message that fighting in the car will not be tolerated. Alternatively, or if the pattern continues to be repeated too many times, the outing could be canceled and the family returns home.

Letting a child know in advance what the consequences for specific misbehaviors will be can be particularly useful. Then, if a violation of a rule occurs, the parents can frame the child's behavior as a choice to experience the particular consequences. This approach can be especially appropriate with older children. For example, the rule in 12-year-old Andrew's house was that in order to sleep overnight at the home of a friend sometime during the weekend, all chores had to be completed by Friday at 4:00 P.M. When Andrew failed to complete his chores on time, his parents' response was, "I guess you have chosen to stay home this weekend."

The imposition of logical consequences also can be selected and framed relative to age-appropriate behavior. For example, a 10-year-old child might be sent to bed earlier than usual when his or her behavior is more consistent with that of a 5-year-old than with what is expected of a 10-year-old. In similar instances, it is important that the parents provide such an explanation for the consequence they are imposing.

In most cases, however, it is important to avoid using a child's bedroom as a place of punishment. This is his or her private space and should be respected as such. Indeed, this is more than likely the place in which he or she has all sorts of toys, games, or other fun things with which to play. Time-out or grounding is more appropriately implemented somewhere that is not very exciting, and preferably where the parents can keep an eye on what is happening. A corner of the dining room or a child-proofed bathroom come to mind as possibilities in this regard.

Finally, just as natural consequences for inappropriate behavior should be enforced on a firm and consistent basis, it is equally important that appropriate behaviors be acknowledged regularly and in a logical manner. Rather than taking for granted the good things children do and only reacting—perhaps overreacting—when there is a problem or a rule violation, parents might be encouraged to find ways to provide age-appropriate affirmation to children for having followed the rules. For example, a child might be allowed to stay up a little later or watch a special video because of general behavior that was very mature. Perhaps a teenager's curfew might be increased slightly following consistent adherence to the parents' rule regarding the time at which the teenager was expected to get home. Accordingly, the child learns that there are logical consequences that follow from all behaviors, not just those considered undesirable by his or her parents.

Throughout the process of establishing rules and expectations and enforcing consequences, it is important for parents to remain firm but calm. They thus remain respectful despite their displeasure, and their style of communication reflects that found in families that flourish. They do not need to raise their voices or demonstrate their anger; indeed, parents probably will be far more effective if they can avoid doing so. In fact, lowering one's voice can be an extremely meaningful form of communicating parental displeasure. In addition, parents also can be advised to remember the wisdom their children possess and to consider consulting them, as appropriate.

Acknowledging Children's Wisdom

As already indicated, it is my belief that children often are wise beyond their years. In therapy I therefore am likely to request input from the younger family members regarding what they consider to be appropriate in terms of their parents' expectations for them. In many cases I have found that children tend to be harder on themselves than are their parents. Even when this is not the case, they generally have a pretty good idea about whether or not their parents are being fair; this, despite the fact that they may not like the rules or the consequences for violating them.

Similarly, the therapist might suggest to parents that as their children get older, they may want to consult them and engage in negotiation around changes in rules and consequences. In this way, the expertise of their children is acknowledged and a sense of ownership on the part of the children is encouraged. Because negotiation is a two-way process, the parents also may learn important information regarding what the children are looking for from them, as well as gain new insights about their children. Certainly this is a process that also may be engaged in during the course of therapy.

An example of this process is provided by the Wilkins family, which included Mom, Dad, and their two teenage sons, Bruce (14) and Ken (16). The Wilkins came to therapy with concerns about Ken's acting-out behavior. Mom and Dad reported that they had struggled with Ken when he was in elementary school, but he had settled down and had been performing well both at school and at home since entering junior high school. Although he still managed to get high grades, recently he had begun to sneak out of the house at night, and on at least one of these occasions it was apparent that he had been drinking. At our first meeting, which included all members of the family, I learned that Mom and Dad were both adamantly opposed to the use of alcohol, period. They thus were deeply hurt that Ken would violate a rule that was so important to them, as if sneaking out of the house weren't bad enough. Both boys acknowledged awareness of their parents' feelings about alcohol use. They also shared their feelings that their parents were much too strait-laced in general, and that they were way too strict with them in particular. When I asked Ken in what ways his parents were too strict with him, he responded that he was hardly allowed to do anything: He could only go somewhere if driven by one of his parents or the parent of a friend of whom his parents approved. His curfew was much earlier than that of his friends. And he wasn't going to be allowed to date until he was 18. He said he was embarrassed by his parents and was often teased by his friends because of them and their rules. Bruce had similar complaints and was very sympathetic to Ken's anger and frustration.

During the course of several conversations that ensued thereafter, I encouraged Mom and Dad to express their concerns and fears, making sure that Ken and Bruce understood their parents' rationale for the various rules. The focus then shifted to a consideration of the ways in which the boys, and particularly Ken, could earn back or demonstrate their increasing maturity so that new rules could be negotiated over time. I emphasized my belief in the importance of parents acting as if they trusted their children so that their children could demonstrate their trustworthiness. I also stated my belief in the need to evolve new rules to match increasing maturity.

When the time came to focus on specific rule changes, I requested that the boys each think about what might be reasonable, given their ages, and both were able to make requests that their parents found acceptable. Indeed, the missing ingredients with this family seemed to be trust in one another as well as parental awareness of the wisdom of the children. When these ingredients were added, the family members became more flexible and the needs of the growing children were able to be accommodated in ways that worked for all. Thus, resilience was facilitated, and the family was able to move forward in a much more positive direction. Although achieving these changes with the Wilkins family was a fairly lengthy process, sometimes much simpler suggestions can be extremely helpful, as is often the case with the utilization of feedforward.

Practicing Feedforward

The typical parental response to even the smallest of undesirable behaviors, especially as children get older, often is criticism, either of the behavior or of the person. Although criticism of a behavior has less potential to hurt the child's self-concept than does criticism of the person, there is an even better way to handle behaviors considered to be unacceptable. The reality is that criticism only tells the recipient what he or she shouldn't have done. Furthermore, because it acknowledges the undesirable behavior, it may serve to maintain that behavior rather than eliminate it (Becvar & Becvar, 1999). Although with criticism there is perhaps an implicit message about what would be more appropriate, it seems to make more sense to request explicitly the behavior that is desired. This approach, in turn, redirects the focus to, and thus is more likely to encourage, actions that are more consistent with what is valued by the family. To act in this manner is to practice *feedforward*.

Feedforward is a communication tool that includes a clear message about what the parent would like the child to do. It (1) avoids shaming or demeaning either the child or his or her behavior, (2) prevents actions that unwittingly may serve to maintain the undesirable behavior, and (3) precludes responses from the child that are consistent with, or logical to, criticism (i.e., criticism of the parent, anger, frustration). Furthermore, it represents an important aspect of the effective communication deemed important both to resilience and the ability to flourish. The following two brief scenarios illustrate the processes that are likely to be set in motion by either criticism or feedforward.

When Jeremy's mother went to her son's room to change the sheets on his bed, she was absolutely appalled at the state of affairs she found. Despite just 2 days earlier having insisted that Jeremy clean his room and straighten out his bureau drawers, she found the freshly laundered, folded clothes she had placed in his room the day before all over the floor, mixed in with dirty clothes. When Jeremy came home from school, his mother greeted him by telling him how angry she was and how hard it was for her to understand his choice to live like a slob. She then informed him that because he was so careless with his clothes, from now on he would have to do his own laundry.

Jenny's father needed to repair a broken piece of furniture and found that it was going to require a board to brace a weak frame. However, when he went to his tool bench to get his saw so that he could cut the board to size, it was missing. Not surprisingly, he was furious. He reined in his anger, however, and asked his wife if she knew where the saw was, but she said that she did not know. He then went to Jenny's room and asked her if she knew anything about the missing saw. Jenny was chagrined, acknowledged that she had taken the saw to school because she was working on a project with some of her friends, and said that she had forgotten to bring it home. As they were getting into the car to go retrieve the saw, Jenny's father said that in the future he would very much appreciate it if she would ask before borrowing a tool and be sure to return it immediately afterward.

In considering the above two scenarios, it is not difficult to imagine the different ways that each would play out. In the first case, it is highly likely that Jeremy would storm up to his room, probably muttering unkind words about his mother under his breath, and slam the door. His mother probably would respond angrily in turn, and things would go from bad to worse. In the second scenario, a relationship of respect between father and daughter is maintained even as Jenny understands clearly that she has disappointed her father *and* what is expected of her in the future. A deviation-amplifying process, which usually culminates in a lose–lose situation between parent and child, is thus avoided. Rather, the outcome is far more to the liking of everyone involved as well as beneficial to the family as a whole—something that also may occur as parents own their impotence, our next topic.

Owning Impotence

As systems therapists we often learn that that one gains influence, or "power," as one gives up power or the ability to influence (Watzlawick et al., 1974). That is, paradoxically, the more the therapist goes one down by owning his or her impotence, the more the client is likely to see the therapist as credible and to follow through on suggestions. Thus, for example, a therapist who honestly states that he or she doesn't have all the answers is likely to be perceived by clients as wise, which has the effect of giving the therapist's words or homework assignments greater meaning. Indeed, there is something about acknowledging our humanness, including our frailties, that seems to make us more believable.

Certainly I also have found this to be the case when working with teenagers, and it is an idea that parents might usefully incorporate into their behavioral repertoires. The reality is that once young people reach a certain age, physical control becomes close to impossible. If a teenager decides to sneak out, or drink, or smoke, or engage in any one of a number of behaviors considered by the parent to be unacceptable, the parent ultimately will be unsuccessful in forceful attempts to prevent the teenager from doing so. What is essential at this point is a relationship of respect. Such a relationship is nurtured from the earliest days of a child's life and tends to really bear fruit during the adolescent years. However, even if parents are late in focusing on this area, the potential for success exists.

Thus, parents can be encouraged to articulate their rules and expectations while also acknowledging that there really is no way they can make the child follow the rules or meet these expectations; all they can do is request that the child behave appropriately, and trust that the child will respond accordingly. Now the responsibility rests with the child, and there is nothing against which to rebel, no power struggle in which to engage. When making these suggestions, the therapist must be sensitive to the fact that parents often find them to be daunting. However, as alternatives are considered, there generally is recognition that there really are few realistic and potentially effective options. Accordingly, I often feel free to share some of my personal and professional experiences with teenagers in this regard.

For example, in my work at a school for children with learning disabilities and related behavioral problems early in my career, I was assigned to the adolescent unit. Most of my clients were male, and many were physically much larger than I am. Despite their bravado, I found them to be very lovable and really enjoyed the time I spent working with them. Needless to say, they certainly attempted to challenge my authority early on, but I chose not to participate in any way with their efforts to engage me in a power struggle. And I will never forget how dismayed they were whenever I acknowledged that I had made an error with a particular assignment or was wrong about something else they were studying. By acknowledging my fallibility, I seemed to have gained their respect, and we generally got along quite well.

Years later, my children certainly provided me with many opportunities to own my impotence. Fortunately, and I believe in part as a function of the time we spent together as a single-parent family, we had very strong relationships with each other, a dimension I now recognize as an important characteristic of families that flourish. There was much mutual love and respect between us, and when push came to shove, my children never failed to demonstrate that they were trustworthy. Although I give them the lion's share of the credit, I know that as a parent some of the credit also is due to me, to my ability to be trustworthy, and to model the same behaviors that I expected of them. And this brings us to a final area in which conversations with parents can be useful.

Modeling Desired Behaviors

It is a well known fact that all of us, including children, learn as much or more from what we see and experience than we do from what we hear. Or, in the words of Dorothy Law Nolte (1972), "Children learn what they live." Therefore, if the goal is to teach, guide, and strengthen, then parents must be as conscious of their own behaviors as they are of the behaviors of their children. Accordingly, they must focus on modeling the behaviors they desire from their children. Such behaviors can be considered in relation to three overlapping categories: honoring commitments, communicating in a congruent manner, and respecting each person. Each of these behaviors supports resilience.

Honoring Commitments

Honoring commitments means making every effort to deliver on whatever promises have been made. Thus, for example, if parents agree that they are going to be at a special event, pick a child up at a certain time, or participate in a particular activity together, then the parents need to do so. Obviously, there are times when circumstances can interfere with the best of intentions. In such cases, parents do whatever they can to let the child know what has happened (something that has become much easier to accomplish in our cell-phone era). Even without a cell phone, the parents find a way to get a message to the child, and at an appropriate time, compensations for missed engagements are created.

This issue can be particularly crucial when parents are separated or divorced and time with the children is negotiated and managed according to visitation agreements. Given the various disruptions in their world, the children may especially need to know that they can count on both parents. For noncustodial parents, honoring commitments also may help to build strong relationships with their children, despite the fact that daily interaction may no longer be possible.

Honoring commitments also means that consequences for inappropriate behaviors are implemented, as promised. Whereas a lessening of restrictions may be negotiated on occasion, for the most part children know that their parents are serious about enforcing their rules, as described. The parents do not back down under pressure from their children, and they do not undermine each other. Rather, they provide a united front that is firm and consistent. By behaving with integrity in both of these areas, children learn several things: (1) They learn that their parents have integrity and are trustworthy; (2) they learn the value of being trustworthy, and how important it is to their parents that they behave in a similar manner; and (3) they learn to trust that their parents are able to provide the structure and security that they need and want.

Communicating in a Congruent Manner

Similarly, children learn effective communication skills as their parents communicate with them in a congruent manner. That is, parents provide messages that are clear, with a match between the verbal and nonverbal levels. They encourage the expression of feelings as well as the need for those feelings to be owned by the person who is speaking. Clarification of ideas is sought and offered, and mutual understanding is attained in a calm and careful manner. The ideas of all are welcomed, and ridicule is avoided. During conversations, the parent/listener gives the child/speaker his or her undivided attention. Parents also provide a reasonable process for resolving conflicts, and they encourage appropriate negotiation. Attention by parents to each of these aspects of effective communication provides a context of learning that is of vital importance to everyone in the family.

Obviously, in order for parents to communicate effectively with their children, as well as with each other, they may need some coaching. Thus the therapist may wish to devote some time to the teaching and learning of each dimension mentioned above (with or without the presence of the children). And always a part of this process is an emphasis on respect.

Respecting Each Person

Respect is conveyed as parents honor their commitments to their children and as they communicate with them in a congruent manner. It also is conveyed as each person is encouraged, appreciated, accepted, and affirmed as a unique individual, as discussed in the previous chapter. In addition, as parents are honest, kind, and tolerant with their children, the latter are more likely to experience themselves as persons worthy of respect. An important part of all of these processes may include an awareness that *fair* is not necessarily *equal*. Fairness is a function of what is appropriate for each person in each specific set of circumstances. Finally, and perhaps most important relative not only to all three categories of behavior discussed in this section, but also to effective parenting in general, the message that is received by the child as the parent models desired behaviors is that he or she is loved unconditionally.

As described above, the ability to encourage effective parenting is an important key to facilitating resilience. With appropriate parenting behaviors in place, families are thus much more likely to flourish. Accordingly, the therapist must be aware of, and respond to, a variety of considerations, as illustrated in the following case example.

Case Example

Marcia and Roy were extremely worried about some of the behaviors of their son Kevin. When Marcia called for an appointment, she reported that Kevin was an only child and that he was cared for before and after school by her husband's mother, who had been living with them since Kevin was born. Of particular concern was the fact that Kevin was becoming more aggressive, often hitting his mother and father when asked to do something or when he didn't get his own way. Recently, his teacher had reported that Kevin was showing some of the same behaviors at school. I requested that everyone in the household—Marcia, Roy, Kevin, and Grandma—come to the first session.

I began the session by requesting that each person tell me a little something about him- or herself. Roy responded by saying that he was 45 years old, that he was an engineer, and that his job required frequent travel and time away from his family. Grandma, who spoke next, said that she was 70 years old, had been a widow for 15 years, and was very grateful that Marcia and Roy wanted her to live with them and help care for Kevin. Marcia, who was 43, said that although she didn't have to travel, she was a busy attorney, and she really appreciated her mother-in-law's assistance with Kevin. Kevin, who had been playing quietly with building blocks while the adults were talking, reported that he was 7, that he was in the second grade, and that his favorite subjects were reading and recess.

Next I asked the family members what brought them to therapy and how they hoped I would be able to help them. Marcia said that she and Roy were very upset because Kevin wouldn't do what they asked him to do, and that recently his teacher had also reported similar problems at school. Roy said that he didn't have anything to add except that he was puzzled that his mother didn't seem to have any difficulty with Kevin. Grandma agreed that Kevin minded her beautifully, and that she couldn't understand the change that came over him when his parents came home from work. She did say that she felt Marcia and Roy were too easy on the boy, but she figured that was their business and tried to stay out of the way when they were at home. By this time, Kevin was hiding his head in Grandma's lap, and when I asked him if there was anything he would like to say, he just shrugged his shoulders.

I then asked the parents and Grandma how discipline was handled on their respective "shifts." Grandma reported that she had very clear rules for Kevin, and that when he didn't follow them, he was given consequences. For the most part, however, she said that things went smoothly. When Kevin came home from school, they had milk and cookies together, she sat with him while he did his homework, and then he was allowed to play out of doors or watch television until dinnertime. Grandma prepared dinner and would eat with the rest of the family when they were there, or just with Kevin when Roy was away and Marcia came home late. After dinner, she went to her room so that Kevin could have time with his parent or parents, depending upon who was home.

Marcia said that by the time she got home in the evening, she just wanted to enjoy time with Kevin. However, he often became angry or upset and would start hitting her when she asked him to do even the simplest of tasks, such as washing his hands before eating, clearing the dinner table, or getting ready for bed. At that point, she would attempt to reason with Kevin, often trying to bribe him to get him to obey. She acknowledged that she felt guilty that she was gone so much and really didn't want to have to yell at Kevin or discipline him too sternly. Often, both she and Kevin went to bed angry and upset with each other.

Roy reported that he believed he and Marcia both should be stricter with Kevin. However, he didn't want to push his wife too hard on that subject, given that he was gone so much and she had to do most of the parenting. He also said that he was guilty of some of the same behaviors, but that what he would do in response to Kevin's hitting was lose his temper, yell at his son, and then storm out of the house, once again leaving Marcia to pick up the pieces. He said that they both loved Kevin very much, but that the boy was out of control and something needed to change.

My story was that it was Marcia and Roy who were "out of control," meaning that they had not been able to communicate their effectiveness as parents to Kevin. Although I didn't say so in so many words, I believed that Kevin was confused by, and angry at, his parents for their seeming inability to handle him, which was in stark contrast to his grandma. I also felt that Kevin had upped the ante by acting out in school, which had worked in terms of pushing his parents to seek outside help.

During the course of several sessions in which I saw only Marcia and Roy, I discussed my perspective on discipline and encouraged them to take small steps to see if they could attain positive results. I acknowledged and affirmed their love and concern for their son and emphasized the importance of their being able to work together as a team. For example, I explained the need always to back each other up in Kevin's presence, although without stepping in or attempting to rescue one another, which would undermine that parent's ability in the son's eyes. Disagreements should be resolved in private so that they presented a united front with Kevin.

I also worked with Marcia and Roy to establish firm rules and consequences around bedtime and hitting behavior on which both agreed. These, I stressed, should be enforced consistently. I assured them that in the long run, Kevin would love and respect them far more if they would follow through rather than cave in when he protested. I explained my feeling that he had too much power for a little boy, and that perhaps rather than being angry, he was frightened.

I also suggested that on the nights when Roy was home, he should be in charge of putting Kevin to bed, taking some time to read with him when the child had gotten to bed on time. Marcia was to follow a similar routine on the nights when she was in charge. What was most important was to show their love to Kevin by demonstration of their ability to handle him. Periodically, I invited Marcia and Roy to bring Kevin with them to therapy; this enabled me to check in with him about what was happening from his perspective and also gave me the opportunity to observe and coach his parents, as appropriate. Over time, Kevin's aggressive behaviors decreased both at home and at school. At a final session that included everyone in the family, there was general agreement that life in their home was much more satisfactory than when they first had come to therapy.

Summary and Reflections

As is often the case, Marcia and Roy came to therapy seeking help for a child who was acting out, who had evidenced problematic behavior both at home and at school. Consistent with my awareness of the logic of behavior in context, I was alerted to consider the ways in which Kevin was being parented and the circumstances in which the acting-out behavior did, or did not, occur. Given the descriptions of the different ways in which Kevin responded, on the one hand, to his grandmother and, on the other hand, to his parents, it seemed most appropriate to work, at least initially, with Marcia and Roy. Indeed, they were well aware that their parenting skills left something to be desired and certainly were open to this focus and to my suggestions.

In my conversations with Marcia and Roy I began by sharing my story about the importance of effective parenting, including a consideration of the expanded meaning of discipline. I then focused primarily on the importance of choosing their responses rather than reacting to Kevin, as they had been doing in the past. In particular, they were encouraged to establish clear rules for Kevin, to explain those rules to him, and to utilize natural/logical consequences when the rules were broken. As part of this process, I was attempting to help them create an effective hierarchy in which they were in charge, supported one another on parenting issues, and presented a united front with Kevin. I also sought to help them model the behaviors they desired from their child, rather than the anger and frustration that previously had been typical of Marcia and Roy's responses. In their case the particularly relevant aspects included encouragement for effective communication as well as respect for each other and their child. I also wanted to help Marcia and Roy create more satisfactory relationships with their son on a one-on-one basis; hence the suggestions regarding Kevin's bedtime routine.

Not surprisingly, as Marcia and Roy engaged in these new, more useful behaviors, Kevin's behavior improved and the family was able to move in the direction of flourishing. This shift toward a flourishing family life can be further facilitated by helping clients create supportive contexts—the subject of the next chapter.

CHAPTER NINE

Creating Supportive Contexts

In well-functioning, predominantly happy families—that is, flourishing families characterized by resilience—meaningful, positive experiences tend to be prevalent. Such experiences are logical to a context in which members feel nurtured, encouraged, strengthened, and supported, even (or perhaps especially) in troubled times. We might think of the families who create such contexts as having a consciousness about devoting energy to all the levels of human needs described by Maslow (1968). That is, basic *survival needs*, including those in the categories of physical well-being, safety and security, love and belonging, and esteem, all receive appropriate attention. In addition, as these survival needs are satisfied, at least to a large extent, the focus broadens to include as well a consideration of *being needs*—that is those needs related to fulfilling one's potential, termed by Maslow as the process of self-actualizing.

Interestingly, the needs of those who are said to be self-actualizing are very similar to the values and traits found to characterize resilient individuals and families. Such being needs include a focus on truth, goodness, beauty, unity, wholeness, the transcendence of opposites, aliveness, uniqueness, perfection and necessity, justice and order, simplicity, experiential richness, effortlessness, playfulness, self-sufficiency, and meaningfulness (Boeree, 2005). Further, people in the self-actualizing category generally are seen as more spontaneous and creative than others, and they tend to be less limited and constrained by cultural stereotypes. In addition, they typically experience moments of great joy, or what are known as peak experiences (Lowry & Maslow, 1979; Maslow, 1968).

In my own musings on human potential, I have embraced the belief that we all have an inherent urge toward growth and wholeness, or a natural inclination toward the achievement of our fullest capability (Becvar, 1997). However, in contrast to Maslow's observation that the process of self-actualizing is primarily a characteristic of older adults, I believe that the creation of contexts that are supportive of the natural tendency to grow can facilitate a sense of wholeness much earlier in life. According to one definition, "A condition of wholeness can be described as one in which a person operates from a unified consciousness of body, mind, emotions and soul" (Raheem, 1991, p. 16). It is my position that at whatever age people attain such a sense of wholeness, they acknowledge a basic connectedness with others (i.e., have a systemic awareness). They are tolerant and accepting of human foibles in themselves and those around them and thus are able to suspend judgment and seek to understand the logic of situations as well as allow time to provide perspective rather than immediately jumping to conclusions. People who operate from a place of wholeness trust that they are supported as a function of access to, or a belief in, a transcendent level, and they are aware of their ability to participate in the creation of their reality. They are more concerned with the utility of their belief systems than the degree to which they represent truth in an absolute sense. In addition, they choose to walk a path with heart. That is, they follow their intuitions about what would be most appropriate for them, have a sense of meaning and purpose, and thus are able to experience joy in their lives.

Regardless of the way in which the process is conceptualized, there is much that families can to do encourage the achievement of the fullest potential of their members and thus of the system as a whole. In this chapter we focus on ways therapists can facilitate the enrichment of family life, in general, with the goal being the creation of supportive contexts. Specific aspects considered include celebrating and having fun, respecting the need for private time and space, enhancing relationships, creating family time, learning how to negotiate and compromise, practicing random acts of kindness, and finding meaning and purpose in life. This chapter also presents a final case example in addition to remarks about the case example described in the previous chapter.

Celebrating and Having Fun

Who hasn't heard the familiar adages about all work and no play making for dull persons, or about a spoonful of sugar helping the medicine go down? Well worn though they may be, as with most such sayings they contain at least a kernel of wisdom. Obviously, there is much about life that requires hard work, that tastes like bitter medicine, that is serious, or that is best served by a task-oriented attitude. Indeed, becoming a mature person certainly requires an ability to handle a myriad of roles and responsibilities, some of them less than pleasant. However, doing so does not necessarily demand perpetual solemnity, nor does it preclude possibilities for spontaneity and humor, for celebrating and having fun. To the contrary, liberal sprinklings of spontaneity, humor, celebrations, and fun often make tasks and responsibilities far more easily accomplished and sometimes even enjoyable.

Spontaneity in families refers to the ability of members to be flexible, to respond in the moment, to welcome an occasional interruption of the usual routine as an opportunity rather than as an annoyance. And although being whisked off for a surprise weekend trip to Paris might be grand and glorious, being spontaneous does not necessarily require large expenditures of either time or money. Rather, all that is needed is a little imagination and a willingness to utilize one's creative instincts. Some simple examples include a spur-of-the-moment decision to have a midwinter picnic dinner on a blanket in the living room; toasting marshmallows or making "s'mores" in the fireplace for dessert; an invitation in the middle of cleaning the house to go for a walk or to a movie; an unexpected early dismissal from school to go on a lunch date with a parent; or acceptance of an invitation to play a game with a child even though one is in the midst of doing something else. Moments such as these make memories that are not soon forgotten, and encouraging families in this regard certainly can prove valuable to them.

Similarly, emphasizing the significance of a sense of humor can be very important. As mentioned early on, I see humor as playing a very important role in our ability to negotiate our life journeys successfully (Becvar, 1997). Indeed, humor and the laughter that goes with it tend to lighten our burdens, ease our tensions, and even ameliorate some of our pain. As Cousins (1979) described, laughter can even be healing. A suggestion that

I have made more than once in the course of therapy is for young siblings to become the "ambassadors of humor" for their family. They are invited to cut out jokes or cartoons and tape them in odd (albeit safe) places around the house, such as the inside of a toilet seat lid or the door to a refrigerator. Alternatively, I might suggest that they decorate the paper napkins used for a meal or put things away wrong (e.g., put the sugar bowl where the salt and pepper shakers usually go, and vice versa). Needless to say, there certainly is a method to the apparent madness of my suggestions. First, siblings, who previously may have been in conflict are encouraged to work together in this way. Second, children generally are tickled by the seemingly whacky ideas I provide. And third, the laughter that everyone is likely to experience can help to shift the focus, at least temporarily, away from problems, and the positive energy that is likely to be generated may make the achievement of solutions more possible.

A larger goal of such suggestions is to encourage a sense of playfulness and the ability to have fun despite life's challenges. Thus I also often encourage family members to celebrate at every appropriate opportunity. Events both small and large can be acknowledged with homemade certificates, photographs, special meals, etc., as described previously. Even difficult times can be eased through a celebratory orientation. What I am suggesting is not a Pollyanna approach but a both/and perspective that recognizes that two seemingly incompatible feelings are not mutually exclusive. Certainly I know firsthand that one can be sad and also feel joy (Becvar, 2001), and that to the extent that one focuses on the latter feeling, the former becomes more tolerable. For example, as I write this I am 1 week away from the observance of what would be my son's 41st birthday, were he still living. Each year on this date my husband and I go with the same friends to my son's favorite restaurant, where we have lunch together. We observe the occasion by celebrating John's birth and life, even as we mourn his death.

While potentially useful with a variety of situations, introducing a both–and perspective can be particularly helpful when the therapist is working with clients who are faced with overwhelming challenges, such as the death of a family member or a diagnosis of cancer. For example, when Courtney and her husband Ed came to therapy at the end of 6 months of chemotherapy that had followed immediately on the heels of a mastectomy for breast cancer, both were terrified about what the future would bring. Although the chemotherapy regimen had been difficult for Courtney, the couple had been so focused on getting through it that they had not had, or taken the time to deal with their fears. Now they were entering that limbo that often is experienced during the 5-year period that must be survived without a recurrence before the cancer patient is considered to be out of the woods. They were seeking help regarding what to do next. Their goal was not only for Courtney to remain healthy but also to find ways to live well despite the cloud that now was hanging over their heads.

In subsequent conversations, we spent a great deal of time considering their illness narratives (Kleinman, 1988)—that is, their stories about what had occurred—as well as their beliefs about death and what happens after we die. We searched for ways they might fulfill dreams and thus experience a sense of purpose in life in an effort to avoid or overcome despair (LeShan, 1990). Although heavy topics, addressing them openly often enables new, less frightening perspectives to evolve and new behaviors to emerge. Therapy also included (1) an admonition to limit discussions on these topics outside of our sessions to an hour a day, and (2) a prescription to do something fun, either together or alone, for at least an hour a day. I particularly encouraged Courtney to rent and watch funny movies, and I suggested that Ed be in charge of creating surprises from time to time. I also recommended that they have an end-of-chemotherapy party and invite all of their friends to celebrate their new life with them. As they followed through with these various suggestions, they saw for themselves how their ability to cope was improved by the inclusion of more fun and lightheartedness. Over time, they were able to decide that they, and not cancer, were in charge of their lives. Indeed, they demonstrated resilience that enabled them to emerge from the cancer experience in a much better, stronger place.

Although often in less dramatic circumstance, there are many other ways in which celebrating and having fun can be encouraged. For example, the individual members of a family can be celebrated by respecting their needs for private time and space, supporting and enabling them to do what they enjoy on their own. The various dyadic relationships in a family can be celebrated as time and energy are devoted to their enhancement in a conscious manner. And the family as a whole can be celebrated as opportunities to be together, perhaps playing, perhaps being serious, are created regularly. Given their distinctions and their importance, each of these topics is addressed separately in the next three sections.

Respecting the Need for Private Time and Space

Included among the many ideas and issues about which personal experience has taught me is the importance of private time and space for individual family members. As I often share with clients, prior to our marriage my husband was a confirmed bachelor, a loner, and a very private person. In order to make the leap and become part of a blended family that included a wife, one teenager, and one preteen, he knew that he was going to need a personal haven to which he could retreat from time to time. Therefore, one of the first things he did in our new home was to make an office for himself, and periodically he would go there to read, work, nap, or just regroup. What I soon recognized was that his need for private time and space had little or nothing to do with me or my children. It was not about rejection of his new family; it was about self-protection and self-care. What is more, over time I benefited as I became aware of how meaningful it was to have an office of my own, a place just for myself and my "stuff," where I could be free to do what I wanted without interruption. Now I regularly discuss with couples their needs for space and time alone and help them to consider whether having a private retreat within their home is feasible and desirable, as well as options for making such a retreat a reality.

There are many other ways in which the need or desire for private time and space can be respected. For example, the members of a couple can agree that each will have opportunities to exercise, to participate in various creative or social activities, or have a regular morning, night, or afternoon out, and that during these times the other will not expect to be included. Family members also can be encouraged to establish a rule about knocking on a closed door before entering. Additional rules about requesting permission before borrowing can be an important topic for consideration. Discussions can include the idea that even in rooms shared by two or more children, rules about honoring each person's belongings can be created and enforced.

Paradoxically, the more that family members are respected as individuals and given some personal freedom, the more likely they are to respect and desire to be with the family as a whole. Given the importance to fostering resilience of a balance between separateness and togetherness in families, therapists are advised to consider this dynamic.

Indeed, it can be a particularly important awareness for parents during their children's teen years, when young people are likely to be extremely sensitive to what they perceive as parental "snooping," in addition to their general tendency to want to disassociate themselves from family activities. Thus, for example, when working with the Richards family, which included Mom, Dad, and their four children, ages 7, 10, 13, and 16, discussing the need for respect of each individual's needs was crucial to the resolution of the problems they had been experiencing with their oldest daughter, Kim. The family home was rather small for a family of six, and the children had to double up in the two bedrooms. In addition, everyone was expected to participate in all family functions, including outings, which for Kim was particularly problematic given that usually the latter were more appropriate for the three younger children than they were for a teenager. The solution suggested was that Kim be expected to join the family for activities at home but that she be given an option to choose whether or not to participate when the family went on an outing, for example, to a movie or to an amusement park. Not surprisingly, once she was given more freedom to choose, Kim participated with the family as often as she opted out.

Similarly, the more that the members of a couple have the freedom to do things that energize them personally, the more likely they will be to want to spend time and participate in activities with each other. And the more energized they are, the more they will bring to the relationship. All of which brings us to a consideration of additional ways in which family members can be encouraged to enhance the various relationships of which they are a part.

Enhancing Relationships

Families that flourish are comprised of both well-functioning individuals and well-functioning relationships. In the case example at the end of Chapter 8, we learned that one of the routines that occurred on a daily basis was that Grandma and Kevin had milk and cookies together when Kevin came home from school. This was an event to which each could look forward, and one that provided an opportunity for sharing and simple pleasure. As part of the therapy, Kevin's parents were invited to create a regular bedtime ritual whereby both would have nightly private time with their son. Consistent rituals such as these provide structure and foster a sense of security for children. They also acknowledge and support the unique dyadic relationships that comprise a family system. For example, in Kevin's family, there are six such relationships: Kevin and Grandma; Kevin and Marcia/Mom; Kevin and Roy/Dad; Roy and Marcia; Marcia and Grandma; and Roy and Grandma.

Additional suggestions for one-on-one time between parents and children can include inviting one child to go along each time a parent needs to run an errand, or designating a special, age-appropriate activity to be done with each child on a regular basis. For example, a parent might be encouraged to take a teenage daughter or son out for breakfast, perhaps on a weekly or a monthly schedule. A younger child might be invited to give each parent a tour of his or her room and all of its contents. A parent might ask an adolescent to explain his or her music preferences, demonstrating a willingness to listen and learn by staying present, without criticizing, and asking meaningful questions.

In blended families it can be particularly important to suggest that the biological parent spend time alone with each of his or her children. In this way relationships that were formed prior to the creation of the new family continue to be nurtured, and a sense of loss about the way things used to be may be precluded or at least alleviated. Similarly, support for time alone for each child with his or her noncustodial parent also may reduce feelings of alienation or hostility, even as this time together may be supportive of these relationships.

For couples, as mentioned early in this book, I regularly suggest that they spend 15–30 minutes together every day doing something fun. I often invite the members of the couple to take turns being in charge of the activity for the day, choosing something each thinks the other would enjoy. Whether or not this is the format selected, I include instructions regarding the exclusion of TV, radio, telephone, newspapers, and children during this time together. In other words, this is to be understood as sacred time, and interruptions can occur only in the case of an extreme emergency, such as fire or illness. Although enforcing this rule is often as hard for the parents as it is for the children, I explain how important it is to nurture the couple relationship that existed before the spouses or partners became parents, a relationship that hopefully will continue once the children have left home. I also encourage the members of a couple to invite each other out on dates, just as they did when they were court-ing each other.

In the case of three-generational families, such as the one in which Kevin was living, it also may be important and useful for the therapist to consider ways in which the relationships between the various adults can be enhanced. Thus, for example, inviting Marcia and Roy to consult with Grandma about her parenting strategies provided useful informa-tion for them. At the same time, it also affirmed Grandma's expertise and offered opportunities for connection that previously had not been created. In addition, Marcia and Roy might have been encouraged to take time separately to go shopping with Grandma or to take her out for lunch, while the other parent stayed at home with Kevin. All such activities honor the various relationships of which the family is com-prised and balance the time and energy that, ideally, is devoted to the larger unit as well.

Creating Family Time

Creating experiences that bring the family together as a whole is as im-portant as nurturing relationships on a one-on-one basis. Such times honor and support a sense of "we-ness," or family nationality—an im-portant characteristic of families that are flourishing. These times to-gether enable members to have a greater awareness of their roots and to be nourished by and learn from the dynamics of the larger system to which they belong. This participation in and nurturing of the group, in turn, is supportive of the ability also to be separate and to grow as an in-dividual. Whereas family time tended to be a given in the not-so-distant past, usually during the evening meal and often at other meals, today the harried, hurried lifestyle characteristic of so many families often requires members to be very intentional in making family time happen.

Given the fact that both parents generally are employed outside the home and children often are involved in a myriad of activities, calen-dars must be consulted and family time planned in advance if it is going to happen on a regular basis. For many parents such a planning process may involve difficult choices and a consideration of priorities, as well as a willingness to be unpopular with the kids when they insist on full participation. As noted previously and reiterated by Doherty (2000), the internet and other media to which young people today seem to have unlimited access often represent significant challenges for families. However, children are best served by an effective parental hierarchy, with authority exercised appropriately. This authority includes affirming the need for all to take part in family activities, at least part of the time.

Whereas focusing on mealtimes can be appropriate for some families, for others this may not be possible. Additional suggestions for family time include a game night or a movie night in which everyone is involved. Weekly family meetings can be suggested as a way to help keep everyone organized and abreast of what is happening as well as provide time to discuss various issues that may affect all members. Perhaps the family might wish to take on a volunteer project together. And a consideration of family vacations also may be appropriate. As the therapist can inform clients, even when money is an issue, short day trips to visit local points of interest or take advantage of free activities generally are possibilities. What is more, inviting everyone to participate in planning either large or small activities and vacations can enhance the significance of the experience as well as foster a sense of belonging to the family as a whole.

Indeed, as the Richards family, mentioned above, gave their daughter more freedom regarding the outings in which she would choose to participate, Kim continued to go along at least half of the time. Then, recognizing that all of their children were growing up, the parents became aware of the need to include everyone in the process of deciding what they would do together. They thus evolved a plan that allowed each family member to take turns picking an activity designed to be fun and to appeal to as many members of the family as possible. This new format also played a part in Kim's decisions to keep participating with the family as a whole.

Accordingly, therapists might do well to raise the issue of family time and to invite consideration of options. Sometimes, however, important information in this regard arises spontaneously. For example, in response to a question I routinely ask regarding what one thing in the family each person would like to see changed, a child immediately expressed a wish that they do some fun things together as a family. However, although the other family members liked the idea, there was much difference of opinion regarding the specific activity to pursue. Indeed, whether the discussion is invited or emerges on its own, and whatever the activity, decision making around plans for family time can provide an opportunity for learning about and practicing the skills of negotiation and compromise.

Learning Negotiation and Compromise

Regardless of the issue at hand, individuals who live in the kind of close contact that generally occurs in families are likely to have more positive interactions overall when they are able to engage in productive negotiations and arrive at meaningful compromises. Hence the inclusion of the ability to negotiate and achieve meaningful compromise as an important process dimension in families that flourish. Therapists are advised to understand the ways in which this topic can be addressed most usefully with families.

Productive negotiations include an implicit acknowledgment that change in a system is a bilateral rather than a unilateral process (Becvar & Becvar, 1997a). There is a recognition that everyone is a participant and that a change in one area affects everyone and everything in the family. For example, the decision by a stay-at-home mother to begin graduate school is likely to reverberate throughout the family, perhaps in unexpected ways, despite the fact that it is acknowledged by all as a positive step. Just a few of the issues likely to arise are questions regarding the redistribution of responsibilities; that is, how children will be transported to school and other activities, who will prepare meals and help out with housework so Mom can attend classes and study, and what will happen when Mom is no longer as available to spend time with family members than previously was the case. Although this example concerns a major decision, even with minor changes similar processes are likely to be set in motion.

Productive negotiations allow for each person's voice to be heard, without judgment or comment, and with respect for the validity of different perspectives. Indeed, it is the creation of a meaningful process rather than the decisions ultimately agreed upon that generally is more crucial. Once everyone has voiced his or her viewpoint, the focus can shift to a consideration of the pros and cons of the various options articulated. For example, in one family with whom I worked, when considering a family vacation the parents wanted to rent a van and drive across the country, one of the children wanted to go somewhere like Disneyland and stay for a week, and another wanted to visit grandparents. As the discussion proceeded, issues such as time available and cost had to be factored into the mix, along with an opportunity to share feelings about the various ideas suggested. Having addressed all of these issues, the family reached a point where a meaningful compromise could be outlined and agreed upon.

Ideally, a compromise represents a win–win situation in which everyone gets at least some of his or her needs met and no one feels cheated or like a loser. Continuing with the above example, it was established that the parents had 2 weeks available for a vacation and that resources were somewhat limited. The family compromise involved agreement to take a car trip with a route that allowed for a 3-day visit with grandparents as well as a 3-day stay near a large amusement park, along with opportunities to have brief excursions along the way to some of the historic sites in which the parents were particularly interested. Not only was each family member pleased with the outcome, but important lessons also were learned regarding ways in which to respond effectively to the needs and desires of everyone involved.

Adults, too, can benefit from suggestions regarding negotiation and compromise. When working with couples or other relationships, for example, negotiation of a quid pro quo (Jackson, 1965), or a something-for-something compromise, can be very useful. According to Watzlawick, Weakland, and Fisch (1974), relationships often run into trouble when there is a tacit agreement or contract, formed early on, about how each will relate with the other or about what will happen in various circumstances. Although neither partner verbalizes these unspoken expectations, both tend to be sensitive to their violation. Thus, making the covert overt by bringing these expectations out into the open can be an extremely important aspect of therapy. Such a process can be followed by clear articulation of what each agrees to do for the other in order to improve the relationship. For example, partner A agrees to let partner B know what time he or she will be home for dinner each evening, and partner B agrees to wait until partner A gets home before serving or eating the meal.

Each of the above forms of negotiation and compromise provides options for behaving in a manner that is kind and respectful of everyone involved. Each also occurred in very well-planned and open ways.

Sometimes, however, acts of kindness can be more random or appropriately covert.

Practicing Random Acts of Kindness

In 1982 Anne Herbert, a waitress working in a restaurant in Sausalito, California, wrote on a placemat the message, "Practice random acts of kindness and senseless acts of beauty" (Random Acts of Kindness, 2005). This message obviously struck a chord in the hearts of many, as it soon appeared on bumper stickers, eventually became a topic of discussion in a profusion of newspaper articles and radio programs, and ultimately led to the publication of a book, *Random Acts of Kindness* (Kingma, 1993), describing true stories of acts of kindness. Using the search engine of Google.com on the Internet, one can access a minimum of 8,640,00 sites devoted to this topic.

The idea is to do some thoughtful act, such as donating to a charity previously not supported, putting money in the pocket of a needy person, or picking up litter on the street just to make the surroundings more pleasant. We are encouraged to behave in accordance with the Dalai Lama, who stated, "My religion is simple. My religion is kindness" (Random Acts of Kindness Home Page, 2005.) A similar concept is captured by Ursula Hegi in her book *Stones from the River* (1994). One of the characters is this book is described as the "unknown benefactor" because from time to time he leaves as gifts various items desired or needed by different people on the doorsteps of their homes. It is not until a great many years later that the identity of the unknown benefactor is revealed.

As therapists we can encourage the same sort of behavior among family members, inviting them to engage in random acts of kindness for one another, to become unknown benefactors. Thus spouses and partners might leave love notes in unexpected places such as a coat pocket, or tucked into a brief case, on a cell phone. Parents also can place love notes in their children's lunch boxes or in a bureau drawer. Putting a family member's favorite candy bar under his or her pillow or bringing home a rose for no reason can go a long way toward engendering or enhancing positive feelings. Similarly, doing a job without being asked, such as emptying the dishwasher, setting the table, taking out the trash, or walking the dog, can be welcomed acts of kindness. The theme of such behaviors is the creation of an atmosphere in which the members of the family suspect others of trying to be supportive, without the need for recognition of the kind act. Not only is everyone likely to feel better, but such acts are not soon forgotten.

Indeed, I can still remember my delight when as a preteen, I had just taken a shower and was preparing to dress to go to a party. Although I had a vague idea about what I was going to wear, certainly an issue of great concern at that age, when I came out of the bathroom and went into my room, I found that my mother had placed a beautiful new outfit, which she had purchased secretly, on my bed. It was a wonderful surprise, especially because it was just exactly the right thing at the right time. Years later, I still enjoy both creating and receiving surprises, whether large or small, and I am aware that the many little things that my husband and I do for each other in this regard help to keep the feeling of courtship alive in our marriage, which is now in its 28th year.

Similarly, as various family members engage in acts of kindness, whether or not they do so anonymously, positive energy is likely to be generated. The benefactor undoubtedly will benefit as much as the recipient of his or her kindness. Further, as the idea catches on and everyone participates, an atmosphere of support is created. Although always an important dimension in families that flourish, attention in this area can be particularly helpful in facilitating resilience following a severe crisis.

To illustrate, when Jane and Doug suddenly lost the younger of their two daughters to meningitis, the family was devastated. Jane felt crushed, Doug was angry at the world, and Jackie, their older daughter, was experiencing sadness, confusion, and guilt for being the survivor. The family members did not know what to say to, or how to behave with, each other, and they seemed to be drifting further and further apart. Over many sessions, during which the feelings of each were validated and their respective needs and desires were articulated, they began to come together again, slowly coming to terms with what had happened. From the beginning, I had suggested that they focus on being kind and gentle with one another. And as tensions began to ease, I encouraged them to become unknown benefactors for each other, in very small ways. My intention was to help them regain a sense of their strength as well as to recognize that not all of the sweetness in life had died with their daughter or sister.

Thus, despite the most stressful circumstances, as detailed in Chapter 4, resilience can be facilitated. Rather than by means of a lecture that often has a strong chance of being ignored, family members can be offered the opportunity to learn experientially the significance and far-reaching ramifications of an attitude of compassion and consideration. This also may be the case when the focus shifts to finding a sense of meaning and purpose in life.

Finding Meaning and Purpose in Life

As emphasized several times, having a sense of meaning and purpose in life generally has been found to be an extremely important contributor to psychological health (Jones, 1995). In therapy, therefore, attention in this area may be quite significant as we seek to support clients on the journey to the achievement of their goals and the ability to flourish. Accordingly, in addition to asking those who come to us for assistance to articulate their specific desired outcomes for the therapeutic process, we also might consider asking them to describe and engage in a conversation about their larger life goals and the values that they hold most dear.

Such conversations may involve an evaluation of the degree to which the work clients are doing expresses what they truly want to be doing, whether they are satisfied with their current level of education, or whether they would like to increase their education or training in any way. Obviously, with discussions such as these may come concerns about available options and the need to consider priorities and realities. Nevertheless, they can be very fruitful questions and issues to ponder.

In my work with Carl, for example, who was nearing retirement age and was concerned about how to plan for the next stage of his life, conversations about several issues proved to be very useful. Carl had not found fulfillment in his current job for several years. Although he didn't want to retire early, which would mean forfeiting some of his benefits, he found himself becoming more and more irritable at home and with his colleagues. He also was worried about having enough money to retire even when he reached the appropriate age. And, like many in the baby boomer cohort, he wasn't ready to take up residence in a rocking chair or sit at home doing nothing once he was able to retire. Rather, he wanted to continue to be productive in some way. We therefore began to consider Carl's interests and to explore possibilities for training that wouldn't be too costly. Carl's wife, Julie, was invited to join us for several sessions in order that her needs might be included as Carl engaged in the process of planning for the future. Indeed, it became apparent that whatever Carl did, it would be important to allow time for travel, a goal shared by both. Eventually, Carl decided to focus on becoming a consultant to other businesses like the one in which he worked, which precluded the need for further training. He thus would be able to do something meaningful on a schedule that he created and without having to be immersed in any one setting for too long a time. At the same time, Carl and Julie began taking Spanish lessons so that when they traveled they would have more options. They thus began to anticipate retirement as an opportunity rather than as a stage of life to be dreaded.

Another area that can be useful for the therapist to address is that of creativity: Are clients satisfied in this regard, or is there something they wish they had done or could be doing? Do they have an unfulfilled dream? As Lawrence LeShan (1990) found in his work with cancer patients, despair and illness can be replaced by hope and health when one is able to make dreams come true rather than lamenting their demise. In order to help clients get in touch with their dreams, the therapist might ask them what they would do if money and other responsibilities were not an issue, or whether there is anything that they deeply value but have not yet fully experienced or realized. In addition, clients might be invited to consider what they would like to have accomplished by the time they reach the age of 75, or by the time they die, that would enable them to feel that their lives had been meaningful. Further, the therapist can question clients regarding their most important beliefs, or consider what gives their lives the most meaning.

A related area, one that certainly is too important to be overlooked (Becvar, 1997), is that of religion or spirituality. I regularly ask clients where they are relative to this realm, and seek to include conversations related to it, as appropriate. If relevant for clients, I may ask whether or not they have developed the religious/spiritual side of their lives to the extent that they desire. We might also consider the degree to which support may or may not be forthcoming from this area, as well as its influence on the achievement of a sense of meaning and purpose. Just having permission to talk about religion or spirituality can be very important for clients, in addition to the fact that it may prove to be a significant source of information. At the same time, it is important to be aware that all of the conversations related to meaning and purpose also may reveal areas of concern.

For example, previously unspoken fears related to one's mortality and death can have a profound impact on relationship problems and other issues. Therefore, as appropriate, in addition to inquiring about what clients would like to have accomplished before they die, the therapist might incorporate questions regarding clients' beliefs about what happens after death, as I did with Courtney and Ed as they struggled following Courtney's treatment for breast cancer. Despite the fact that at first glance such a focus may seem morbid, discussions in this realm, preferably before being confronted with a life-threatening illness, are likely to facilitate a much greater appreciation for the present: "Every day is my best day; this is my life; I'm not going to have this moment again" (Siegel, 1995, p. 39). Or, in words attributed to George Santayana, "The dark background that death supplies brings out the tender colors that life supplies in all their purity."

As answers to questions related to the above issues are articulated, therapists might seek to support clients in the pursuit of a sense of meaning and purpose by helping them to focus on and utilize their unique gifts and skills, perhaps in ways not previously exercised. Therapists also might encourage them to listen to their own inner voices and wisdom— a very important ability we all have if nurtured appropriately. Indeed, it is crucial to help clients achieve a sense that they are living in integrity with themselves as they seek understanding of and make choices consistent with their personal truth. This represents what I call walking a path with heart (Becvar, 1997).

As clients cultivate a sense that their lives have meaning and purpose and that they are on a path that feels right for them, everyday existence may take on a magical quality. This does not mean that problems won't arise or that challenges will be overcome instantly. Rather, it means that life has a qualitatively different feel to it, that one constantly feels nurtured and supported. Individuals on such a path also are better able to nurture and provide support for others, even as they are able to handle more effectively the challenges with which they are faced. They are self-actualizing, they are resilient, and they are flourishing. In all likelihood, so also are their families.

Case Example

The Brooks family was referred to me by an elementary school social worker, who had been working for some time with the oldest child, Duane, because of his bullying behavior. When Duane's parents were called in to discuss what was going on, it became clear that they were having some serious struggles of their own that were far beyond the limits of the social worker's purview. The social worker therefore encouraged them to consider family therapy and then made the initial contact with me. Shortly thereafter Pam Brooks called for an appointment. I suggested that Pam and her husband Tony first come in by themselves and that we would figure out together how to proceed once we had had a chance to meet.

As I learned during our first meeting, Pam and Tony had been married for 13 years and had three children: Duane, age 11, Donald, age 9, and Denise, age 7. Pam worked weekends as a nurse, and Tony was a physician. Although both parents acknowledged their concerns about Duane, the focus of our discussion very quickly shifted to their marriage. Each described their relationship as having been troubled and conflicted for many years. Recently, things had come to a head when Tony revealed that he had had an extramarital affair. Although the couple had agreed to try to work through their problems, much anger and frustration with one another was still quite evident. Specifically, Tony was very unhappy about Pam's housekeeping and her inability to take charge of, and discipline, the children. Pam was equally as unhappy with what she perceived as Tony's lack of involvement with the family, and she was struggling with trust issues in the aftermath of the affair. However, each professed love for the other, and both were committed to making their marriage work. The goals they articulated included regaining trust, rebuilding their relationship, and becoming effective parents to their children, whom they realized were being affected by what was happening between them.

At the end of the first session, I suggested that we wait awhile before having them bring the children with them to therapy. I also made my fairly standard homework assignment of spending 15–30 minutes doing something fun together on a daily basis, or at least as often as possible. Regarding issues around trust, I explained that it certainly would take time to regain, but that there were steps they could begin taking that could help the process. I encouraged Pam to act as if she trusted Tony, and I encouraged Tony not only to behave in a trustworthy manner, but also to go out of his way to keep Pam informed of his whereabouts. She was not to check on him; he was to give her no reason to feel she needed to do so. Finally, I requested that they avoid discussing their problems with each other, or with anyone else. If those who already knew about the problems asked either Pam or Tony about what was happening, they were to respond by thanking them for their interest and telling them not only that they were getting professional assistance, but that they had been instructed not to talk about their issues outside of therapy. In addition, I suggested that they let their children know that they had decided to get help both for their marriage and for the family, and that at some point they might want them to go with them to see the therapist.

At the next session, Pam and Tony reported that things had been much calmer during the previous week. They felt that not discussing their problems, either between themselves or with others, had been a really good idea because it freed them up to enjoy other areas of their life. They also had enjoyed their fun times together, although they had only managed to make it happen on three occasions. Pam also said that Tony had been great about calling her during the day and letting her know where he was and what time he would be home. And Tony was relieved because Pam had stopped monitoring him so closely. What is more, Duane's behavior at school was reported by the social worker to have improved. I complimented the couple for the amazing number of changes they had managed to make in such a short time and expressed my belief that they had much about which to feel hopeful.

I then said that I would like to shift focus for a bit, and I asked them to describe what each initially had fallen in love with about the other. I also asked them to discuss the things they used to do together that each enjoyed. Interestingly enough, both Pam and Tony reported an almost idyllic courtship full of much fun and affection, with many creative ways to spend time with each other. Next, I followed up with questions about how they had handled conflict in the early days of their relationship. Once again, they agreed that they really hadn't experienced much conflict until after the children arrived. However, over the years, their increasing dissatisfaction with the way that the other was behaving had come to be expressed in loud, verbal assaults that rarely resulted in meaningful resolution. I therefore suggested that from this point on when a problem arose, they were to use the timer technique of 5 minutes for each to speak, 30 minutes of reflection, and then a repeat of the process until they had achieved a solution both felt good about (described in Chapter 6). I also suggested that they remember the foundation of love and respect on which the relationship had originally been built. Accordingly, they were encouraged to establish a boundary that each would refuse to violate in terms of their behavior with one another; this boundary included no verbal assaults or inappropriate language or behavior toward each other or the children. Finally, in addition to continuing with the suggestions of the previous week, I asked each to make a list of the expectations he or she had for all aspects of their marriage. They were not to share their lists with each other until our next meeting.

At the third session, Pam and Tony reported that things were continuing to go well and that they were having some success in their ability to handle conflict more effectively. However, and happily, they also found that now that they were behaving more thoughtfully toward one another, they had not had as many problems to try to resolve. At the same time, there was still unhappiness on the part of both regarding several of the other issues described in the first session. I responded by saying that was exactly why I had requested that they get in touch with their expectations, and I invited them to get out their lists. Not surprisingly, given their very different family backgrounds, Pam and Tony had very different ideas about how a family should operate and how they would like their lives together to be.

Despite her knowledge of a physician's lifestyle, Pam expected Tony to come home at a regular time every night, eat dinner with the family, and then have time to play with the children after dinner. She also wanted to be doted on as her father had doted on her mother, and to be taken out on dates occasionally. In addition, she wanted her husband to be less of a fierce disciplinarian and to curb his anger toward the children as well as toward her. Her desire was that they would talk with the children regarding inappropriate conduct when it occurred and use reason to get them to behave appropriately. Further, when she went to work on the weekends, she wanted Tony to care for the children rather than always having to get baby-sitters.

Tony, on the other hand, expected Pam to keep the house clean and to be sure that toys and clothes, etc., were picked up and put away by the time he got home. He definitely wanted to be able to spend more time with Pam and the children but didn't quite know how to do it, given their busy schedules. In terms of parenting, he felt that they both should be firm with the children and that there are points beyond which reasoning should be replaced by consequences. He appreciated the fact that Pam wanted to work but said that they really didn't need the income, and that he just could not always be available to take care of the children on the weekends.

Most important in all of this, from my perspective, was giving each an opportunity to hear where the other was coming from, which then could be followed by a process of creating realistic expectations that worked for both. Ultimately, it was agreed that Pam would improve on her housekeeping and that Tony would make arrangements that allowed him to get home for dinner at least three times a week. He also agreed to stay home with the children one weekend a month. Relative to parenting, I encouraged them to create a united front, meaning that they would discuss issues together, agree on rules and consequences, and then support each other in maintaining them. Neither would undermine the authority of the other in front of the children, and any problems perceived would be discussed in private. In addition to continuing with time together during the week, I also suggested that they have a once-a-month date night, arranged in advance so that all schedules could be accommodated.

During the next several meetings, the focus remained on the progress that Pam and Tony were making on these issues. We spent a fair amount of time discussing and seeking resolution related to the areas of anger and resentment, and I shared my beliefs about affairs happening when there are problems in the relationship. Although certainly not condoning the affair, providing a story that enabled the couple to understand the logic of the inappropriate behavior helped them in their efforts to come to terms with what had happened. Several discussions also were devoted to considering ways in which Pam and Tony could continue to improve their parenting as well as family life, in general. As part of this process, they agreed on regular bedtimes for the children, limits on the amount of time spent in front of the TV or a computer, small celebrations for successes, implementation of logical consequences, and modeling the respectful behavior they desired from their children. Throughout, I continued to inquire about Duane and was gratified to learn that he was continuing to do well both in school and at home.

During one of our discussions, both Pam and Tony lamented the fact that they had no religious affiliation, primarily because they had never found a church that fit their beliefs, despite the fact that this was an area of importance to them. Together we considered options, finally coming up with the idea of devoting a part of every Sunday evening to spiritual practices of their choice, and allowing the children to help create their home church service. The practices that ultimately were chosen included reading from various devotional sources, discussing together what they read, singing together, and praying together. Ultimately, this became a time to which all looked forward.

After about a dozen sessions, Pam and Tony seemed to have reached a point where I could introduce the possibility of their participating in an activity designed to help them move beyond the feelings of hurt and betrayal each had experienced as a function of the behavior of the other. I thus shared with them an activity I call the Ritual of Forgiveness and Letting Go (see Appendix C), giving both a copy of the written instructions and asking them to consider whether or not they felt ready to do such an activity. The ritual includes a period of preparation in which each member of the couple considers whether forgiveness and letting go of the past is possible as well as whether there is a willingness to focus on the present and to create a more meaningful life together in the future. When ready to proceed they are each to write a statement of forgiveness, choose a small item that represents the hurts, grudges and angry feelings to be let go, and compose a statement of recommitment. During the ritual the members of the couple share their statements of forgiveness and give each other the symbol chosen to represent what they are willing to let go, having first placed it in a small box. They then share their pledges to recommit to the relationship. After each disposes of the box given to him or her by the other, they are encouraged to celebrate with a meal together.

After a thorough discussion, Pam and Tony both agreed that the activity seemed to be a good idea. It was further agreed that they would plan it and make it happen at a time that seemed right for them. I would wait to hear from them to schedule the next appointment until after they had had an opportunity to complete the ritual.

I met with Pam and Tony again about a month later and was pleased to learn how much thought they had given to doing the ritual and how useful they had found it in terms of helping them let go of past hurts and focus on what they had together that was good. They had chosen to do the ritual on their wedding anniversary, and in order to create the space and time needed, they had taken the children to stay with Pam's parents for the evening, which allowed them to be at home. They reported that they had followed the instructions faithfully, doing the ritual in the living room in front of a fire, into which they each threw their boxes. They then restated their marriage vows to each other as a way of emphasizing a new beginning. Finally, they celebrated by going out to their favorite restaurant for dinner. The couple radiated a happiness that was in stark contract to the despairing faces that had greeted me at our first meeting.

Having come this far, I told Pam and Tony that I thought they were well on their way to recreating their relationship in a very positive manner. At the same time, I reminded them that there were no guarantees and that continuing to remain conscious about, and care for, their relationship would be essential. In addition, I invited them to bring the children in for the next session, so that I could check in with them, and they could see the person with whom their parents had been working. This session also went well, and after spending some time getting acquainted, most of the conversation focused on how things had changed for the better. Thereafter, I encouraged the couple or the family to come in for monthly relationship checkups, just to ensure that things remained on track. Although the intervals between appointments have increased over the years, I still meet with this family occasionally, although for the most part they are doing fine on their own.

Summary and Reflections

Helping Pam and Tony achieve their goals in ways that also facilitated resilience involved a focus on several dimensions, including helping them to create a supportive context for their family. The homework assignment of spending time together each evening doing something fun, discussions of their courtship, and suggesting a regular date night were all intended to help enhance their relationship and generate energy by reminding them of the positive aspects of their life together. They also were encouraged to behave respectfully toward each other, particularly in terms of their language. In addition, it was extremely important for this couple to find better ways to handle conflict and resolve their problems. By means of both a specific process according to which they would discuss differences, as well as the articulation and consideration of their expectations, they were able to negotiate win–win compromises that were respectful of the needs and desires of both.

Parenting issues also were a crucial consideration, given Duane's problematic behaviors at school. Hence the conversations and suggestions regarding the children's bedtimes, TV and computer time, the implementation of logical consequences, modeling behaviors desired, and celebrating successes. Encouraging them to become a united front when interacting with their children was significant to their effectiveness in each of these parenting areas. What is more, creating meaningful family time devoted to spiritual practices of their choice also seemed to be welcomed by all of the family members. Indeed, as with other families, attention to the transcendent dimension enhanced their ability to flourish.

Finally, as always when dealing with the betrayal of trust that an affair represents, it was important to recognize its significance and to avoid moving too quickly. Accordingly, I provided Pam and Tony with my story of the logic of such behavior at the same time that I acknowledged the pain associated with it. Helping Pam to act as if she trusted Tony and Tony to act in a trustworthy manner was consistent with my general approach to helping couples regain their trust—a process that can be slow and painful. When the couple seemed to have resolved their anger and were satisfied that they were back on track, we could then look for ways to bring closure to the chapter that included the affair/betrayal and find ways to begin writing a new relationship story. It was at this point that they were invited to consider implementing the Ritual of Forgiveness and Letting Go. Once this ritual was successfully completed, I felt it appropriate to see the family as a whole and then move to periodic checkups on an as-needed basis. Indeed, this family had survived a major crisis and were now stronger than before. The family members had demonstrated resilience, and the partners were flourishing in ways that had not been in evidence since before the children were born.

CHAPTER TEN

Conclusion

$\mathbf{A}$s noted at the outset, the approach described and illustrated in each of the preceding chapters may be thought of or summarized as a story about stories (Becvar & Becvar, 1994b). A second-order cybernetics/postmodern meta-perspective provides the larger, overarching story, the theoretical context consistent with which therapists attempt always to operate as they help clients achieve their goals in ways that facilitate resilience. This larger story speaks to a basic stance, describing a "lens" though which therapists view clients as well as the means by which they attempt to understand their stories. At the same time, it invites therapists to utilize a variety of more specific theories or stories. Thus it provides the guidelines for therapists' efforts to help clients rewrite their stories in such a way that their desired goals can be achieved and they can flourish. Such guidelines also encourage therapists to behave in the most respectful manner possible.

Accordingly, the actions of therapists are grounded in, and arise from, such fundamental assumptions as the importance of self-referential consistency; the inevitability of subjectivity; the reality of recursion and mutual influence, or the interconnectedness of all people and stories; the significance of theoretical relativity; and the imperative to adhere conscientiously to the highest ethical standards. Therapists therefore are cognizant of the need to make sure that what they do and what they say are consistent with their beliefs, and they are careful to avoid, or at least be aware of, various pathologies of epistemology. They recognize that all they have are their stories, and that knowledge of the truth in an absolute sense is not available to them. Further, they understand that what they perceive and say about their clients is as much a comment about them and how they think as it is about the clients. Therapists also understand that separateness is an illusion and that whatever anyone does or says has an impact on the others in his or her world, as well as on the world itself, and vice versa. Therapists therefore view all as involved in each other's destiny, a perspective that encourages them to be very sensitive to the effect of their behavior on others. What is more, they search for the utility to be found in the many theories, or professional stories, available to them as therapists. The specific stories they generally utilize include those that focus on family form and structure, various therapeutic approaches, both individual and family development and enrichment, and diverse culture and ethnicity issues. Also extremely important to these therapists are the variety of ways in which flourishing, in general, and resilience, in particular, can be experienced and storied.

Consequently, as therapists go about the process of selecting and accessing stories that they believe may be appropriate or useful in terms of helping clients achieve their goals, they attempt to do so in a manner that enables them not only to resolve the current problem or issue successfully, but also to "land on their feet," knowing that they are stronger than they were when they first sought help. In maintaining this dual awareness, therapists hope that in the future their clients will not need their services. Indeed, their goal is to "work themselves out of a job," at least in terms of the clients' ability to deal effectively with similar kinds of problems or issues in the future. At the same time, therapists certainly view the capacity to recognize the need for professional assistance as a strength and thus also encourage both periodic checkups and a return for therapeutic "booster shots" on an as-needed basis.

Whether during the first visit or as part of a return visit, an important part of the therapy process involves acknowledging and validating the experience and wisdom of clients. Therapists recognize that they have expertise in terms of their skills, knowledge, and years of experience, and that is what clients are looking for when they come to therapy. At the same time, therapists believe that part of their expertise also includes helping to create a context in which clients can recognize that they, too, have expertise, and that they can all work together as colleagues or team members. Therapists also strive to help clients become aware of the skills and knowledge they possess in relation to their own lives that can be called upon as they address the challenges with which they are faced. Although they may be stuck in the moment, they are better equipped than they realize to participate in the process of becoming unstuck as they seek, with assistance, to cocreate more useful stories consistent with the goals they have articulated.

Isomorphic to this process, therapists' larger story provides them with the option of considering different stories that they might access if those they are using are not as effective as they would like them to be in terms of both helping clients achieve their goals and facilitating resilience. Therapists first may reflect and check in with themselves regarding other approaches that they have found useful in similar situations. They also may consider consulting some of the many professional books and journal articles that are available on specific therapeutic issues. In addition, they may turn to a colleague, consultant, or supervisor, a resource which all clinicians are advised to make recourse no matter how long they have been practicing. Indeed, *practicing* is what therapists are doing, and thus they may never outgrow the need for assistance.

Fortunately for me, I have ready access to the colleagues with whom I share office space. In addition, I am married to someone who can act as a consultant any time that I am stuck. It may be useful to note that contrary to what many tend to think, my family therapist husband and I rarely talk about client cases in our daily life together. At the same time, when needed, we are available to each other, and often are able to shed new light on a situation, offering to each other different perspectives, or alternative ways to story the therapeutic process. This is similar to what we do with those whom we supervise more formally. For me, consultation is particularly helpful when the questions I have relate to ethical and legal issues.

As I often remind my students and supervisees, I don't believe there is any aspect of therapy that does not have ethical overtones or implications. Rather than giving attention to this area only when a major ethical dilemma arises, it behooves us all to be alert constantly to such equally important issues as value conflicts, cultural insensitivity, theory imposition, and lack of access for clients in terms of money, time, or transportation. My own sensitivity in this regard has been heightened as a function of the ethical codes of the professions of which I am a member as well as of my theoretical orientation. In addition, as a member of the Missouri Board of Licensed Marital and Family Therapists for the past 10 years, I have become acutely aware that licensure is primarily about protection of the public, and protection of the public is best achieved by means of ethical behavior in the broadest sense.

As part of an ethical stance it is important to recognize that there may be many equally effective approaches to helping clients. For example, let us consider my therapy with the Brooks family, sessions with whom were summarized in the case example at the end of the previous chapter. As described, I chose to work primarily with Pam and Tony, the marital couple. This choice was based on their emphasis on the problems in their relationship as well as on my agreement that the couple's struggles were affecting their three children, particularly their oldest son, Duane, who was behaving inappropriately at school. I therefore chose to trust that as Pam and Tony were able to resolve their marital problems, the children would feel more secure and Duane would stop, or at lease reduce the frequency of, his bullying behavior. Further, I was hopeful that as Pam and Tony felt better about their relationship they would be able to work together more effectively as parents. Given that this approach seemed to be working, I also opted to include the children in therapy only sporadically. And this was done primarily as a means to check in with them and to reassure them that their parents were indeed getting help.

Although the approach I utilized with the Brooks family worked very well, I believe that any one of a number of other approaches might have been equally as effective. Consequently, I can claim nothing more for my approach than that it was effective for me with this family at this time. Alternatively, however, I might have chosen to work with the whole family, or I might have decided to work primarily with Duane, with similar results. What is more, relative to either of these two alternatives, there are many additional theories to which I might have made recourse as I attempted to help this family overcome their problems and experience themselves as flourishing, as ultimately they did. Not surprisingly, therefore, a typical directive that students in my family practice classes are likely to receive on a final exam involves having to tell the story of a case situation, which I give to them, from the perspective of all of the following: a psychodynamic family therapist, a Bowenian family therapist, a strategic family therapist, a communications family therapist, an experiential family therapist, and a behavioral/cognitive family therapist. My goal with this assignment is to reinforce the importance of recognizing the potential utility to be found in many different therapeutic approaches—that is, professional stories.

In addition, I also emphasize the valuable resource that may be available in terms of personal stories. That is, during the course of therapeutic conversations I am likely to utilize self-disclosure just as I have done throughout this book. I often share, as appropriate, experiences that I have had that I think may be supportive of clients' achieving their goals. Obviously this self-disclosure must be done carefully, with concern for the maintenance of appropriate boundaries. What is more, I certainly don't believe that therapists have to have experienced every type of situation with which clients present in order to be effective. For example, despite the fact that people often wondered how my husband could do marital therapy during his bachelor years, he was able to work quite successfully with many, many couples prior to our marriage. At the same time, however, I have found that my credibility in the eyes of my clients often has been enhanced when I have let them know that I have faced and overcome challenges similar to those they currently are experiencing. And the longer I live, the more stories I have to share in this regard.

Indeed, I find that there are many advantages to the opportunity to grow older, in addition to the obvious fact that most of us would see it as better than the alternative. That is, the more experiences we have, the more we are invited to learn. And whatever we learn personally ultimately can be woven into our work with clients. For example, the ending of my first marriage and my experiences as a single parent were critical catalysts to my choice to study families and to train to become a social worker/family therapist. My second marriage taught me much about both the blessings and the challenges of life in a blended family, information that certainly helps in my interactions with clients living in similar kinds of families. The death of my son led to an exploration of religion and metaphysics that ultimately informed the creation of what I think of as a spiritual orientation in counseling and therapy (Becvar, 1997). In addition, my search to come to terms with this loss also resulted in my choosing to gain greater expertise in the realm of death, dying, and bereavement (Becvar, 2001), an area that I now claim as a specialization. A similar desire and ability to work with others experiencing life-threatening illnesses grew out of my firsthand knowledge of breast cancer.

Lest you think that learning can be gained only from such challenging experiences, let me assure you that this certainly is not the case. For example my thinking, and thus my approach to therapy, also have been strongly influenced by the many positive events that occurred as a function of being a parent. Indeed, as much as I treasure my professional work, I am fond of saying that parenting is the job that I have loved most and done best. Having the opportunity to nurture and act as a mentor for two remarkable young people has been the highlight of my life. And running a close second is the experience of a deeply fulfilling and loving relationship with my second husband. Although life is never perfect, and we all certainly have dealt with difficult moments in our relationships, the stories gained from events and encounters in my own wonderful family often dot the landscape of my professional work.

Another positive aspect of my daily life that is a great source of satisfaction comes from my role as a teacher in an academic setting. Not only is this role enhanced by examples drawn from my clinical work, but interactions with students over the course of many years have taught me a great deal that I find useful in therapy. Indeed, students who are seeking to learn ask good questions, and such questions push me as a teacher to come up with meaningful answers. Often, the results of this teaching / learning process find their way into my thinking as I work with clients.

This interweaving of personal experience also occurs in the areas of healing, wellness, and self-care. Thus I frequently share with clients stories about the ways in which I go about maintaining good health. I realize that this information may be particularly helpful to clients who are dealing with life-threatening illnesses. As a cancer survivor of many years, I recognize that I may be perceived as an important role model who provides hope regarding what may be possible for them. At the same time, this information also may be relevant for other clients who are dealing with less challenging conditions.

In addition to incorporating explicit information about healing and wellness into my work with clients, I also believe that my ability to be effective as a therapist focused on facilitating resilience is enhanced to the degree that I am healthy in body, mind, and spirit. Indeed, it is my belief that burnout is best prevented by giving due attention to each of these areas. Such a focus is consistent with the healthy selfishness in which I encourage my clients to engage. It also is consistent with the adage, "Physician, heal thyself." Thus my positive experiences, this time in terms of healing, are woven into, and have an influence on, my work, however implicitly.

At the same time, I would be remiss if I did not also note that just as the personal experiences of therapists may influence the direction taken relative to professional approaches or the creation of useful stories to be shared with clients, clients certainly have a tremendous impact on therapists, both personally and professionally. Indeed, there is much that clients may teach us, particularly in regard to resilience. As I have stated previously in relation to my work in the area of death, dying, and bereavement,

> I am awed . . . by the spirit of the parents who have lost both of their children to the same disease and yet are able not only to get up each morning but also to focus on providing support for others in a similar situation. I am humbled by the ability of a woman to make a memory book for her young child, knowing that she will not be around when he is able to read it. And I have the deepest admiration for the client who walked into my office, announced he was dying, and asked for assistance both with maintaining the quality of his life and with support for his wife in light of his choice to forego further treatment given his poor prognosis. (Becvar, 2003, p. 475)

Similarly, I have been privileged to witness the remarkable courage, not to mention miraculous recoveries, on the part of some who have been diagnosed with a terminal illness such as cancer. I am grateful to have been part of the journey many of my clients have taken as they demonstrated their ability to surmount the challenges involved with diagnoses of mental illness, creating meaningful and productive lives for themselves and their families with the support of their loved ones. I applaud the couples who have managed to prevent betrayal and other serious problems from destroying their relationships, honoring the love and commitment that brought them together, and working to reestablish trust and achieve workable solutions. I also applaud the couples who decided it was best to part but nevertheless found ways to continue to work together in order to coparent their children effectively.

Indeed, I probably could go on and on, given that another of the benefits of longevity, both personal and professional, is the opportunity to work with a myriad of clients and client situations. However, I know this is not necessary. Rather, what is most important in all of this is a recognition of the strengths and potentials inherent in families and of the lessons they can teach us even as we seek to help them. Ideally, all that we have learned from all sources ultimately can be distilled into wisdom that can be shared with other clients and with other professionals.

And so we have come to the end of my story, at least as it has evolved to this point, and relative to those aspects relevant for inclusion in this telling of it. However, I trust that I will continue to evolve and grow, and that as I do so, other versions of my story will emerge. In the meantime, I am hopeful that others will find in these pages information and stories that will assist them as they seek to facilitate resilience and thus participate in the support and creation of many families that flourish.

Appendices

APPENDIX A

Sensate Focus/Pleasuring Exercise

The activity in which you are invited to engage is referred to as a pleasuring session, which is exactly what it should be. This kind of activity
is sometimes also referred to as a massage or body rub, but that terminol-
ogy may miss the point. Although massage certainly has its place, in this
assignment the focus is not on loosening tired, aching muscles. Rather,
the idea is to convey to your partner through your tactile senses—that is,
by using your hands and fingers—your love and caring. This is a nondemand activity sexually, and intercourse as a part of it is not the object.

On your way home, or as soon as possible, stop at a drug store and visit
the lotion counter. Once there, sample the smell and feel of a number of
lotions and pick one to buy that you think you both would enjoy, or pick
one for each of you. A relatively heavy lotion is suggested, but you may
vary in your preferences. The name and type of lotion is immaterial; however, it should be pleasing to you and should be nonallergenic, particularly if either of you is inclined toward a skin rash or irritation.

After obtaining the lotion, one of you might ask the question, "When
shall we have a pleasuring session?" Please keep in mind that it should
be held at a time when you can devote about 2 uninterrupted hours, and
should be done only if you both really want to participate at that time.
However, once the time is agreed upon, it should be viewed as a defi-
nite commitment. In other words, both of you will be present and actually
ready to begin the pleasuring session at the agreed-upon time. (It is suggested that you both bathe before the time agreed upon for the pleasuring session.)

The setting is important to the success of pleasuring. Given that pleasuring is done in the nude, the room should be warmed to at least 75°. It would be well to set the thermostat up about a half hour before your session is scheduled to begin. It is preferable to choose a room other than the bedroom for this activity, but in any case it should not be done on the bed. The living room floor is suggested, perhaps in front of the fireplace, if you have one. Lay a blanket or pillows on the floor both for comfort and to avoid lotion spills on the rug. The lights should be dimmed, and if you do not have a rheostat on the light switch, perhaps you might use a single lamp, or even better, candles. Turn on the radio, or if you have them, pick out several of your favorite tapes or CDs. Burning incense, if you like it, also might be a pleasing addition. Draw the drapes and take the phone off the hook. Anticipate and remove the possibility of interruptions as far as possible.

After bathing, you might enjoy a drink of your favorite beverage, such as an after-dinner drink, a glass of wine, a cup of tea or hot chocolate. Sitting close to one another, enjoy your drink and engage in conversation, or just sit quietly with each other. You might discuss the happenings of the day, your expectations for the pleasuring session, or your present feelings. This also is the time when you should decide who will be pleasured first.

When you are ready, the person to be pleasured first should lie down on his or her stomach, in a comfortable position, and the person doing the pleasuring should sit astride him or her at about the hips. Before proceeding, a word of caution. *Lotion should never be poured directly on the person being pleasured.* You should pour a little into your hand, then rub your hands together before applying lotion to your partner. This will warm the lotion sufficiently and also will economize on the amount used.

Start pleasuring your partner at the back of the neck, remembering that this is not a massage but that you are trying to express your love and caring. Do not hurry. Take plenty of time to express your feelings. Move down your partner's body across the shoulders, down the backs of the arms, down the back and torso, pleasuring the buttocks, thighs, and calves of the legs to the feet. At this point you should ask if there is any spot your partner would like you to go over again. If there is, you should redo that area. Once you have done this, the partner being pleasured will turn over and the pleasurer will start at the feet, paying particular attention to the soles of the feet, the area between the toes, and across the top of the feet. The same attention should be paid to the other extremities. You should then move up the shins and the front of the thighs. At this point it will not be surprising if a male partner has an erection, but pay no attention to this. Remember that this is a nondemand activity sexually, and there should be no touching of the genitals during this activity. You will proceed to the abdomen, stomach, chest, arms, and neck. Here the pleasurer should again ask if there is a part the partner would wish to have pleasured again. If so, this request should be complied with.

Next, the pleasurer should move around and cradle his or her partner's head in his/her lap, pleasuring the face and neck. Pay particular attention to the area around the mouth and lips, the nose, the eyelids and eyes, the ears and earlobes, the forehead and temples, and the sides of the neck. At this time you should verbally express your feelings for your partner. When you have finished, your partner should lie on his or her side, and you should lie beside him or her in what is sometimes referred to as "spoon fashion," with your stomach against his or her back. You should place your arm across his or her torso so that you can feel his or her breathing, and you should try to synchronize your breathing with that of your partner. This may seem a bit difficult at first but can quickly be mastered. You should lie this way for 3 or 4 minutes. This is a time for feeling close.

Following this quiet time, partners should exchange original positions. The pleasurer becomes the pleasured, and his or her partner will proceed to pleasure him or her in the same manner and in the same order as he or she was pleasured.

Systemic Analysis/Multidimensional Assessment

I. Describing the Client System

A. Name, ages, and your story about the developmental stages and other relevant information regarding both individual members and the system.

B. Strengths and resources of members/system
   1. As perceived by the clients
   2. As perceived by you

C. Genogram
   1. Include names, birth dates, and information about marriages, divorces, remarriages, deaths, education, ethnicity, geographic locations, health and illness patterns, occupations, religion/spirituality
   2. Discuss trends/patterns you infer from genogram.

II. Describing the Client Context

A. Patterns of interaction
   1. Discuss system rules and boundaries you infer from family interactions.
   2. Describe your story about the interpretive frameworks of family members.
   3. Describe your story about the way in which communication occurs.

B. Other systems involved
1. Describe your perspective about the way in which the referral was made.
2. If court ordered, discuss the reasons for (story about) involvement with the court.
3. Describe the larger network of the client system.
C. Ecomap
1. Include other systems impinging on the client system.
2. Describe trends/patterns you infer from ecomap.

III. Describing the Presenting Problem
A. Problem(s) as defined by each member
1. Describe the problem as original contact person described it.
2. Describe the problem as each person defined it during the course of the first meeting.
3. Describe reactions of members to each other's descriptions.
B. Attempted solutions
1. When the problem has been experienced, describe the ways in which other members say they responded to the identified client.
2. Describe other attempts to seek professional assistance.
3. Describe clients' stories about the decision to come to you for therapy.
C. Logic of presenting problem(s)
1. Describe the way(s) in which the presenting problem(s) "fits" or "makes sense," given the particular client context.
2. Describe the patterns that must change in order for a new context to emerge.

IV. Reflecting on the Process of Analysis
A. Describe the story that you were telling yourself about the clients during each step in the process to this point.
B. Describe your influence on the unfolding of events.
C. Describe the impact that other stories might have had on the unfolding of events.

V. Establishing Goals

A. Describe the clients' views about what would be going on if things were the way they would like them to be.
B. Describe resources available relative to the clients' needs and desires both from your perspective and that of the clients.
C. Describe your influence on the selection of goals.

VI. Implementing Interventions/Perturbing the System

A. Describe behaviors chosen to facilitate the cocreation of a new context within which the presenting problem is no longer logical, and desired outcomes fit.
B. Describe the process of contracting with the client relative to specific assignments/interventions aimed at achieving goals.
C. Describe your thinking and its impact on the intervention process.

VII. Evaluation

A. Describe what happened when interventions were implemented.
B. Describe the impact of feedback on the process; what you and the client did with information received.
C. Describe the stories you and the client were telling yourselves about successes or failures.

VIII. Reflecting on the Process of Analysis/Assessment as a Whole

A. Describe the impact of your field of practice and setting.
B. Describe the impact of time.
C. Describe the impact of practice modality/approach selected.
D. Describe the impact of therapist–client characteristics relative to class, ethnicity, gender, age, sexual orientation, physical challenges.
E. Describe the impact of value and ethical issues.
F. Create a brief summary/story about this case as a whole.

APPENDIX C

Ritual of Forgiveness and Letting Go

Please read through the entire set of directions before proceeding.

Preparation

Spend some time thinking about the following questions:

1. Can I forgive my partner for not living up to my expectations?
2. Can I let go of whatever hurts, grudges, angry thoughts, etc.—however justified they may be—continue to draw us back to the past?
3. Can I make a commitment to myself, my partner, and our relationship to live in the present in such a way that we can create a more satisfying and meaningful life for ourselves now and in the future?

When you are able to respond in the affirmative to the above three questions, you are ready to do the following:

1. Write a statement that expresses your willingness to forgive and let go consistent with your answers to #1 and #2 above.
2. Find, make, or buy something small that represents all of the hurts, grudges, angry thoughts, etc., that you are willing to let go.
3. Write a statement of recommitment to your partner in which you offer your pledge to him or her, consistent with your answer to #3 above.

When you are ready to participate fully in a Ritual of Forgiveness and Letting Go, let your partner know.

Context

When each of you has informed the other that you are ready, choose a time and place where you can be alone and undisturbed for at least 3 hours. If you decide to stay at home, farm the kids out, take the phone off the hook, do whatever is necessary to ensure your privacy.

It is important to come to the appointed time with a sense of the seriousness of what it is you are about to do. Laughter is not bad, but the solemnity and significance of the occasion also need to be acknowledged. In order to set the mood, spend some time together creating and marking the chosen space in a manner that signifies and honors its sacredness. If you are at home, you may want to have a fire in the fireplace. Other options, regardless of where you are, include lighting candles, playing soft music, burning incense, putting fresh flowers in the room, etc.

Next, place a small rug or blanket large enough for both of you to sit on in your space, preferably on the floor. (You also may want to provide two pillows or cushions for sitting on the rug or blanket.) Place two small white cardboard boxes with lids and two pieces of white ribbon in the center of the rug or blanket.

The Ritual

Seat yourself so that you are facing each other, with knees nearly touching but with the boxes between you. Close your eyes and spend a few moments in quiet reflection or prayer. When you are ready to proceed, open your eyes. When both of you are ready, take turns doing the following:

1. Read your written statement that expresses your willingness to forgive and let go.
2. When both of you have read your statements, place the object that represents all of the hurts, grudges, angry thoughts, etc., which you are willing to let go, in one of the small white boxes in front of you

while saying the following: "*I bless and release the past and give thanks for the sorrows as well as the joys we have shared. I give thanks for all that we have learned in our journey together to this point. I respect and give thanks for our ability to forgive and let go.*"

3. Place a lid on the box with your object in it, tie it with a piece of white ribbon, and give the box, as a gift of love, to your partner.
4. Thank your partner and place his or her box behind your back.
5. Move close enough so that your knees touch and take each others' hands. Offer your pledge of recommitment to yourself, your partner, and your relationship to live in the present in such a way that you can create a more satisfying and meaningful life for yourselves now and in the future.
6. Spend some time just being together in whatever way feels appropriate for you.
7. When you are ready, decide how long each of you will need to dispose of your partner's box without saying how you plan to dispose of it. Establish a time to come together again.
8. Dispose of your partner's box. (Suggestions include burying, burning, immersing.)
9. At the appointed time, go out for or, prepare and eat, a celebration meal together.
10. Enjoy!

References

Abbott, P. (1981). *The family on trial.* University Park: Pennsylvania State University.

American Psychiatric Association. (1994). *Diagnostic criteria from DSM–IV™.* Washington, DC: Author.

Andersen, T. (1987). The reflecting team: Dialogue and meta-dialogue in clinical work. *Family Process, 26,* 415–428.

Andersen, T. (1991). *The reflecting team: Dialogues and dialogues about the dialogues.* New York: Norton.

Andersen, T. (1992). Reflections on reflecting on families. In S. McNamee & K. J. Gergen (Eds.), *Therapy as social construction* (pp. 54–68). Newbury Park, CA: Sage.

Andersen, T. (1993). See and hear: And be seen and heard. In S. Friedman (Ed.), *The new language of change: Constructive collaboration in psychotherapy* (pp. 303–322). New York: Guilford Press.

Anderson, H., & Goolishian, H. A. (1986). Problem-determined systems: Towards transformation in family therapy. *Journal of Strategic and Systemic Therapies, 5,* 1–13.

Anderson, H., & Goolishian, H. A. (1988). Human systems as linguistic systems: Preliminary and evolving ideas about the implications for clinical theory. *Family Process, 27,* 371–393.

Anderson, H., & Goolishian, H. A. (1990). Beyond cybernetics: Comments on Atkinson and Heath's "Further thoughts on second-order family therapy." *Family Process, 29,* 157–163.

Attneave, C. (1982). American Indians and Alaska native families: Emigrants in their own homeland. In M. McGoldrick, J. K. Pearce, & J. Giordano (Eds.), *Ethnicity and family therapy* (pp. 55–83). New York: Guilford Press.

Azrin, N., Nastor, B., & Jones, R. (1973). Reciprocity counseling: A rapid learning-based procedure for marital counseling. *Behavior Research and Therapy, 11,* 365–383.

Bach, R. (1977). *Illusions: The adventures of a reluctant messiah.* New York: Delacorte Press.

Bandler, R., Grinder, J., & Satir, V. (1976). *Changing with families.* Palo Alto, CA: Science and Behavior Books.

Barger, R. N. (2000). A summary of Lawrence Kohlberg's stages of moral development. Retrieved June 3, 2005, from http://www.nd.edu/~rbarger/kohlberg.html

Barnhill, L., & Longo, D. (1978). Fixation and regression in the family life cycle. *Family Process, 17,* 469–478.

Bateson, G. (1972). *Steps to an ecology of mind.* New York: Ballantine Books.

Bateson, G. (1979). *Mind and nature.* New York: Dutton.

Becvar, D. S. (1984a). *The family and society in the context of American society: A systems theoretical perspective.* Unpublished doctoral dissertation, St. Louis University, St. Louis, MO.

Becvar, D. S. (1984b). Models for religious education in whole family systems. *Family Perspective, 18*(4), 157–165.

Becvar, D. S. (1984c). Family clustering for growth and development. In M. H. Hoopes, B. L. Fisher, & S. Barlow (Eds.), *Structured family facilitation programs* (pp. 261–269). Rockville, MD: Aspen Systems.

Becvar, D. S. (1985). Creating rituals for a new age: Dealing positively with divorce, remarriage, and other developmental challenges. In R. Williams, H. Lingre, G. Rowe, S. Van Zandt, P. Lee, & N. Stinnett (Eds.), *Family strengths* (Vol. 6, pp. 57–65). Lincoln, NE: University of Nebraska Press.

Becvar, D. S. (1997). *Soul healing: A spiritual orientation in counseling and therapy.* New York: Basic Books.

Becvar, D. S. (Ed.). (1998). *The family, spirituality and social work.* New York: Haworth.

Becvar, D. S. (2000a). Euthanasia decisions. In F. W. Kaslow (Ed.), *Handbook of couple and family forensics* (pp. 439–458). New York: Wiley.

Becvar, D. S. (2000b). Families experiencing death, dying and bereavement. In W. C. Nichols, M. A. Nichols, D. S. Becvar, & A. Y. Napier

(Eds.), *Handbook of family development and intervention* (pp. 453–470). New York: Wiley.

Becvar, D. S. (2000c). Human development as a process of meaning making and reality construction. In W. C. Nichols, M. A. Nichols, D. S. Becvar, & A. Y. Napier (Eds.), *Handbook of family development and intervention* (pp. 65–82). New York: Wiley.

Becvar, D. S. (2001). *In the presence of grief: Helping family members resolve death, dying and bereavement issues.* New York: Guilford Press.

Becvar, D. S. (2003). The impact on the family therapist of a focus on death, dying and bereavement. *Journal of Marital and Family Therapy, 29*(4), 469–477.

Becvar, D. S., & Becvar, R. J. (1994a). *Hot chocolate for a cold winter's night: Essays for relationship development.* Denver, CO: Love.

Becvar, D. S., & Becvar, R. J. (1999). *Systems theory and family therapy: A primer* (2nd ed.). Lanham, MD: University Press of America.

Becvar, D. S., & Becvar, R. J. (2006). *Family therapy: A systemic integration* (6th ed.) Boston: Allyn & Bacon.

Becvar, R. J., & Becvar, D. S. (1994b). The ecosystemic story: A story about stories. *Journal of Mental Health Counseling, 16*(1), 22–32.

Becvar, R. J., & Becvar, D. S. (1997a). *Pragmatics of human relationships.* Iowa City, IA: Geist & Russell.

Becvar, R. J., & Becvar, D. S. (1997b). The client–therapist relationship: Comparison of second order family therapy and Rogerian therapy. *Journal of Systemic Therapies, 16*(2), 181–193.

Beer, S. (1974). Cybernetics. In H. von Foerster (Ed.), *Cybernetics of cybernetics* (pp. 2–3). Urbana, IL: Biological Computer Laboratory, University of Illinois.

Bernal, G. (1982). Cuban families. In M. McGoldrick, J. K. Pearce, & J. Giordano (Eds.), *Ethnicity and family therapy* (pp. 187–207). New York: Guilford Press.

Bernal, G., & Shapiro, E. (1996). Cuban Families. In M. McGoldrick, J. Giordano, & J. K. Pearce (Eds.), *Ethnicity and family therapy* (2nd ed., pp. 155–168). New York: Guilford Press.

Bigner, J. J. (2000). *Gay and lesbian families.* In W. C. Nichols, M. A. Nichols, D. S. Becvar, & A. Y. Napier (Eds.), *Handbook of family development and intervention* (pp. 279–298). New York: Wiley.

Billingsley, A. (1968). *Black familes in white America.* Englewood Cliffs, NJ: Prentice-Hall.

Boeree, D. G. (2005). *Abraham Maslow.* Retrieved December 9, 2005, from http://www.ship.edu/~cgboeree/maslow.html

Boldt, D. (2000, Sept. 3). State of family rises as public concern. *Philadelphia Inquirer.* Retrieved January 6, 2006, from http://www.alliancefor marriage.org/site/News2?page=NewsArticle&id=5586

Boss, P. (2006). *Loss, trauma, and resilience: Therapeutic work with ambiguous loss.* New York: Norton.

Boszormenyi-Nagy, I., & Spark, G. (1973). *Invisible loyalties: Reciprocity in intergenerational family therapy.* New York: Harper & Row.

Boszormenyi-Nagy, I., & Ulrich, D. (1981). Contextual family therapy. In A. S. Gurman & D. P. Kniskern (Eds.), *Handbook of family therapy* (pp. 159–186). New York: Brunner/Mazel.

Bowen, M. (1976). Theory in the practice of psychotherapy. In P. J. Guerin (Ed.), *Family therapy: Theory and practice* (pp. 42–90). New York: Gardner Press.

Bowen, M. (1978). *Family therapy in clinical practice.* New York: Jason Aronson.

Boyd-Franklin, N. (2003). *Black families in therapy: Understanding the African American Experience* (2nd ed.). New York: Guilford Press.

Bronowski, J. (1978). *The origins of knowledge and imagination.* New Haven, CT: Yale University Press.

Carter, E. A., & McGoldrick, M. (Eds.). (1980). *The family life cycle: A framework for family therapy.* New York: Gardner Press.

Carter, E. A., & McGoldrick, M. (Eds.). (1988). *The changing family life cycle.* New York: Gardner Press.

Casper, L. M., & Bianchi, S. M. (2002). *Continuity and change in the American family.* Thousand Oaks, CA: Sage.

Chamberlain, P., Patterson, G., Reid, J., Kavanaugh, K., & Forgatch, M. (1984). Observation of client resistance. *Behavior Therapy, 15,* 144–155.

Combrinck-Graham, L. (1990). *Giant steps: Therapeutic innovations in child mental health.* New York: Basic Books.

Conger, R. D., & Conger, K. J. (2002). Resilience in Midwestern families: Selected findings from the first decade of a prospective, longitudinal study. *Journal of Marriage and Family, 64,* 361–373.

Cousins, N. (1979). *Anatomy of an illness.* New York: Norton.

De Haan, L., Hawley, D. R., & Deal, J. F. (2002). Operationalizing family resilience: A methodological strategy. *American Journal of Family Therapy, 30,* 275–291.

Dell, P. E. (1986). Why do we still call them paradoxes? *Family Process, 25,* 223–235.

de Shazer, S. (1985). *Keys to solution in brief therapy.* New York: Norton.

de Shazer, S. (1988). *Clues: Investigating solutions in brief therapy.* Norton.

de Shazer, S. (1991). *Putting difference to work.* New York: Norton.

de Shazer, S. (1994). *Words were originally magic.* New York: Norton.

Dinkmeyer, D. C., & McKay, G. D. (1996). *Raising a responsible child: How to prepare your child for today's complex world.* New York: Fireside. (Original work published 1973)

Doherty, W. J. (2000). *Take back your kids: Confident parenting in turbulent times.* Notre Dame, IN: Sorin Books.

Duvall, E. (1962). *Family development.* Philadelphia: Lippincott.

Elkins, D. (1990). On being spiritual without necessarily being religious. *Association for Humanistic Psychology Perspective,* June, 4–5.

Epston, D. (1994). Extending the conversation. *Family Therapy Networker, 18*(6), 30–37, 62–63.

Erikson, E. (1963). *Childhood and society.* New York: Norton.

Falicov, C. J. (1982). Mexican families. In M. McGoldrick, J. K. Pearce, & J. Giordano (Eds.), *Ethnicity and family therapy* (pp. 134–163). New York: Guilford Press.

Falicov, C. (1996). Mexican families. In M. McGoldrick, J. Giordano, & J. K. Pearce (Eds.), *Ethnicity and family therapy* (2nd ed., pp. 169–182). New York: Guilford Press.

Falicov, C. J. (1998). *Latino families in therapy.* New York: Guilford Press.

Featherstone, J. (1976). *What schools can do.* New York: Liveright.

Frankel, C. (1963). The family in context. In F. Delliquadri (Ed.), *Helping the family in urban society* (pp. 8–22). New York: Columbia University Press.

Freud, S. (1955). *The interpretation of dreams.* (J. Strachey Ed. & Trans.). NY: Basic Books. (Original work published 1900)

Garcia-Preto, N. (1982). Puerto Rican families. In M. McGoldrick, J. K. Pearce, & J. Giordano (Eds.), *Ethnicity and family therapy* (pp. 164–186). New York: Guilford Press.

Garcia-Preto, N. (1996). Puerto-Rican families. In M. McGoldrick, J. Giordano, & J. K. Pearce, (Eds.), *Ethnicity and family therapy* (2nd ed., pp. 183–199). New York: Guilford Press.

Garfield, R. (1982). Mourning and its resolution for spouse in marital separation. In J. C. Hansen & L. Messinger (Eds.), *Therapy with remarriage families* (pp. 1–16). Rockville, MD: Aspen.

Gergen, K. J. (1991). *The saturated self.* New York: Basic Books.

Gibran, K. (1983). *The prophet.* New York: Knopf. (Original work published 1923)

Gilligan, C. (1982). *In a different voice.* Cambridge, MA: Harvard University Press.

Glasser, P. H., & Glasser, L. N. (1970). Adequate family functioning. In P. H. Glasser & L. N. Glasser (Eds.), *Families in crisis* (pp. 290–301). New York: Harper & Row.

Greeff, A. R., & Human, B. (2004). Resilience in families in which a parent has died. *American Journal of Family Therapy, 32,* 27–42.

Grzywacz, J. G., & Bass, B. L. (2003). Work, family, and mental health: Testing different models of work–family fit. *Journal of Marriage and Family, 65,* 248–262.

Gutman, H. (1976). *The black family in slavery and freedom.* New York: Vintage Books.

Haggan, P. (2002). Family resilience through sports: The family as a team. *Journal of Individual Psychology, 58*(3), 279–289.

Haley, J. (1963). *Strategies of psychotherapy.* New York: Grune & Stratton.

Haley, J. (1973). *Uncommon therapy.* New York: Norton.

Haley, J. (1976). *Problem-solving therapy.* San Francisco: Jossey-Bass.

Haley, J. (1980). *Leaving home.* New York: McGraw-Hill.

Haley, J. (1984). *Ordeal therapy.* San Francisco: Jossey-Bass.

Hareven, T. K. (1971). The history of the family as an interdisciplinary field. In T. K. Rabb & R. I. Rotberg (Eds.), *The family in history: Interdisciplinary essays* (pp. 211–226). New York: Harper & Row.

Harper, J., Scoresby, A., & Boyce, W. (1977). The logical levels of complementary, symmetrical and parallel interaction classes in family dyads. *Family Process, 16,* 199–210.

Hartman, A., & Laird, J. (1983). *Family-centered social work practice.* New York: Free Press.

Hartshorne, T. S. (2002). Mistaking courage for denial: Family resilience after the birth of a child with severe disabilities. *Journal of Individual Psychology, 58*(3), 263–278.

Hawley, D. R., & De Haan, L. (1996). Toward a definition of family resilience: Integrating life-span and family perspectives. *Family Process, 35,* 283–298.

Hegi, U. (1994). *Stones from the river.* New York: Scribner.

Heiman, J., LoPiccolo, L., & LoPiccolo, J. (1981). The treatment of sexual dysfunction. In A. S. Gurman & D. P. Kniskern (Eds.), *Handbook of family therapy* (pp. 592–627). New York: Brunner/Mazel.

Helmstetter, S. (1986). *What to say when you talk to yourself.* New York: Pocket Books.

Hill, R. B. (1971). *The strengths of black families.* New York: Emerson Hall.

Hinde, R. A., Finkenauer, C., & Auhagen, A. (2001). Relationships and the self-concept. *Personal Relationships, 8*(2), 187.

Hines, P. M., & Boyd-Franklin, N. (1982). Black families. In M. McGoldrick, J. K. Pearce, & J. Giordano (Eds.), *Ethnicity and family therapy* (pp. 84–108). New York: Guilford Press.

Hines, P. M., & Boyd-Franklin, N. (1996). African American families. In M. McGoldrick, J. Giordano, & J. K. Pearce (Eds.), *Ethnicity and family therapy* (2nd ed., pp. 66–84). New York: Guilford Press.

Ho, M. J. (1987). *Family therapy with ethnic minorities.* Newbury Park, CA: Sage.

Hoffman, L. (1993). *Exchanging voices: A collaborative approach to family therapy.* London: Jearnat.

Hoopes, M. M., & Harper, J. M. (1987). *Birth order roles and sibling patterns in individual and family therapy.* Rockville, MD: Aspen.

Howard, G. S. (1999). Culture tales. *American Psychologist, 46,* 187–197.

Husserl, E. (1965). *Phenomenology and the crisis of philosophy* (Q. Lauer, trans.). New York: Harper & Row.

Jackson, D. D. (1965). Family rules: The marital quid pro quo. *Archives of General Psychiatry, 12,* 589–594.

Jackson, L. E., Gregory, H., & Davis, M. G. (2004). NTU psychotherapy and African American Youth. In J. Ancis (Ed.), *Culturally responsive interventions: Innovative approaches to working with diverse populations* (pp. 49–70). New York: Brunner-Routledge.

Jacobson, D. S. (1979). Stepfamilies: Myths and realities. *Social Work, 24*(3), 203–207.

Johnson, K., Bryant, D. D., Collins, D. A., Noe, T. D., Strader, T. N., & Berbaum, M. (1998). Preventing and reducing alcohol and other drug use among high-risk youths by increasing family resilience. *Social Work, 43*(4), 297–308.

Jones, J. W. (1995). *In the middle of this road we call our life.* New York: HarperColllins.

Kaplan, H. S. (1974). *The new sex therapy: Active treatment of sexual dysfunctions.* New York: Brunner/Mazel.

Kaslow, F. (1982). Profile of the healthy family. *The Relationship, 8*(1), 9–25.

Keeney, B. P. (1983). *Aesthetics of change.* New York: Guilford Press.

Kegan, R. (1982). *The evolving self: Problem and process in human development.* Cambridge, MA: Harvard University Press.

Keith, D. V., & Whitaker, C. A. (1982). Experiential/symbolic family therapy. In A. M. Horne & M. M. Ohlsen (Eds.), *Family counseling and therapy* (pp. 43–74). Itasca, IL: F. E. Peacock.

Kingma, D. R. (1993). *Random acts of kindness.* York Beach, ME: Conari Press.

Klass, D. (1988). *Parental grief: Solace and resolution.* New York: Springer.

Kleinman, A. (1988). *The illness narratives: Suffering, healing and the human condition.* New York: Basic Books.

Knapp, R. (1986). *Beyond endurance: When a child dies.* New York: Schocken.

Koch, S. (1981). The nature and limits of psychological knowledge. *American Psychologist, 36*(3), 257–269.

Kohlberg, L. (1981). *The philosophy of moral development.* San Francisco: Harper & Row.

Kragh, J. R., & Huber, C. H. (2002). Family resilience and domestic violence: Panacea or pragmatic therapeutic perspective? *Journal of Individual Psychology, 58*(3), 290–304.

Kuhn, T. (1970). *The structure of scientific revolutions.* Chicago: University of Chicago Press.

LaFarge, P. (1982). The joy of family rituals. *Parents, 57*(12), 63–64.

Lasch, C. (1975, Nov. 13). The family and history. *New York Review of Books*, Nov. 13, 33–37.

Lasch, C. (1979). *Haven in a heartless world.* New York: Basic Books.

Lee, E. (1996) Asian-American families: An overview. In M. McGoldrick, J. Giordano, & J. K. Pearce (Eds.), *Ethnicity and family therapy* (2nd ed., pp. 227–248). New York: Guilford Press.

LeShan, L. (1990). *Cancer as a turning point: A handbook for people with cancer, their families, and health professionals.* New York: Penguin Books.

Levi-Strauss, C. (1956). The family. In H. L. Shapiro (Ed.), *Man, culture, and society* (pp. 261–285). New York: Oxford University Press.

Lewis, J. M., Beavers, W. R., Gosset, J. T., & Phillips, V. A. (1976). *No single thread.* New York: Brunner/Mazel.

Lowry, R. J., & Maslow, B. G. (Eds.). (1979). *The journals of A. H. Maslow.* Monterey, CA: Brooks/Cole.

Mair, M. (1988). Psychology as story-telling. *International Journal of Personal Construct Psychology, 1,* 125–138.

Marsh, D. T., & Johnson, D. L. (1997). The family experience of mental illness: Implications for intervention. *Professional Psychology: Research and Practice, 28*(3), 229–237.

Martin, E. P., & Martin, J. M. (1975). *The black extended family.* Chicago: University of Chicago Press.

Maslow, A. H. (1968). *Toward a psychology of being* (2nd ed.). Princeton, NJ: Van Nostrand Reinhold.

Masters, W. H., & Johnson, V. E. (1970). *Human sexual inadequacy.* Boston: Little, Brown.

Maturana, H., & Varela, F. (1987). *The tree of knowledge.* Boston: New Science Library.

McAdam, R. K. (1986). Cognitive behavior therapy and its application with adolescents. *Journal of Adolescence, 9,* 1–15.

McAdoo, H. P. (1980). Black mothers and the extended family support network. In L. Rodgers-Rose (Ed.), *The black woman* (pp. 125–144). Beverly Hills, CA: Sage.

McCubbin, H. I., McCubbin, M. A., Thompson, A. I., & Thompson, E. A. (1998). Resiliency in ethnic families: A conceptual model for predicting family adjustment and adaptation. In H. I. McCubbin, E. A. Thompson, A. I. Thompson, & J. E. Fromer (Eds.), *Resiliency in native American and immigrant families* (pp. 3–48). Thousand Oaks, CA: Sage.

Minuchin, S. (1974). *Families and family therapy.* Cambridge, MA: Harvard University Press.

Minuchin, S. (1984). *Family kaleidoscope.* Cambridge, MA: Harvard University Press.

Minuchin, S., & Fishman, H. C. (1981). *Family therapy techniques.* Cambridge, MA: Harvard University Press.

Minuchin, S., Rosman, B. L., & Baker, L. (1978). *Psychosomatic families: Anorexia in context.* Cambridge, MA: Harvard University Press.

Moshman, D. (1994). Reason, reasons and reasoning: A constructivist account of human rationality. *Theory and Psychology, 4*(2), 245–260.

New Solutions for Non-Traditional Families Facing Financial Concerns. (2005). Retrieved May 6, 2005, from http://www/newyorklife.com/cda/0,3254,14473,00.html

Nichols, W. C., Nichols, M. A., Becvar, D. S., & Napier, A. Y. (Eds.). (2001). *Handbook of family development and intervention.* New York: Wiley.

Noam, G. G. (1993). "Normative vulnerabilities" of self and their transformations in moral action. In G. G. Noam & T. E. Wren (Eds.), *The moral self* (pp. 209–238). Cambridge MA: MIT Press.

Nolte, D. L. (1972). *Children learn what they live.* Retrieved December 2, 2005, from http://www.empowermentresources.com/info2/children learn-long_version.html

O'Hanlon, W. H. (1993a). Possibility therapy: From iatrogenic injury to iatrogenic healing. In S. Gilligan & R. Price (Eds.), *Therapeutic conversation* (pp. 3–17). New York: Norton.

O'Hanlon, W. H. (1993b). Take two people and call them in the morning: Brief solution-oriented therapy with depression. In S. Friedman (Ed.), *The new language of change: Constructive collaboration in psychotherapy* (pp. 50–84). New York: Guilford Press.

O'Hanlon, W. H., & Wiener-Davis, M. (1989). *In search of solutions: A new distinction in psychotherapy.* New York: Norton.

O'Hanlon, W. H., & Wilk, J. (1987). *Shifting contexts: The generation of effective psychotherapy.* New York: Guilford Press.

Oswald, R. F. (2002). Resilience within the family networks of lesbians and gay men: Intentionality and redefinition. *Journal of Marriage and Family, 64,* 374–383.

Oxford University Press. (2005). *Compact Oxford English dictionary.* Retrieved November 18, 2005, from http://www.askoxford.com/concise_oed/discipline?view1uk

Parappully, J. (2002). Thriving after trauma: The experience of parents of murdered children. *Journal of Humanistic Psychology, 42*(1), 33–70.

Patterson, G. M., Reid, R. B., Jones, R. R., & Conger, R. E. (1975). *A social learning approach to family intervention: Vol. I. Families with aggressive children.* Eugene, OR: Castalia.

Patterson, J. M. (2002a). Integrating family resilience and family stress theory. *Journal of Marriage and Family, 64,* 349–360.

Patterson, J. M. (2002b). Understanding family resilience. *Journal of Clinical Psychology, 58*(3), 233–246.

Perrin, E. (2004). *Panel discusses differences in growing up with gay parents.* Retrieved July 4, 2005, from http://www.tuftsdail.com/vnews/display.v/ART/2004/11/23/41a2dbfla7d30?in_archive51

Phillips, J. L. (1969). *The origins of intellect: Piaget's theory.* San Francisco: Freeman.

Piaget, J. (1955). *The language and thought of the child.* New York: World Publishing.

Pinderhughes, E. (1982). Afro-American families. In M. McGoldrick, J. K. Pearce, & J. Giordano (Eds.), *Ethnicity and family therapy* (pp. 108–122). New York: Guilford Press.

Raheem, A. (1991). *Soul return: Integrating body, psyche and spirit.* Lower Lake, CA: Aslan Publishing.

Random Acts of Kindness. (2005). Retrieved December 30, 2005, from http://www.auscharity.org/kind/htm

Random Acts of Kindness Home Page. (2005). Retrieved December 30, 2005, from http://www.noogenesis.com/malama/kindness/

Riskin, J. (1982). Research on non-labeled families: A longitudinal study. In F. Walsh (Ed.), *Normal family processes* (pp. 67–93). New York: Guilford Press.

Ricoeur, P. (1981). *Hermeneutics and the human sciences.* (J. Thompson, Trans.). New York: Cambridge University Press.

Robbins, M. S., Schwartz, S., & Szapocznik, J. (2004). Structural ecosystems therapy with Hispanic adolescents exhibiting disruptive behavior disorders. In J. Ancis (Ed.), *Culturally responsive interventions: Innovative approaches to working with diverse populations* (pp. 71–99). New York: Brunner-Routledge.

Robbins, R., & Harrist, S. (2004). American Indian constructionist family therapy for acculturative stress. In J. Ancis (Ed.), *Culturally responsive interventions: Innovative approaches to working with diverse populations* (pp. 23–47). New York: Brunner-Routledge.

Rober, P. (2005). Family therapy as a dialogue of living persons: A perspective inspired by Bakhtin, Volosinov and Shotter. *Journal of Marital and Family Therapy, 31*(4), 385–397.

Roberts, N. H., & Escoto, E. R. (2002). "Our child won't go to bed!": A functional assessment and intervention from a family resilience perspective. *Journal of Individual Psychology, 58*(3), 245–249.

Roer-Strier, D., & Sands, R. G. (2001). The impact of religious intensification on family relations: A South African example. *Journal of Marriage and Family, 63,* 868–880.

Rogers, C. R. (1947). Some observations on the organization of personality. *American Psychologist, 2,* 358–368.

Ryan, E. B., Short, E. J., & Reed, W. A. (1986). The role of cognitive strategy training in improving the academic performance of learning disabled children. *Journal of Learning Disabilities, 19,* 521–529.

Sandau-Beckler, P. A., Devall, E., & de La Rosa, I. A. (2002). Strengthening family resilience: Prevention and treatment for high-risk substance-affected families. *Journal of Individual Psychology, 58*(3), 306–327.

Satir, V. (1964). *Conjoint family therapy.* Palo Alto, CA: Science & Behavior Books.

Satir, V. (1972). *Peoplemaking.* Palo Alto, CA: Science & Behavior Books.

Satir, V. (1982). The therapist and family therapy: Process model. In A. M. Horne & M. M Ohlsen (Eds.), *Family counseling and therapy* (pp. 12–42). Itasca, IL: F. E. Peacock.

Satir, V., Stachowiak, J., & Taschman, H. (1975). *Helping families to change.* New York: Jason Aronson.

Sawin, M. M. (1979). *Family enrichment with family clusters.* Valley Forge, PA: Judson Press.

Sawin, M. M. (1982). *Hope for families.* New York: Sadlier.

Schwartz, J. P. (2002). Family resilience and pragmatic parent education. *Journal of Individual Psychology, 58*(3), 250–262.

Shapiro, E. R. (2002). Chronic illness as a family process: A social–developmental approach to promoting resilience. *Journal of Clinical Psychology/In Session: Psychotherapy in Practice, 58*(11), 1375–1384.

Shon, S. P., & Ja, D. Y. (1982). Asian families. In M. McGoldrick, J. K. Pearce, & J. Giordano (Eds.), *Ethnicity and family therapy* (pp. 208–228). New York: Guilford Press.

Siegel, B. (1995). Love: The work of the soul. In R. Carlson & B. Shields (Eds.), *Healers on healing* (pp. 39–44). Los Angeles: Jeremy P. Tarcher.

Singer, D. G., & Revenson, T. A. (1978). *A Piaget primer: How a child thinks.* New York: New American Library.

Stuart, R. B. (1969). Operant-interpersonal treatment of marital discord. *Journal of Consulting and Clinical Psychology, 33,* 675–682.

Stuart, R. B. (1980). *Helping couples change.* New York: Guilford Press.

Sutton, C. T., & Broken Nose, M. A. (1996). American Indian families: An overview. In M. McGoldrick, J. Giordano, & J. K. Pearce (Eds.), *Ethnicity and family therapy* (2nd ed., pp. 31–449). New York: Guilford Press.

Thomas, A. J. (1998). Understanding culture and worldview in family systems: Use of the multicultural genogram. *Family Journal, 6*(1), 24–32.

Thomas, W. I., & Thomas, D. S. (1928). *The child in America.* New York: Knopf.

Thompson, E. A., McCubbin, H. I., Thompson, A. I., & Elver, K. M. (1998). Vulnerability and resiliency in native Hawaiian families under stress. In H. I. McCubbin, E. A. Thompson, A. I. Thompson, & J. E. Fromer (Eds.), *Resiliency in native American and immigrant families* (pp. 115–132). Thousand Oaks, CA: Sage.

Thornton, A., & Young-DeMarco, L. (2001). Four decades of trends in attitudes toward familiy issues in the United States: The 1960s through the 1990s. *Journal of Marriage and Family, 63*(4), 1009–1037.

Varela, F. J. (1979). *Principles of biological autonomy.* New York: Elsevier North Holland.

Visher, E., & Visher, J. (1982). Stepfamiles in the 1980s. In J. C. Hansen & L. Messinger (Eds.), *Therapy with remarriage families* (pp. 105–119). Rockville, MD: Aspen.

Walsh, F. (1982). *Normal family processes.* New York: Guilford Press.

Walsh, F. (1998). *Strengthening family resilience.* New York: Guilford Press.

Walsh, F. (2003a). Family resilience: A framework for clinical practice. *Family Process, 42*(1), 1–18.

Walsh, F. (2003b). *Normal family processes: Growing diversity and complexity* (3rd ed). New York: Guilford Press.

Watzlawick, P., Weakland, J. H., & Fisch, R. (1974). *Change: Principles of problem formation and problem resolution.* New York: Norton.

Weigert, A. J., & Hastings, R. (1977). Identity, loss, family and social change. *American Journal of Sociology, 82*(6), 1171–1185.

Whitaker, C. A. (1975). Psychotherapy of the absurd: With a special emphasis on the psychotherapy of aggression. *Family Process, 14*(1), 1–16.

Whitaker, C. A. (1976a). A family is a four-dimensional relationship. In P. J. Guerin (Ed.), *Family therapy: Theory and practice* (pp. 182–192). New York: Gardner Press.

Whitaker, C. A. (1976b). The hindrance of theory in clinical work. In P. J.

Guerin (Ed.), *Family therapy: Theory and practice* (pp. 154–164). New York: Gardner Press.

Whitaker, C. A., & Keith, D. V. (1981). Symbolic–experiential family therapy. In A. S. Gurman & D. P. Kniskern (Eds.), *Handbook of family therapy* (pp. 187–225). New York: Brunner/Mazel.

Whitaker, C. A., & Malone, T. P. (1953). *The roots of psychotherapy.* New York: Blakiston.

White, M. (1991). Deconstruction and therapy. *Dulwich Centre Newsletter, 3,* 21–40.

White, M. (1995). *Re-authoring lives.* Adelaide, Australia: Dulwich Centre.

White, M., & Epston, D. (1990). *Narrative means to therapeutic ends.* New York: Norton.

Wilkinson, D. (1999). Reframing family ethnicity in America. In H. P. McAdoo (Ed.), *Family ethnicity: Strength in diversity* (2nd ed., pp. 15–69). Thousand Oaks, CA: Sage.

Wilson, M. N., Kohn, L. P., & Lee, T. S. (2000). Cultural relativistic approach toward ethnic minorities in family therapy. In J. F. Aponte & J. Wohl (Eds.), *Psychological intervention and cultural diversity* (2nd ed., pp. 92–109). Boston: Allyn & Bacon.

Wolin, S. J., & Bennett, L. A. (1984). Family rituals. *Family Process, 12*(3), 401–420.

Zimmerman, S. L. (1979). Reassessing the effect of public policy on family functioning. *Social Casework, 59,* 451–457.

Index